Collins

AF513247

Breeze 4

Semester 1

Collins

Breeze 4

Semester 1

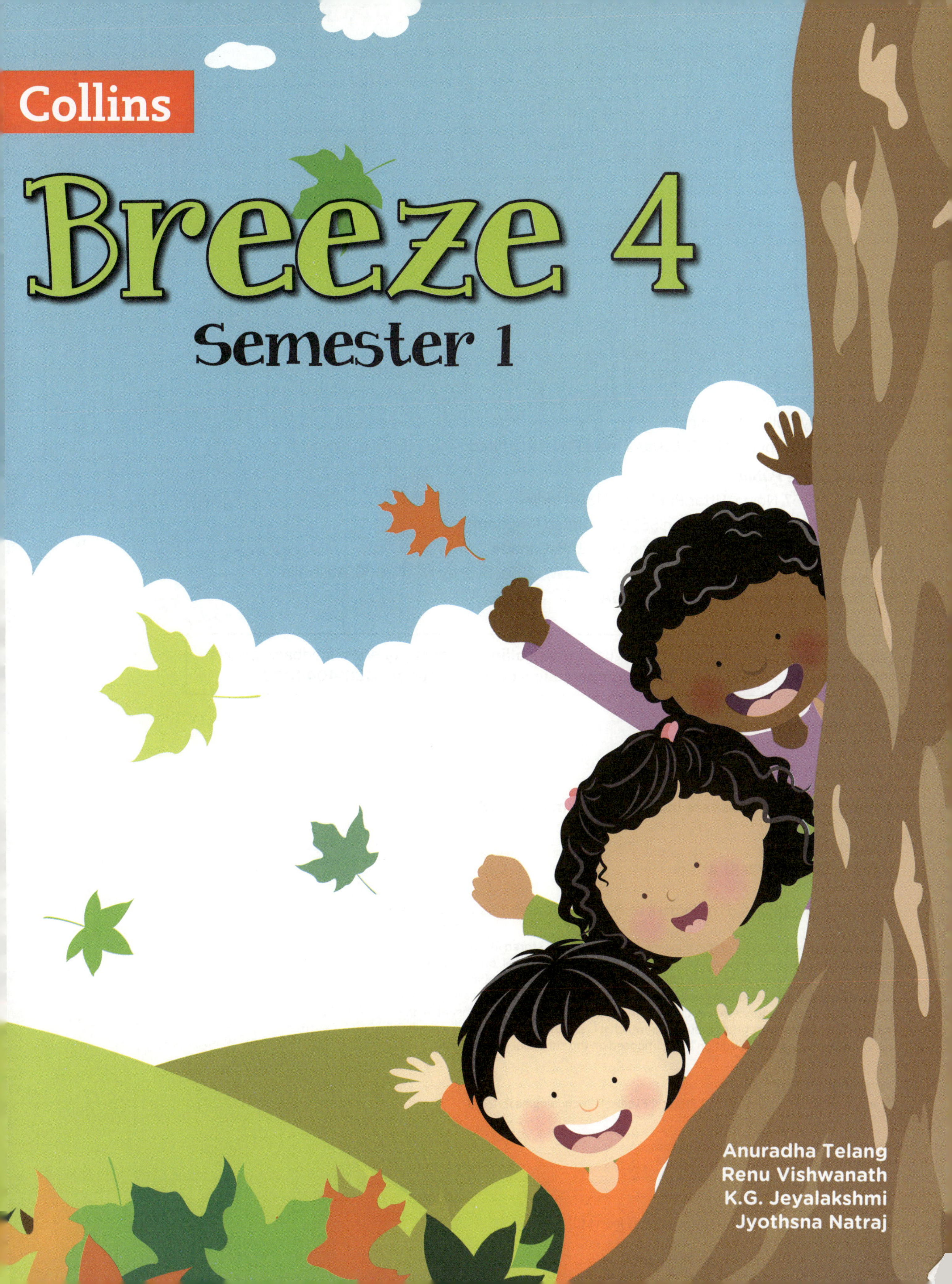

Anuradha Telang
Renu Vishwanath
K.G. Jeyalakshmi
Jyothsna Natraj

Published by Collins Learning
A division of HarperCollins*Publishers* India Private Limited

HarperCollins *Publishers*
A-75, Sector 57, Noida, Uttar Pradesh 201301, India
1 London Bridge Street, London SE1 9GF, United Kingdom
2 Bloor Street East, Toronto, Ontario M4W 1A8, Canada
Lvl 13, 201 Elizabeth Street (PO Box A565, NSW, 1235), Sydney NSW 2000, Australia
195 Broadway, New York, NY 10007, USA

Browse the complete Collins catalogue at **www.collins.in**. For any queries/feedback, please write to us at **SCHOOLSUPPORT@harpercollins.co.in** or call us on **0120-4044800**.

First edition 2018

Latest reprinted edition 2020

Reprint: 10 9 8 7 6
ISBN: 978-935-277481-4

Content development:
Mathematics and Environmental Studies: Excelsoft Technologies Pvt. Ltd.

Typesetting and layout by Recto Graphics

Cover by Manish Kumar

Printed and bound in India by Thomson Press India Ltd.

Preface

Breeze—an integrated semester course for classes 1 to 5 provides a comprehensive learning experience. This series of ten semester books teach lessons in an integrated manner, combining all the core subjects—English, Mathematics, Environmental Studies/Science, Social Studies and General Knowledge/Value Education. The lessons facilitate an interactive session in class for the learner's holistic development.

Breeze provides learning experiences with sufficient opportunity for exploration to young minds in their formative stage. The interactive approach of this series integrates multiple intelligences applied in every classroom across all levels.

Cross-curricular links have been created across the areas of learning for experiential and comprehensive development. The enquiry and skill based approach of the books contributes to the trans-disciplinary structure and comprehension. The books maintain a good balance between teacher-led and learner-initiated activities.

Breeze enables learners to understand the interdisciplinary nature of knowledge and apply this approach to problem solving. The well-graded course materials develop a link between natural, cultural and social environment. The course content across the subjects develop basic language skills through analysis, application and appreciation; develop critical and analytical thinking; enhance scientific temperament and create a strong sense of human values.

Some of the pedagogical elements integrated across all subjects include

- Learning Objectives
- Warm up
- New Words
- Do it Yourself
- Think and Answer
- Eco Zone
- Life Skills
- Value Zone
- Activity and Connect for cross-curricular links

Breeze series aims to develop 21st century skills including critical and creative thinking skills, effective communication skills, interpersonal and collaborative skills, and information and media skills in the young learners. This series is supported by comprehensive teacher's resources in the form of an interactive e-book with animations and interactivities, answer keys, lesson plans and a Test Generator for creation of quick test.

We value any feedback on this series. Please e-mail us at schoolmarketing.collins@harpercollins-india.com

Key Features

English

- **Warm-up:** A wide variety of activities at the beginning of chapters to ensure the learners' active engagement in the lesson
- **Reading:** A well-chosen selection of picture stories and comic strips from a wide range of literary genres
- **Comprehension:** Plenty of exercises including factual, inferential and extrapolative questions
- Cross-curricular boxes (*Science Scan, Maths Magic, Earth Speaks, Looking Back, and Fact File*) highlight topics interrelated with other subjects taught in the same grade
- **Glossary:** All new words in the text highlighted and their meanings provided along with a separate glossary for literary devices and literary terms
- **Life Skills and Values:** Separate thematic section on life skills and values
- **Vocabulary:** Boxed explanations of new vocabulary words and topics followed by a variety of exercises
- **Grammar:** Grade-appropriate grammar with detailed explanations and rules in simplelanguage
- **Listening and Speaking:** A wide variety of communicative activities and pronunciation covered in this section
- **Writing:** A well-graded section with a variety of creative-writing exercises including informal and formal letters, diary entries, flow charts, posters, stories, biographies, notices, reports, travelogues, character sketches, book reviews, recipes, acrostic poems, articles, and picture-based compositions
- **Activities:** A fun activity accompanying each poem
- **Projects:** Cross-curricular projects linked to topics taught in the particular grade in other subjects

Mathematics

Concepts explained in simple and easy-to-understand language

- **Exercises and Revision Exercise** within each chapter to recall and revise the concepts learnt
- **Mental Maths** to help practise calculation skills and deductive reasoning
- **Worksheets** to reinforce practice with fun exercises
- **Cross-curricular Links** to integrate knowledge across subjects
- **HOTS (Higher Order Thinking Skills)** and **Challenge** to sharpen the thinking skills beyond textual knowledge
- **Maths Lab Activity** to test skills for investigation, observation and analysis

Science

- **Revise and Recall, Think and Answer** test application of the concepts learned.
- **Science in Context** gives interesting extra information on the topic being discussed.
- **Summary** provides snapshot of the chapter content which helps students in quick revision.
- **Cross-curricular learning link** integrates knowledge across subjects.
- **Life Skills** test awareness, empathy and attitude towards self and others.
- Relevant **activities** hone experimental and deduction skills.
- **Project** questions link the concept learned to real-life applications.

Social Studies

- **Observe and Reflect** has pre-reading tasks that allow the learners to infer and relate to the topic.
- **Fact Zone** provides interesting titbits of information and **Find Out** tasks encourage referencing skills.
- **Do It Yourself** contains application-based activities for experiential learning.
- **Eco Zone** sensitizes learners towards conservation of environment.
- **Remember** and **Review Zone** at the end of the units facilitate understanding, recall and reinforcement, and assessment.
- **Think Zone** focuses on Higher Order Thinking Skills.
- **Life Skills Zone** equips learners with the basic skills they need to excel in life and **Value Zone** helps to build the right attitudes and values in learners.
- **Activity Zone** has varied creative tasks.

General Knowledge

- Each task comprises at least two kinds of inputs to help learners arrive at the answers and acquire knowledge at the same time.
- Special themes are an exciting mixed bag of environment education, life skills, values, India, sports, our world, science, language, art, personalities and entertainment to make learners become well-rounded individuals.
- **Activity pages**, aim to hone and cement specific verbal, visual and logical aptitudes through the common lens of general knowledge
- **Life skills**, draws attention to the science behind the safety measures we should take
- **Fact zone**, brings a good dose of fun to learning
- **India-specific content**

Value Education

- **Discuss** are warm up exercises, **Think and Say** are situations to test the application of the value taught and **Read Along** provides a story or poem related to the value being discussed in the chapter
- **Be smart** are exercises based on multiple intelligences
- **Remember** provides brief pointers that the learners can incorporate in their behaviour
- **Figure Out** are questions based on the story or poem taught and **Relate** are real life situations for problem solving
- **Create** provides creative tasks, **Enjoy** suggests media that communicates the value discussed, **Project** provides projects based on the values taught

Acknowledgements

English

The publishers wish to thank and acknowledge the following for granting us permission to use copyright material:

Ruskin Bond for The Cherry Tree; Gareth Lancaster for I'm Late for School; Bruce Lansky for Liza & the Lost Letter © 2010 by Bruce Lansky. Reprinted from Girls to the Rescue: Lion on the Prowl with the permission of Meadowbrook Press; The Will (English), translated by Pragya Gopinath, based on original story Vaseeyat (Urdu), written by Aniz Azmi, illustrated by Juhi Agarwal, supported by P.A.N.I Foundation, published by Pratham Books (© Pratham Books, 2015) under a CC BY 4.0 license on StoryWeaver; The Potter by Chitra Padmanabhan [© Pitara.com]

Every effort has been made to trace copyright holders and to obtain their permission for the use of copyright material. However, in some instances, we have been unable to trace the owners of the copyright pieces published here. The authors and publishers will gladly receive any information enabling them to rectify any error or omission in subsequent editions.

Images and Photographs

winhorse, miya227, jiratto, mura, zeremski, sergio_kumer, twinsterphoto, alessandrocatta, Prajwalkm, sabirmallick.

Science

All illustrations AptaraCorp Ltd.

Images

MR. SUWIT GAEWSEE-NGAM, apiguide, Jakkrit Orrasri, Sealstep; CoolKengzz, O lympus, Super Prin, Kokhanchikov; Grigorev Mikhail, Ruud Morijn Photographer, roundstripe; Nelson Sirlin, Nithid Memanee; asif waseem, themorningglory, wichitpong katwit, Pakhnyushcha; a9photo, Decha Thapanya, dabjola, Julia Pivovarova; Nithid Memanee, a9photo, Nelson Sirlin, Kokhanchikov, wichitpong katwit; Nithid Memanee, Grigorev Mikhail, Decha Thapanya; outdoorsman, Daniel Prudek, Gillian Holliday; Xavier MARCHANT, worldswildlifewonders, MNSKumar, rickyd; Wanchai Orsuk; FourOaks, Ratchapol Yindeesuk, Stephane Bidouze, Cathy Keifer; neelsky; Gillian Holliday, Daniel Prudek, Xavier MARCHANT, outdoorsman, Cathy Keifer, MNSKumar, Stephane Bidouze, Ratchapol Yindeesuk; Multiart, glasscuter, v.s.anandhakrishna, highviews, Anna Breitenberger, windu, mygoodpix, Elena Larina; EvgeniaSh., Hurst Photo; Robyn Mackenzie, zkruger, Kondor83, Hong Vo, Dancestrokes, Tischenko Irina, Evgeny Karandaev, Elena Schweitzer, Christine Langer-Pueschel, Ljupco Smokovski, Laborant, grynold, Madlen, monticello; Kondor83, Robyn Mackenzie, Elena Schweitzer, Tischenko Irina, Evgeny Karandaev, Dancestrokes, Christine Langer-Pueschel, Hurst Photo; tacar, Freer, VladislavGudovskiy, Dancestrokes, Elena Schweitzer, Tischenko Irina

Social Sciences

All illustrations Quadrum Solutions

Images

strmko; fotoVoyager; schita, Aelita17; Mykhailo Muzyka; Gannet77, Rafal Cichawa, Rattham, Shweitank; Bartosz Hadyniak, Danielrao, Danielrao; PeteDraper; Lya_Cattel; Marcus Lindstrom; UdayanSankarPal, Rattham, Danielrao; Luciano Mortula; pixelfusion3d, shylendrahoode, werusq, mrinalnag; davidevison; mwphotos; f9photos; DavorLovincic, djgunner; OSTILL, Roberto A Sanchez; EcoPic, photka; RichardHayman13, naveen0301; pjmalsbury, mahroch; AravindTeki, iannomadav, girishacf; spyder24; Sujay Govindaraj; yaseenin, turtix, siraanamwong, cinoby; powerofforever, FaraAk, Aleynikov; RNMitra; SoumenNath, menonsstocks; LSP1982, gehringj, yanikap; thinair28; intst; ertyo5, DamianPEvans; botulinum21, Anna Bryukhanova, pjrimages; VasukiRao; yogesh_more; fabio lamanna, vesnyanka; TarpMagnus, MosayMay, sandsun, Yurchello108; voraorn, kokouu; sandsun; julianwphoto; mshch, Tatiana Belova; mshch, skhoward, apomares; julianwphoto, Jeremy Richards; Musat; L.L. Prasanna Ranatunga, Anna Yu, CornelisNienaber_, eROMAZe, yoglimogli, Zwilling330, Andyworks, girishacf, girishacf; Maps © Collins Bartholomew Ltd 2016

General Knowledge

All illustrations Henu Studio

Rafflesia f ower-GettyImages/Christian Ziegler, Taj Mahal-istock/cinoby; Corbett National Park-iStock/tabidally; Golden Temple-istock/Holger Mette; Phiran-GettyImages/TAUSEEF MUSTAFA; Phulkari-GettyImages/Th e India Today Group; Kullu Cap-GettyImages/The India Today Group; House Boat-istock/mariusz_prusaczyk; Lakshman Jhoola-istock/catshiles; Chikan Embroidery-Joey Berzowska -originally posted to Flickr; Christ Church, Shimla-istock/heckepics;

Contents

English

Mathematics

Science

Social Studies

GK

VALUE EDUCATION

ENGLISH

1 I'm Late for School

Self and friends

OBJECTIVES

In this chapter, we will:
- *read and understand a humorous poem.*
- *learn rhyming words.*
- *know about our friends.*

WARM-UP

Work in pairs. Look at the picture of Rohan's room. Discuss the picture with your partner.

READING

Read this funny poem by Gareth Lancaster about a boy who wakes up late one day, and find out what happens.

I got up late for school today,
And nearly missed the bus!
I hurried down the stairs,
Wolfed my toast, and caused a fuss!

I quickly threw books in my bag,
My pens, my lunch, and shorts.
Grabbed my coat from out the cupboard,
Took my bat and ball for sports.

I slid across the kitchen floor,
And hopped around the cat!
Then expertly rolled over,
Jumped back up and grabbed my hat!

I belted out of our front door,
Spun round and swung it shut.
Saw the bus was waiting for me,
I felt I had time to strut!

wolfed: ate quickly and greedily
belted: moved somewhere very quickly
strut: to walk in a proud way with your head held high and your chest out

I climbed aboard and then froze still,
And knew that things weren't right!
My friends fell down in fits of fun,
And pointed with delight!

My face went red, I couldn't breathe,
For in my haste I knew!
I'd forgotten to wear trousers,
Jumper, shirt, my socks, and shoes!

jumper: a warm knitted piece of clothing which covers the upper part of your body and your arms

COMPREHENSION

A. Choose the correct option.

1. The poet got up
   a. early for school.
   b. late for school.
   c. quickly for school.
2. The poet's coat was kept in the
   a. bag.
   b. box.
   c. cupboard.
3. The bus
   a. had left.
   b. was late.
   c. was waiting for the poet.
4. The poet's friends
   a. laughed at him.
   b. praised him.
   c. ignored him.

B. Read the lines from the poem and answer the questions.

1. *I hurried down the stairs,*
   Wolfed my toast, and caused a fuss!
   a. Who hurried down the stairs?
   b. What does 'wolfed my toast' mean?
2. *My friends fell down in fits of fun,*
   And pointed with delight!
   a. Why did the poet's friends fall down?
   b. What did the poet's friends point to?

C. Answer the questions.

1. What did the poet put in his bag in a hurry?
2. What things did he carry for sports?
3. When did the poet realise that things were not right?
4. Why did the poet's face go red?

Life Skills and Values

Empathy and friendship

1. Do you think it is right to make fun of someone's mistake? How should we react when someone makes a mistake?
2. What would you do if your friend wore a pair of mismatched socks to school by mistake? Would you laugh or do something else?
3. Friends are very special people. Discuss how friends play an important role in our lives.

VOCABULARY

Rhyming words

- The words *bus* and *fuss* have similar final/ending sounds. When two words have similar final/ending sounds, we say they **rhyme**.

Find three more pairs of words in the poem that rhyme.

1. ....
2. ....
3. ....

ACTIVITY

Get to know a little more about three of your good friends. Talk to them and fill in the table.

Name of friend			
Hobbies (any two)			
Favourite books (any two)			
Favourite films (any two)			
Favourite sports (any two)			
Strengths (any two)			
Weaknesses (any two)			

2 Everything Is Possible

Helping others

OBJECTIVES

In this chapter, we will:

- *read a story about helping others.*
- *learn to use compound words.*
- *learn to spell words correctly.*
- *learn to use articles a, an, and the, and prepositions of time.*
- *listen to a poem and fill in the blanks.*
- *learn to create a chain-story.*
- *write a paragraph on helping others.*

WARM-UP

Complete the graphic organiser. Write the things which make you happy.

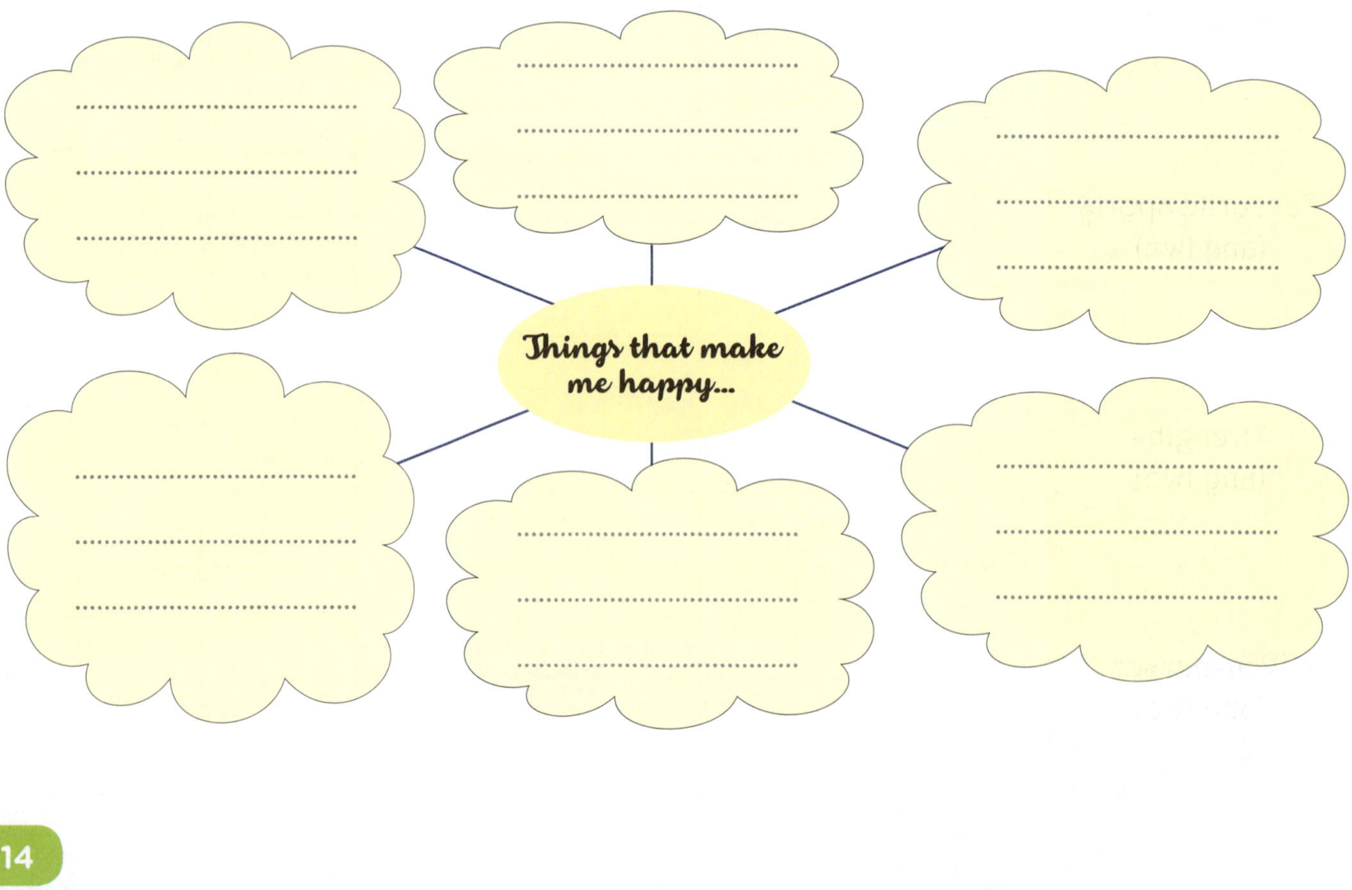

READING

Read this story about Anjali and her friend Pinky, who proved that if you set your mind to it, everything is possible.

Anjali's parents had moved to Junagarh a month ago. Her father, Ashish, was the commissioner of the city. Her mother, Suman, worked with a bank. Anjali had simply fallen in love with the lush green city. She especially enjoyed the lion safari at the Sasan-Gir Sanctuary, which was just two hours' drive away from Junagarh.

Anjali was eager to join her new school. It was Friday and the school was to reopen on Monday after the vacation. She went to the living room and flopped herself on the settee, her favourite haunt to read storybooks.

Late in the afternoon, she heard someone enter her house. Mother informed her that it was Raghuram. He was the gardener who lived in the outhouse located in the mango orchard behind their home. He had brought some fresh mangoes.

Anjali loved mangoes and jumped up with joy. 'Hurrah!' She grabbed a mango in each hand and ran off to the garden swing to enjoy the juicy fruit. As she was swinging, she saw a timid face peep from behind the tree.

She called out, 'Who are you?'

Fact File

- Sasan-Gir or Gir National Park is a wildlife sanctuary. It is the only place in Asia where Asiatic lions are found.
- Lions are found in only two continents – Africa and Asia.
- Asiatic lions are a highly endangered species, and less than 400 of them are left in Sasan-Gir.

commissioner: the head of a city administration
lush: lush gardens have a lot of green grass or plants
safari: a trip to see wild animals
flopped: sat down heavily and suddenly
settee: a long seat with a back and arms
haunt: a place frequently visited by a person
outhouse: a building such as a shed that is built on or in the grounds of a house
timid: showing a lack of courage and confidence

'I am Pinky. My father works in the mango orchard.'

Anjali invited her to play with her on the swing and shared a mango with her.

Many days went by and both the girls became very good friends. One day, Anjali asked, 'I have never seen you go to school. Why?' Pinky looked very uncomfortable. She did not answer and simply ran away.

Anjali was puzzled. The next day, too, there was no sign of Pinky. Anjali missed her friend, and decided to go with her mother and meet Pinky at the outhouse.

As they were walking to Pinky's house, Anjali saw some men put up a new hoarding across the compound wall. It read: **Each One, Teach One**.

Anjali read it and remembered, 'Our teacher has taught us rhyming words. *Teach* and *each* is a pair of rhyming words, but I wonder what this sentence means?'

Suman smiled at her daughter and said, 'It means every person can help another person to read and write.'

'It is a very nice idea!' exclaimed Anjali.

'Yes, indeed it is,' said her mother.

Suman and Anjali reached the outhouse. Pinky met them and shyly said, 'I ran away that day because I thought you would make fun of me. You see, I never went to school and do not know how to read and write. It is impossible that I can learn now.'

'Nothing is impossible, Pinky. In fact, everything is possible if you set your mind to it,' said Anjali's mother and put her arms around the child.

Anjali exclaimed, 'I have an idea. Why don't you come home every afternoon after I return from school? I will help you learn how to read and write.'

Fact File

'Each one, teach one' is a proverb which originated in the United States of America during the time African slaves were denied education. When one of these slaves managed to get an education, it was his or her duty to teach another person to read and write.

uncomfortable: worried or nervous

Anjali was true to her word and Pinky never missed a day. During the monsoon showers, both the girls stayed indoors and practised reading and writing.

Anjali introduced Pinky to the world of stories. There were many kinds of stories – fairy tales, mythological stories, and Aesop's Fables. Every day, Anjali would bring new books from the school library and read them to Pinky. She even gave Pinky all her old storybooks.

Pinky was unstoppable. She was hard-working and slowly started to read on her own. One day, Suman told Anjali, 'I think now the time has come that Pinky can be admitted to a school.' Anjali was very excited at the idea. 'Do you think she can come to my school?' asked Anjali. Suman enquired and finally Anjali's school was ready to admit her.

Pinky was nervous, but Anjali held her hand firmly and walked her up to her classroom on the first day. There was a slight hint of a tear in Pinky's eyes when Anjali finally waved her goodbye.

That day, Anjali was eagerly waiting near the school gate to know how Pinky had fared on her first day at school. She saw Pinky rushing outside excitedly. She was shouting with joy, 'I did it! I can read, write, and play! I enjoy going to school.'

Just guess! Who was the happiest person? It was Anjali. She felt as if she had cleared an exam! The two girls sang in chorus, 'Everything is Possible!'

mythological: relating to, based on, or appearing in myths or mythology
Aesop's Fables: animal stories with a moral by Greek slave and storyteller Aesop who lived on the island of Samos during the sixth century BC
enquired: asked for information
fared: performed (at a particular task)

COMPREHENSION

A. Choose the correct option.

1. Anjali and her parents had shifted
   a. to Junagarh from another city.
   b. from Junagarh to another city.
   c. to Junagarh from Mumbai.
2. Which of the given statements is true?
   a. Anjali's mother was the commissioner and her father worked in a bank.
   b. Anjali's father was the commissioner and her mother worked in a company.
   c. Anjali's father was the commissioner and her mother worked in a bank.
3. Raghuram was
   a. a gardener who worked in a mango orchard.
   b. an officer who worked in a bank.
   c. Pinky's uncle.
4. Anjali introduced Pinky to
   a. the world of animals.
   b. the world of books.
   c. the world of plants.

B. Answer the questions.

1. What did Anjali's father do?
2. What was one of the many things that Anjali liked about Junagarh?
3. How did Anjali help Pinky learn to read and write?
4. Do you think Anjali did the right thing by giving her old books to Pinky? Why?
5. How do you think Anjali felt after helping Pinky to learn reading and writing?
6. How do you think Pinky's life changed after Anjali helped her? What would have happened if Anjali had not met Pinky?

Life Skills and Values

Helping others

Anjali was the happiest when Pinky started going to school. Why do we feel happy when we help others? Think of an incident when you helped somebody and felt happy. Narrate the incident in class.

VOCABULARY

Compound words

A **compound word** is a word formed by combining two words. For example:

bed + room = bedroom *foot + ball = football* *lap + top = laptop*

A. Choose words from Column A and match them with those in Column B to form compound words.

Column A	Column B
1. fairy	a. bow
2. news	b. cake
3. pan	c. land
4. rain	d. paper
5. up	e. sheet
6. work	f. side

B. Fill in the blanks with the compound words above.

1. The .... gives us the latest news.
2. There is a beautiful .... in the sky.
3. The .... on grammar was very easy.
4. I visited .... in my dream last night.
5. My mother made a delicious .... for me yesterday.
6. Anjali was unable to solve the puzzle because the blocks were placed .... down.

DICTIONARY SKILLS

Circle the correct spelling. You may use a dictionary for help.

1. a. axcited	b. exceted	c. excited
2. a. preised	b. praised	c. praized
3. a. treasure	b. treazure	c. treesure
4. a. fevourite	b. faworite	c. favourite
5. a. magazine	b. magezine	c. magajine

GRAMMAR

Articles

- **Articles** indicate whether a noun is specific or general.
- There are two types of articles—indefinite article and definite article.

Indefinite article

- The indefinite article is *a/an*. It is used when we don't specify the things or the people we are talking about. For example:

  I met a friend.

- The indefinite article is always used with a singular noun when it is used for the first time. For example:

  I saw a cat outside my house.

- The indefinite article *a* is used before consonant sounds. For example:

  The dogs lived in a shelter.

- The indefinite article *an* is used before vowel sounds. For example:

  It is an allergy.

Definite article

- The definite article is *the*. It is used when we talk about a specific thing that both the speaker and the listener know. For example:

  The President is visiting the Taj Mahal.

Some rules

- When we speak of someone or something for the first time, we use *a* or *an*. The next time we repeat that noun, we use *the*. For example:

  A boy came in. The boy had a puppy in his hands.

- Do not use articles with names of countries, states, cities, lakes, and mountains. For example:

  He lives in Manali. He is training to climb Mount Everest.

- If a country is a collection of states, we use the definite article. For example:

  the United States *the United Kingdom*

- Do not use articles with plurals and uncountable nouns. For example:

  She writes books. *He loves classical music.*

A. Fill in the blanks with suitable articles.

1. The boy bought .... apple-shaped plate.
2. Pinky found .... storybook on the shelf.

3. One day, Anjali noticed .... new hoarding outside her house.
4. He put his cat on the sofa. .... angry cat scratched the sofa.
5. Anjali went on .... safari. .... safari was .... great experience.

Prepositions of time

- We use prepositions to describe a relationship between a noun and the other words in a sentence.
- Prepositions used with time expressions are called **prepositions of time**.
- The words *at*, *in*, and *on* are three common prepositions of time.
- *In* is used
  - to talk about years.
    He was born in 1994.
  - to talk about months.
    I visited Delhi in December.
  - to talk about decades.
    The film was released in the seventies.
  - to talk about centuries.
    The machine was invented in the eighteenth century.
  - to talk about seasons.
    We wear warm clothes in winter.
  - to talk about periods of time.
    The bridge was built in six months.
- *On* is used
  - to talk about days.
    He returned on Tuesday.
  - to talk about the morning/afternoon/evening/night of a certain day.
    He called me on Monday morning.
  - to talk about dates.
    Independence Day is celebrated on 15 August.
- *At* is used
  - to express an exact time of the clock.
    I have a music class at one o'clock.
  - to talk about holiday periods.
    He will come home at Christmas.
  - with the words *night, sunrise,* and *sunset*.
    Owls hunt at night.
  - to talk about meal times like lunchtime and dinner time.
    The canteen is crowded at lunchtime.

B. Fill in the blanks with suitable prepositions of time.

1. His birthday falls .... 12 May.
2. Where will you go .... Sunday?
3. It rained heavily .... July this year.
4. The supermarket is closed .... night.
5. I will meet my friend .... 11 a.m.
6. Anjali's old books were lying .... the attic.
7. Riya went home .... lunchtime as she was unwell.
8. Did you attend the dance class .... your birthday?
9. The world made great progress .... the twentieth century.
10. Will we be able to travel to Mars .... the twenty-first century?

LISTENING AND SPEAKING

Listening

A. Listen to the poem *The Arrow and the Song* by Henry Wadsworth Longfellow and fill in the blanks.

The Arrow and the Song

I shot an .... into the air,
It fell to ...., I knew not where;
For, so swiftly it flew, the ....
Could not .... it in its flight.

I breathed a .... into the air,
It .... to earth, I knew not where;
For who has sight so .... and strong,
That it can follow the .... of song?

Long, long afterward, in an ....
I .... the arrow, still unbroke;
And the ...., from beginning to end,
I found again in the .... of a friend.

Speaking

B. Divide the class into groups of ten. Each team will create a chain-story.

Here are the rules for the players:

- Each person can say only one sentence and the story must continue.
- The first player begins the story by saying 'Once there lived a young girl in the city of Mumbai…' and completes the sentence.
- The next player will continue the story in a meaningful way.
- This process continues until it reaches the last player in the team.
- The last player will conclude the story in one sentence.

Choose any one of the following as the theme of your story.

1. Friendship   2. Sharing   3. Kindness   4. Helping others

WRITING

Chotu, an orphan, works in a tea-stall. Write a paragraph on how you would help him so that he can stop working and go to school.

I see him every day.

3 Shadow and Carly

Animal friends

OBJECTIVES

In this chapter, we will:

- *read a story about love for animals and friendship with them.*
- *learn to use friendship terms and idioms.*
- *learn to identify the subject and the predicate.*
- *learn to punctuate sentences.*
- *listen to a story and fill in the blanks.*
- *learn to make requests and respond to requests.*
- *practise writing an informal letter.*

WARM-UP

Do you have a pet? Identify the pets shown below and tick the pet you have. If you do not have a pet, tick the one you would like to adopt.

READING

Read this story about how caring and loving cats can be, and what it means to have a home where you are loved and cared for.

'Goodbye, Shadow,' Paige said as her family dropped me off at the cat shelter. 'I know you'll find a good home soon. I'm sorry, I'm allergic to you.' She held me tight and her tears hit my fur. I couldn't bear to see her so sad, so I told myself it was the allergy that made her eyes so wet.

'Always remember that I love you, and I want you to find another special human. The shelter is nice, but a cat needs a *forever home*. A cat needs to *belong* somewhere,' she said.

After she left, my eyes were overflowing somehow. Maybe I was allergic to the other cats. They were everywhere.

A cat sniffed me, then nudged my side. 'Are you okay?' she asked.

'Of course,' I said, backing away.

She looked me straight in the eye, and I knew she understood me. I was embarrassed that she saw me cry.

'I had a cold when I came in too,' she said.

'It's an allergy,' I replied.

'Well, you'll feel better tomorrow and better each day after that. I'm Carly.'

'I'm Shadow.' We touched noses to complete the introduction.

Science Scan

- Cats, tigers, lions, jaguars, leopards, and cheetahs all belong to the cat family.
- Pet cats and small wild cats are called *small cats*, while the others are called *big cats*.
- All cats are carnivores.

allergic: caused by or related to an allergy
allergy: extreme sensitivity to a substance, especially a food, pollen, fur, or dust, which causes the body to react to it causing discomfort
embarrassed: felt shy or ashamed

'I'll show you around. I've been here almost two years,' she said.

Two years! I knew I couldn't be without a family for that long.

Carly introduced me to everyone: Isabel, Theo, Scamp.

She said. 'You'll like it in here. We aren't kept in cages and we can stay until we find *forever homes*, even if it takes years.'

I settled in and found a bed next to a cat tree. I felt odd; I was used to sleeping by Paige.

The next morning a boy and his mom came in. The boy petted me, then walked away. I knew he must be filling out the adoption papers. I just imagined hands would pick me up and put me in a carrier, but, the boy picked up Isabel.

Of course, he would want her. She was beautiful. My colours are in odd patterns.

'Congratulations, Isabel! I'll miss you, but I'm happy for you,' I said.

'Maybe we need to groom some more,' I suggested to Carly.

The next morning I groomed until my tongue was as dry as fresh litter. A girl and her dad came in. The girl threw a fur mouse and I pounced on it to prove I was a good mouse catcher. They walked away.

I just knew hands would pick me up and put me in a carrier, but, the girl picked up Theo. Of course, she would want him. He was talkative.

'Congratulations, Theo! I'll miss you, but I'm happy for you,' I said.

I made more friends, but lost them when they found homes. Carly was always there to play with me, though.

Every time I think of how much I wanted a home and a special human friend, that old allergy comes back to my eye. Then, I remembered what Paige told me – that someone would adopt me, and Paige never, ever lied to me.

We tried to get adopted. We saw lots of people, but no one chose us. One early spring morning, Carly woke me up with 'Happy Anniversary! You've been my friend for a year.'

cat tree: an artificial structure made of wood and covered with carpet for cats to play, exercise, and relax on
petted: stroked or patted lovingly
adoption: the action of legally taking up another's child or an animal and bringing it up as one's own
carrier: (here) a basket-like case for transporting small pets
groom: to clean the fur or skin by licking
litter: absorbent material, used to line a shallow container in which a cat can urinate and defecate when indoors

She meant to be nice, but I wasn't happy. How had I not found a home in a whole year? I decided to sleep all day.

Around lunchtime a human sat down and put me on her lap. I refused to snuggle.

I heard a carrier door jangle, but I wouldn't look to see which friend was leaving.

'Bye, Shadow! I finally have a home. But I'll really miss you. You're my best friend.'

I couldn't congratulate her. I couldn't say goodbye.

Instead, I did something I'd never done before. I extended my claws and scratched. I scratched the couch, the wallpaper. I scratched everything I could, except a cat or a human. Even when I'm upset, I never hurt anyone.

Someone called my name. I just knew I was in trouble. A pair of hands picked me up and put me in a carrier. At last, I was being adopted.

'He's the cutest, sweetest cat here,' said the girl whose lap I had been on.

'Our other new cat is cute and sweet too,' said the boy. 'I'd say it's a tie.'

They took me to the car and Carly was already there. We were being adopted together! She winked at me. I winked back. And amazingly, we never got 'allergies' again.

Fact File

- There is a saying that *a cat has nine lives.* This is because a cat's collarbones are not attached to any other bones but connected to its shoulders only by muscles. This gives cats great flexibility and freedom of movement. They can squeeze into what seem like small openings and don't get hurt even after falling from heights.
- Cats can also drink seawater and survive droughts. This is because their kidneys can filter seawater and remove the salt content from it!

snuggle: to settle into a warm, comfortable position
jangle: to make or cause to make a ringing metallic sound

COMPREHENSION

A. Choose the correct option.

1. Whose family dropped Shadow off at the shelter?
   a. Carly's family
   b. Paige's family
   c. Theo's family
2. Shadow told himself that it was the
   a. fever that made Paige's eyes wet.
   b. allergy that made Paige's eyes wet.
   c. strong wind that made Paige's eyes wet.
3. Who was Shadow's first friend at the shelter?
   a. Carly b. Paige c. Theo
4. Who was adopted first?
   a. Isabel b. Scamp c. Shadow
5. For how long were Shadow and Carly not adopted?
   a. For a fortnight b. For a month c. For a year

B. Answer the questions.

1. Why did Shadow feel odd after settling in at the cat shelter?
2. Why, according to Shadow, was Theo adopted by the girl?
3. Why was Shadow upset when Carly wished him a happy anniversary?
4. How did Shadow react when Carly was adopted? Why?
5. What happened to Shadow and Carly in the end?
6. What do you think actually caused tears in Paige's eyes when her family dropped off Shadow at the cat shelter?
7. Do you think Shadow is a nice, likeable cat? Give reasons to support your answer.
8. What kind of person did Paige want Shadow to be adopted by? What does that show about Paige?

Life Skills and Values

Empathy for animals

1. Paige loved Shadow, even though she could not keep him as a pet. It is not possible for everyone to adopt pets. In what other ways can we show our love for animals?
2. Many people abandon their pets on streets when the pets grow old or catch a disease. What would you say to those people?

VOCABULARY

Friendship terms

- Shadow and Carly were *best friends*.
- There are various kinds of friends. For example:
  - best friend: a friend who you are closest to
  - companion: a person with whom you spend a lot of time
  - confidant: a friend whom you trust and who you share your secrets with
  - mate: your friend or companion
  - acquaintance: someone you know slightly, but who is not a close friend

A. Fill in each blank with the most appropriate term from the ones defined above.

1. Shadow and Carly remained .... forever.
2. Carly was Shadow's .... as she shared all her problems with him.
3. Shadow never knew that he would meet a new .... at the shelter.
4. Shadow an Theo were ....
5. I met an .... after many months.

Idioms

- An idiom is a phrase or group of words whose meaning is different from the meanings of the individual words. Here are some examples of sight idioms:
  - a sorry sight: when something is in a bad state and it makes you feel sad
  - at first sight: when you see something for the first time
  - catch sight of: when you see something momentarily
  - lose sight of: when something that could be seen cannot be seen anymore
  - no end in sight: when you cannot see an end to troubles or work
  - set one's sight on: when you decide to focus or aim on achieving something

B. Fill in each blank with a suitable idiom from the ones given above.

1. Though the offer looks attractive ...., it has too many conditions.
2. As I opened the window, I .... a dove flying over the mountain.
3. The boatman started his journey and soon .... land.
4. The poor man's damaged house is ....
5. To achieve success in life, one should .... the goal.
6. There is .... to the water scarcity problem we have been facing since last month.

GRAMMAR

Subject and Predicate

- The **subject** of a sentence is the person or thing the sentence talks about.

  Anjali loved mangoes.

  Anjali is the subject of the above sentence, as the sentence talks about Anjali.

- The **predicate** is the sentence part that tells us something about the subject. It includes a verb.

  Anjali loved mangoes.

  What does the above sentence tell us about Anjali? It says that she loved mangoes. So, *loved mangoes* is the predicate in the sentence.

  Virat Kohli made a century in the final match.

  In the above sentence, *Virat Kohli* is the subject and the rest of the sentence is the predicate.

A. Choose a suitable subject from the box and complete each sentence.

A doctor | *Her friend* | *My mother* | *The big spider* | *The buzzing bee*

1. .... gave her a new pen.
2. .... spun a web above the door.
3. .... sucked nectar from the flower.
4. .... was very happy when I helped her.
5. .... visited our school yesterday for students' routine check-up.

B. Choose a suitable predicate from the box and complete each sentence.

barked all night | landed the aircraft safely | fluttered in the wind | has a long trunk | watered the plants regularly

1. The flag ....
2. The dogs ....
3. The pilot ....
4. The gardener ....
5. The elephant ....

Punctuation

- We use certain marks or signs in writing to make our meaning clear. These marks are called **punctuation marks**.
- The **comma (,)**, the **full stop (.)**, the **question mark (?)** and the **exclamation mark (!)** are some common punctuation marks.
- The system of using punctuation marks is called **punctuation**.

- The comma is used to separate the items in a list. For example:

  I bought apples, grapes, guavas, and *strawberries.*

- The comma is also used after the word that refers to the listener. For example:

  Uncle, where are you going?

  This is for you, Lina.

- The full stop is used at the end of a sentence that tells us something. For example:

  I have a toy car.

  Navit lives in Delhi.

- The question mark is used at the end of a sentence that asks a question. For example:

  When are you leaving for Shillong?

  Are Sangita and Mukul studying?

- The exclamation mark is used at the end of a sentence that expresses a strong or sudden feeling like happiness, pain, fear, surprise, etc. For example:

  How beautiful the stars look!

  What a shot he hit!

- Each sentence begins with a capital letter. For example:

  Tigers hunt at night.

C. The passage has errors in each line. Rewrite it correctly by using punctuation marks and capital letters appropriately.

once a mother goat and her kid lived ....

in a cave in a jungle? one day an elephant ....

passed by their cave, The kid was afraid ....

to see the elephant. it said, 'how big that animal is ....

It will eat us alive. What should we do Should we get ....

out and run away.' The mother goat said, 'Relax ....

elephants don't eat meat. they eat green leaves ....

grass sugarcane and fruits.' ....

LISTENING AND SPEAKING

Listening

A. Listen to what happens to Shadow and Carly after they are adopted and fill in the blanks.

1. Shadow and Carly were adopted by Jenny and her ...., Jim.
2. They lived in a .... near the sea.

3. They went to the .... every evening and played there.
4. Jenny took care of .... and Jim took care of ....
5. Sleeping by ...., Shadow often remembered ....

Speaking

Making a request

- It's important to be polite when you ask people for something or request them to do something for you.
- You can make a request using the following sentence structures.

  Can you please ...?

  Could you please ...?

  Will you please ...?
  Would you mind ...?

  Could you/Can you/Would you/Will you please open the door for me?

  Would you mind opening the door for me?

Things to remember

- *Could* is more polite than *can*.
- Use the word *please* to make your request polite.

Responding to a request

- Here are some of the ways in which you can respond to a request.

Positive Response	Negative Response
Yes, of course. *With pleasure.* *Sure, here you are.*	*I'm sorry I can't.* *I'm afraid I can't.* *I'm sorry, I need it myself.*

B. Work in pairs. Make suitable requests for the given situations. Your partner will respond to the requests appropriately. Perform the activity taking turns.

1. You want to borrow your partner's pen.
2. You need your partner's notebook to complete your schoolwork.
3. Your partner is going to a stationery store. You need to buy a pen.
4. You are thirsty. Ask your partner for a glass of water.
5. The window is shut and it is hot in the room. Request your partner to open the window, since he/she is standing near it.

WRITING

Imagine you are Paige. Write a letter to Shadow's new parents. Mention how you miss Shadow and how happy you are to hear that he has found a home with two loving and caring children.

4 The Fox's Wedding

Animal friends

OBJECTIVES

In this chapter, we will:

- *read a poem based on a folklore.*
- *learn to use cardinal and ordinal numbers.*
- *learn to make wind chimes.*

WARM-UP

Work in pairs and discuss with your partner.

1. When a story or belief is passed through the generations by word of mouth, it becomes a folklore. Discuss any one folklore from your region.
2. Do you remember getting a special gift ever? Draw the gift and write down what made it special?

READING

There is a common folklore in the Indian sub-continent, many African countries, Brazil, France, and Japan that when the sun shines during the rain, a fox gets married. Let's read this folk poem by Harindranath Chattopadhyay about a fox's wedding and find out who all attend it.

The cloud is dropping
It's rain in the sun,
For the Fox's wedding
Has just begun.

From forest and plain
And mountainside,
Guests bring gifts
For the Fox and the bride.

Here comes the first:
A grinning hyena,
Who brings a charming
Bowl from China.

Here comes the second:
A lion bold,
Whose gift is a mirror
Of African gold.

Here comes the third:
A crocodile,
Whose gift is a silver
Cup from the Nile.

Here comes the fourth:
A long-necked camel,
Whose gift is a casket
Of Indian enamel.

grinning: smiling broadly
casket: a small box or chest for keeping jewels, letters, or valued objects
enamel: a glossy substance applied on metallic or hard surfaces as a protective coating

Here comes the fifth:
A monkey who writes,
His gift is a book,
The Arabian Nights.

Here comes the sixth:
A she-wolf vain,
Who brings for the bride
A scarf from Spain.

Here comes the seventh:
A polar bear,
Whose gift is a beautiful
Russian chair.

Here comes the eighth
To the Fox's marriage:
A horse who has brought him
A five-wheeled carriage.

Here comes the ninth:
A jackal who brings
The bride and the bridegroom
Two diamond rings.

Here comes the tenth:
If you please, uninvited;
The guests at the wedding
Are getting excited.

He comes from somewhere
And teaches zoology.
What is his gift?
An empty apology.

vain: arrogant; extremely proud
zoology: the scientific study of animals
empty apology: saying sorry without meaning it

But why has he come
To the Fox's feast?
It is most ill-mannered
To say the least.

The Fox then addressed
The guests who were present:
'Let us be friendly,
Let us be pleasant.

'Let us be civil
And not make a fuss
Since Man, after all,
Is a beast like us.'

The guests of a sudden,
Ceased to complain;
The clouds of a sudden,
Forgot to rain.

The sun came out
Both gay and splendid;
The Fox's wedding
Was happily ended.

ceased: stopped
splendid: wonderful

COMPREHENSION

A. Choose the correct option.

1. The guests had gathered to attend
   a. the hyena's wedding.
   b. the crocodile's wedding.
   c. the Fox's wedding.
2. It started raining
   a. before the wedding ceremony began.
   b. just after the wedding ceremony began.
   c. after the wedding ceremony was over.

3. The lion brought as a gift
   a. a bowl made of African gold.
   b. a plate made of African gold.
   c. a mirror made of African gold.
4. The eighth guest was
   a. a horse.
   b. a monkey.
   c. a she-wolf.
5. The uninvited guest was
   a. a bird.
   b. a snake.
   c. a man.

B. Answer the questions.

1. How many guests attended the Fox's wedding?
2. Who was the fifth guest? What did he bring?
3. Who was the long-necked guest? What did he bring?
4. Can you guess what the Nile is? Which gift was brought from there?
5. What did the Fox say to the other guests about the uninvited guest?

Life Skills and Values

Courtesy

1. How would you have behaved with the uninvited guest if you were in place of the Fox?
2. Going to a party without an invitation is considered rude and impolite. Have you ever gone to a birthday party without being invited?

VOCABULARY

Cardinal and ordinal numbers

- Numbers like *one, two,* and *three* are called **cardinal numbers**. Cardinal numbers do not show the order or position. They just mention the number of people or things. For example:

  Do you have two pens?

  There are seven notebooks on the table.

- Numbers like *first, second,* and *third* are called **ordinal numbers**. Ordinal numbers express the order or position of something in a series. For example:

  The hyena was the first to arrive.

  The seventh to arrive was the polar bear.

A. Here is the list of the animals that attended the Fox's wedding. However, their order is jumbled. Write the order of their arrival using ordinal numbers and then spell them out.

1. camel	....	2. crocodile	....
3. horse	....	4. hyena	....
5. jackal	....	6. lion	....
7. polar bear	....	8. she-wolf	....

B. There is a mistake of cardinal and ordinal numbers in each sentence. Correct and rewrite the sentences. Also, say whether the numbers in your new sentences are ordinal or cardinal.

1. The three chair from the left is broken.

   .... (ordinal/cardinal)

2. There are twentieth benches in the classroom.

   .... (ordinal/cardinal)

3. Tom was so hungry that he ate fifth sandwiches.

   .... (ordinal/cardinal)

4. I won the one position in the painting competition.

   .... (ordinal/cardinal)

5. Zeenat was sitting in the two row at the magic show.

   .... (ordinal/cardinal)

ACTIVITY

Do you like receiving and giving gifts? Follow the instructions and make simple wind chimes, which you can gift to a family member or a friend.

Things required

- a stick
- simple strings
- metallic washers
- colourful paper clips

Procedure

- Take a stick. You may paint it if you wish.
- Take a few metallic washers and colour them.
- Use paper clips and set them on the washers. They will look like petals of a flower.
- String the washers on a string and hand them in different sizes.
- Hang the wind chimes on a tree, on a windowsill, or simply on a pole. See how the chimes produce sound in the breeze.

5 The Samurai Warrior and the Tea Master

Finding solutions

OBJECTIVES

In this chapter, we will:

- *read a story about overcoming difficulties.*
- *learn adjective-noun collocations.*
- *learn to use subjective, objective, and reflexive pronouns.*
- *listen to a description of Ninja warriors and mark sentences as true or false.*
- *learn to spot and describe differences between the given pictures.*
- *learn the different sounds of ough.*
- *practise writing a recipe.*

WARM-UP

Look at the picture clues and fill in the blanks.

bullet train

kimono

Mount Fuji

samurai

kendo

sushi

1. .... is Japan's highest mountain.
2. .... is a popular Japanese rice dish.
3. Japan's high speed train is called the ....
4. The .... were traditional Japanese military soldiers.
5. .... is the traditional dress worn by Japanese women.
6. .... is a Japanese form of fencing with two-handed bamboo swords, originally developed as a safe form of sword training for the samurai.

READING

Many centuries ago in Japan, there was a warrior community known as the samurai. The samurais were the master of their mind and body, and skilful swordsmen. Read this story of one such samurai, Lord Yamanouchi.

Lord Yamanouchi was a wise man and a respectable lord at the emperor's court. A tea master worked in the service of Lord Yamanouchi.

The Japanese tea ceremony is a graceful ritual of preparing green tea. The utensils, the sitting arrangement for both the guests and the host, the steps of preparing, serving, and drinking tea are all predefined.

Once, Lord Yamanouchi and the tea master went on business to the great city of Edo. One evening, the tea master and his friends were taking a stroll.

ceremony: a formal and traditional occasion, one celebrating an event
ritual: a solemn ceremony that consists of a series of actions performed as per a prescribed order
predefined: defined or established in advance

imposter: a person who is pretending to be someone else in order to trick people
duel: a formal fight with weapons between two people to settle a point of honour
robes: long loose outer garments reaching to the ankles

At Lord Yamanouchi's palace...

The next day, the tea master did exactly what Lord Yamanouchi asked him to do.

confident: feeling sure about one's abilities

COMPREHENSION

A. Choose the correct option.

1. Who was Lord Yamanouchi?
    a. A king
    b. A samurai warrior
    c. A poor tea master
2. Which city did Lord Yamanouchi and the tea master visit?
    a. Edo
    b. India
    c. Japan

3. What did the samurai warrior want?
   a. A gift from the tea master
   b. A duel with the tea master
   c. A gold coin from the tea master
4. What was the tea master very good at?
   a. Riding a horse
   b. Fighting with a sword
   c. Performing the tea ceremony

B. Answer the questions.

1. Why did Lord Yamanouchi give the tea master the rank of a samurai warrior?
2. What happened in the city of Edo?
3. What advice did the tea master's friends give him?
4. How was the tea master able to defend himself against the samurai warrior?
5. Do you think the tea master was a man of courage and self-esteem? Give reasons to support your answer.
6. Why do you think Lord Yamanouchi advised the tea master to maintain peace of mind?

Life Skills and Values

Focusing on goals

1. Do you think it was the tea master's quality of focusing on his goal that helped him achieve great success in life? Explain.
2. Imagine you have an exam tomorrow. Your father is watching the final of an important cricket tournament on television and you are tempted to join him. What would you do in that situation? Why?

VOCABULARY

Collocations: adjectives and nouns

- A **collocation** is two or more words that are frequently used together. For example:

  This is strong coffee.

  Here 'strong coffee' is a collocation.

  However, we cannot say 'powerful coffee', even if 'strong' and 'powerful' mean the same thing. We need to know which words will work together to make the word combinations sound correct.
- There are several different word combinations that can make up a collocation. *Strong coffee* is an example of an **adjective + noun collocation**. Some more examples of adjective + noun collocations are: *fierce duel* *foul smell*

Choose the correct adjectives to form correct collocations.

1. He has a *rich/high* **vocabulary**.
2. A *strong/powerful* **wind** was blowing.
3. The mother has *deep/high* **love** for her children.
4. The noise of *loud/heavy* **traffic** can drive you crazy.
5. He spoke with a *heavy/strong* **American accent**.
6. I took the *express/quick* **train** to the airport to save time.

GRAMMAR

Pronouns

- A **pronoun** is a word used in place of a noun that has already been mentioned. This is done to avoid repeating the noun. For example:

  Paige was tired, so she went to bed.

- Personal pronouns are used in place of nouns referring to specific people or things. For example, *I, me, you, he, she, it, him, her, we, us, they,* and *them* are pronouns. These pronouns are divided into different categories according to their usage and role in a sentence.

Subjective pronouns

- The pronouns I, you, he, she, we, it, and they are known as **subjective pronouns** because they act as the subjects of verbs or subjects of sentences. For example:

  She saw Paige.

  We drove Vicky home.

  I waved at her.

Objective pronouns

- The pronouns me, you, us, him, her, it, and them are known as **objective pronouns** because they act as the objects of verbs and prepositions. For example:

  Paige saw her.

  Vicky drove us home.

  She waved at me.

- Here's a table of different forms of pronouns for your easy reference:

	SINGULAR		PLURAL	
	Subjective	**Objective**	**Subjective**	**Objective**
first person	I	me	we	us
second person	you	you	you	you
third person	he/she/it	him/her/it	they	them

- Notice that the pronouns you and it stay the same, whether used in the subjective or objective roles.

Reflexive Pronouns

- A **reflexive pronoun** refers back to the subject of the sentence. Myself, himself, herself, itself, yourself, yourselves, ourselves and themselves are reflexive pronouns. For example:

  He hurt himself while playing volleyball.

  I don't like to praise myself.

  She is preparing herself for the long journey.

Fill in each blank with the correct pronoun.

1. Why are .... crying, Amit?
2. .... have submitted our notebooks.
3. I know that boy. .... is my neighbour.
4. Raman is absent because .... has a fever.
5. Look at the flowers. How beautiful .... look!
6. She did not attend the phone but I have sent .... a message.
7. He looked at .... in the mirror after putting on his new shirt.
8. The king loved his daughter very much. He never scolded ....

LISTENING AND SPEAKING

Listening

A. Listen to a description of Ninja warriors. Then mark the statements as true (T) or false (F).

1. Ninja warriors lived in China 200 years ago. ☐
2. Ninjas were not only fighters, they were spies too. ☐
3. Ninjas worked for themselves. ☐
4. Their main weapon was a sword. ☐
5. A ninja usually wore white clothes. ☐
6. Japanese people believe that Ninjas had magical powers. ☐

Speaking

B. Work in pairs. Spot the differences between the two pictures and describe them to your partner.

Picture A

Picture B

Pronunciation

C. Look at the table below and find out eight ways to say words with 'ough'.

like ***o*** in **go**	like ***oo*** in **too**	like ***off*** in offer	like ***uff*** in suffer	like ***ow*** in flower	like ***aw*** in saw	like ***a*** in above	like **up** in **up**
th**ough**	thr**ough**	c**ough**	r**ough**	pl**ough**	b**ough**t	bor**ough**	hicc**ough**
alth**ough**		tr**ough**	t**ough**	dr**ough**t	f**ough**t	thor**ough**	
d**ough**			en**ough**		th**ough**t	thor**ough** fare	
d**ough**nut					**ough**t		

D. Fill in each blank with the correct word from the box above.

1. We need .... to bake a cake.
2. He needs a medicine for his ....
3. I do not have .... money to buy a cycle.
4. The farmer uses his .... in the field.
5. The samurai warrior was a .... person.

WRITING

Find out how to make lemon ice tea and write down the recipe in simple steps. You can also draw or paste a picture for each step.

PROJECT 1

UNDERSTANDING CULTURE AND RITUALS

Traditional ceremonies are an important aspect of all cultures. In India, every community has its own unique ceremony held to celebrate special occasions. Such ceremonies are called rituals. Rituals help us bond with one another. They also pass on the tradition to the next generation.

Speak to your parents about one ritual that is held in your family or community. Write about the ritual on a sheet of chart paper or in a scrapbook. Follow the format given:

- The name of the ritual
- The occasion on which it is performed
- Guests invited
- Things required to perform it
- Steps followed
- Time taken
- Any special feast that follows the ritual

Paste pictures of the ceremony being performed to make your presentation colourful and attractive. Display your work in the class.

6 See It Through

Focusing on Goals

OBJECTIVES

In this chapter, we will:

- *read and understand a poem on dealing with difficult situations.*
- *learn about the literary device refrain.*
- *describe our goals through pictures and writing.*

WARM-UP

Imagine you are being constantly bullied by a classmate of yours. What would you do? How would you face the bully?

Work in pairs and discuss it. Then choose the option(s) which you think will help you face the problem.

- [ ] You decide to walk away every time.
- [ ] You ignore and avoid that classmate.
- [ ] You seek the help of your teacher.
- [ ] You ask your friend to help you.
- [ ] You decide you will not be afraid but be brave to face the bully.
- [ ] You tell the bully you are not afraid.
- [ ] You reason out with the bully and explain it to him that it is not right.

READING

Read this poem by Edgar Albert Guest to learn what we should do when we are facing troubles.

When you're up against a trouble,
Meet it squarely, face to face;
Lift your chin and set your shoulders,
Plant your feet and take a brace.
When it's vain to try to dodge it,
Do the best that you can do;
You may fail, but you may conquer,
See it through!

Black may be the clouds about you
And your future may seem grim,
But don't let your nerve desert you;
Keep yourself in fighting trim.
If the worst is bound to happen,
Spite of all that you can do,
Running from it will not save you,
See it through!

Even hope may seem but futile,
When with troubles you're beset,
But remember you are facing
Just what other men have met.
You may fail, but fall still fighting;
Don't give up, whate'er you do;
Eyes front, head high to the finish.
See it through!

squarely: directly
brace: a firm position
vain: useless; that does not produce the result you want
dodge: to move quickly to one side to avoid something; to avoid doing something
conquer: to defeat; to succeed in dealing with or doing something
grim: unpleasant and depressing
nerve: the courage to do something difficult or dangerous
desert: to go away; to leave
trim: in good condition
futile: having no purpose because there is no chance of success; pointless
beset: affected in an unpleasant or harmful way

COMPREHENSION

A. Fill in the blanks with words from the box to complete the paragraph.

futile feet fail trouble through dodge give running bravely

There are times in our life when we have to face .... When problems arise, we must face them .... We should stand with our .... firm on the ground. It may be difficult to .... the trouble and at times we may .... but we need to see it .... You cannot save yourself by .... away from the situation.

It is important to never .... up even when it seems .... You may fall but nevertheless you must always see it through.

B. Choose the correct option.

1. The poet says that we must
   a. run away from our troubles.
   b. brace ourselves and face the troubles bravely.
   c. hide in a dark place.
2. In the poem, 'lift your chin and set your shoulders' means
   a. preparing to deal with any kind of situation courageously.
   b. doing physical exercise.
   c. looking straight ahead.
3. The 'black clouds' refer to
   a. cloudy weather.
   b. heavy rainfall.
   c. a troublesome situation.
4. Even when you fail, the poet insists,
   a. you should continue to fight.
   b. you should give up.
   c. you should accept defeat.

C. Answer the questions briefly.

1. What does 'But don't let your nerve desert you' mean?
2. What is meant by the expression 'see it through'?
3. What is the main message of the poem?

Life Skills and Values

Focusing on the goal

1. What would you do if you were not scoring well in a subject repeatedly, even after trying your best?
2. Imagine you are a soldier who is climbing a mountain. While you are halfway through the climb, it starts to snow. What would you do?

VOCABULARY

Literary device: Refrain

In the poem, the line 'See it through' is repeated several times. How many times has it been repeated exactly?

Where is the line repeated: at the beginning of the stanza, in the middle of a stanza, or at the end of the stanza? Why do you think it has been repeated?

Some lines are usually repeated in a poem to give a musical effect to the poem, or to emphasise an idea.

When a line or some lines are repeated at the end of every stanza, we call it a refrain.

Read the poem and identify the refrain in it.

Because I am on a Holiday,
The bell is ringing for the last time!
The entire six weeks in front of me...
No more homework and getting up late!
Searching for all the old playmates,
Because I am on a holiday!

I wonder what the summer will bring?
Climbing trees or reading books,
Or simply collecting pebbles from the sand
When the sun is shining brightly...
Whatever the weather is, I shall be happy
Because I am on a holiday!

ACTIVITY

Have you ever dreamt of achieving something big—maybe doing well in academics, sports, or extra-curricular activities? What should you do to make your dream come true?

Express your goal through pictures and writing.

Draw at least four pictures to show how you will achieve your goal. Each picture should show a stage in your journey to your goal. Give captions to each picture saying what it shows.

....

....

....

....

....

....

....

....

MATHEMATICS

1 Place Value of Large Numbers

Learning Objectives

- To read, write and expand 5-digit and 6-digit numbers
- To round off numbers to the nearest 10, 100, 1000 and 10,000

Let's Get Started

We have studied about numbers from 1 to 9999 in earlier classes. Let us recall some important concepts.

Place Value: It is the value of digits in different places (ones, tens, hundreds and thousands) of a number.

Example: Consider the number 7286. The place value of each digit is shown here.

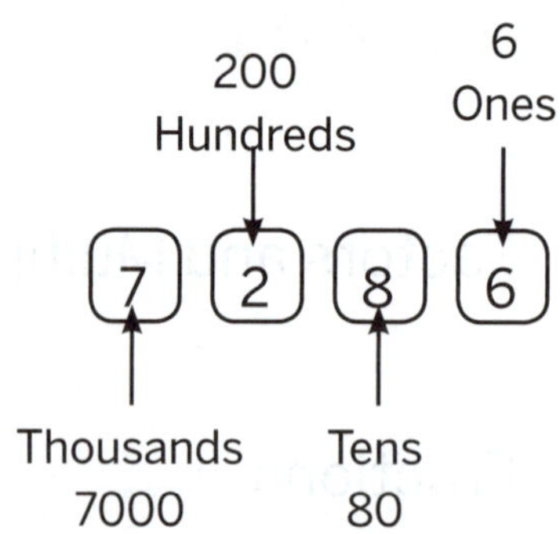

Expanded Form: It is the way in which a number is written to show the sum of the values of its digits. For example: 7286 = 7000 + 200 + 80 + 6

Number Name: It is the name of a number when written based on its place value. For example: Seven thousand two hundred eighty-six

Comparison of numbers: Two numbers can be compared by comparing the digits at different places of the numbers. For example, when we compare the numbers 825 and 2701, we find that 2701 is bigger than 825 as 2701 has 2 thousands whereas 825 has no thousands.

5-DIGIT NUMBERS

Read the following statements and recognize the numbers.

- Sachin Tendulkar scored 18,426 runs in 463 one-day internationals.
- Goa is the state with the least area of 3702 square kilometres, followed by Sikkim (7096) and then Tripura (10,492).

Could you read all the numbers?

The numbers 18,426 and 10,492 are numbers which have more than four digits.

We know that 9999 is the largest 4-digit number. On adding 1 to it, you will get the next number, that is, 10,000. Recall that adding 1 to a number will give its successor. Therefore, 10,000 is the successor of 9999. In other words, 9999 is the predecessor of 10,000. This number has five digits and the new place added is known as **ten thousands** place.

Th	H	T	O
9	9	9	9

	Th	H	T	O
1	0	0	0	0

→

TTh	Th	H	T	O
1	0	0	0	0

This place is known as **ten thousand** and it is written as **TTh**.

The numbers with five place values—ones, tens, hundreds, thousands and ten thousands—are known as 5-digit numbers.

Reading 5-digit Numbers

In order to make the reading easy, the digits are grouped into periods. The ones digit, the tens digit and the hundreds digits are grouped to form the ONES period. The thousands digit and the ten thousands digit are grouped to form the THOUSANDS period.

In order to read a number:

Step 1: Read the digits in the THOUSANDS period together.

Step 2: Then, read the digits in the ONES period.

Thousands period

TTh Th H T O

Ones period

Examples:

18,426 – Eighteen thousand four hundred twenty-six

45,608 – Forty-five thousand six hundred eight

Use of Commas in Writing 5-digit Numbers

Commas are used to distinguish the periods in a number. A comma is placed after the THOUSANDS period to distinguish it from the ONES period. In the number 18426, a comma has to be placed after 18, so the number is written as 18,426.

Examples:

64429 is written as 64,429.

10350 is written as 10,350.

Place Value and Expanded Form

The place value of the ten thousands digit is 10,000. The place values of other digits of 5-digit numbers can be written in the same way as written for the 4-digit numbers. Consider the examples given below.

TTh	Th	H	T	O
1	2	5	4	8
↓	↓	↓	↓	↓
10,000	2000	500	40	8

Number: **12,548**

Number name: Twelve thousand five hundred forty-eight

Expanded form: 10,000 + 2000 + 500 + 40 + 8

TTh	Th	H	T	O
9	0	0	0	9
↓	↓	↓	↓	↓
90,000	0	0	0	9

Number: **90,009**

Number name: Ninety thousand nine

Expanded form: 90,000 + 9

6-DIGIT NUMBERS

The largest 5-digit number is 99,999.
What number would you get if you add 1 to it?

9 + 1 = 10

99 + 1 = 100

999 + 1 = 1000

9999 + 1 = 10,000

99,999 + 1 = ________

On adding 1 to 99,999, you get the number **1,00,000**.

Note that the number has six digits. It is read as **One lakh**.

The new place is known as the **lakhs** place and it is denoted by **L**.

The lakhs place is a new period.

A comma is used after the lakhs digit to distinguish the digit from other periods.

Example: 1,00,000 – One lakh

1,15,264 – One lakh fifteen thousand two hundred sixty-four
7,06,990 – Seven lakh six thousand nine hundred ninety
2,00,008 – Two lakh eight
9,99,999 – Nine lakh ninety-nine thousand nine hundred ninety-nine

Thousands period (TTh Th)

L TTh Th H T O

Lakhs period (L) **Ones period** (H T O)

Place Value and Expanded Form

Consider the examples given below.

L	TTh	Th	H	T	O
3	4	8	1	2	9
↓	↓	↓	↓	↓	↓
3,00,000	40,000	8000	100	20	9

Number: **3,48,129**

Number name: Three lakh forty-eight thousand one hundred twenty-nine

Expanded form: 3,00,000 + 40,000 + 8000 + 100 + 20 + 9

L	TTh	Th	H	T	O
4	1	0	0	8	6
↓	↓	↓	↓	↓	↓
4,00,000	10,000	0	0	80	6

Number: **4,10,086**

Number name: Four lakh ten thousand eighty-six

Expanded form: 4,00,000 + 10,000 + 80 + 6

Exercise 1.1

1 **Write the numbers represented on the spike abacus and also write their number names.**

(a)

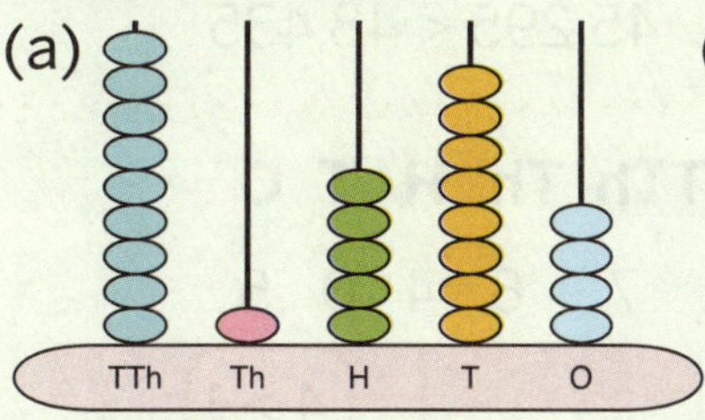

Number: ________

Number name: ________

(b)

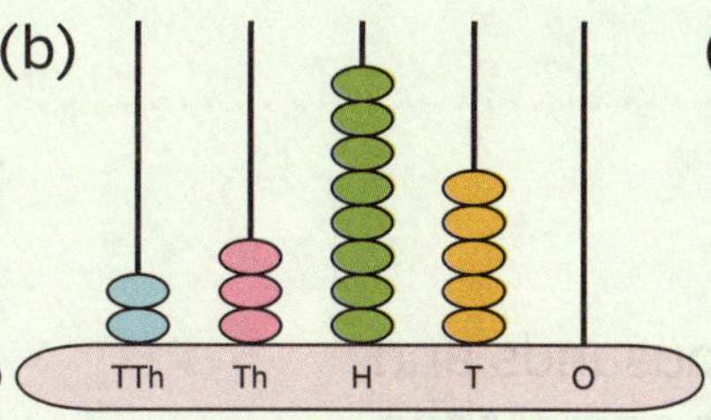

Number: ________

Number name: ________

(c)

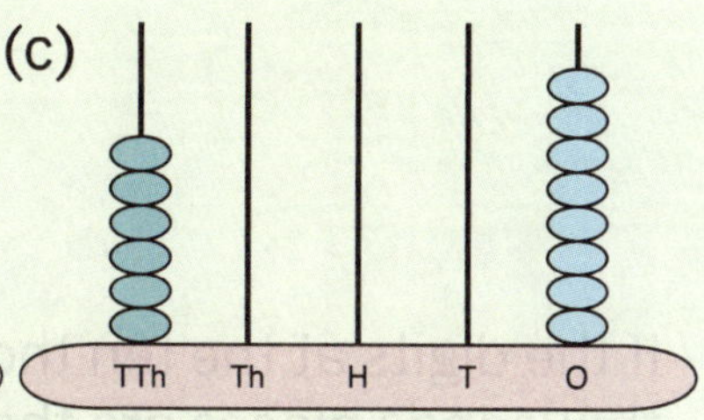

Number: ________

Number name: ________

2 **Write the numbers corresponding to the given number names and expanded forms.**

(a) Forty-five thousand six hundred ninety-five = ________

(b) 1,00,000 + 200 + 10 + 9 = ________

(c) Two lakh sixty thousand eighty-two = ________

(d) 80,000 + 6000 + 500 + 40 + 2 = ________

3 **Write the place value of the underlined digits.**

(a) 40,93<u>**6**</u> ________ (b) 9,<u>**2**</u>1,456 ________ (c) <u>**7**</u>,10,581 ________

(d) 8,12,<u>**7**</u>35 ________ (e) 1,27,3<u>**5**</u>5 ________ (f) 4,0<u>**9**</u>,453 ________

COMPARISON OF NUMBERS

Comparison of 5-digit Numbers

Two or more 5-digit numbers can be compared by comparing the digits at different places, starting from the ten thousands place to the ones place of the two numbers.

Example: The balance in the savings account of Aarav and Aarna are ₹17,895 and ₹21,435 respectively. Let us find who has more money.

TTh	Th	H	T	O
1	7	8	9	5

TTh	Th	H	T	O
2	1	4	3	5

1 < 2

Hence, 17,895 < 21,435
or 21,435 > 17,895
So, Aarna has more money in her account.

If the digits at the ten thousands place are the same, then compare the digits at the thousands place.

TTh	Th	H	T	O
4	5	2	9	5

5 < 8

TTh	Th	H	T	O
4	8	4	3	5

45,295 < 48,435

If the digits at the ten thousands and thousands places are the same, then compare the digits at the hundreds place.

TTh	Th	H	T	O
7	6	4	0	5

4 > 1

TTh	Th	H	T	O
7	6	1	8	2

76,405 > 76,182

If the digits at the ten thousands, thousands and hundreds places are the same, then compare the digits at the tens place.

TTh	Th	H	T	O
3	4	6	8	1

8 > 2

TTh	Th	H	T	O
3	4	6	2	9

34,681 > 34,629

If the digits at the ten thousands, thousands, hundreds and tens places are the same, then compare the digits at the ones place.

TTh	Th	H	T	O
9	3	7	8	4

4 < 6

TTh	Th	H	T	O
9	3	7	8	6

93,784 < 93,786

Brain Teaser

I am a 5-digit number. All my digits are the same and the sum of my digits is 40. Who am I?

Comparison of 6-digit Numbers

Consider the examples given below.

The number with the greater digit at the lakhs place is greater than the other number.

284351 507258

2 < 5

2,84,351 < 5,07,258

If the digits at lakhs place are the same in both the numbers, then compare the digits at the ten thousands place.

474056 438451

7 > 3

4,74,056 > 4,38,451

If the digits at the lakhs and ten thousands places are the same in both the numbers, then compare the digits at the thousands place.

362859 368754

2 < 8

3,62,859 < 3,68,754

If the digits at the lakhs, ten thousands and thousands places are the same in both the numbers, then compare the digits at the hundreds place.

172952 172450

9 > 4

1,72,952 > 1,72,450

If the digits at the lakhs, ten thousands, thousands and hundreds places are the same in both the numbers, then compare the digits at the tens place.

9 0 4 7 6 2   9 0 4 7 3 8

6 > **3**

9,04,762 > 9,04,738

If the digits at the lakhs, ten thousands, thousands, hundreds and tens places are the same in both the numbers, then compare the digits at the ones place.

7 0 0 0 0 2   7 0 0 0 0 8

2 < **8**

7,00,002 < 7,00,008

Brain Teaser

I am a 6-digit number. All my digits are the same and their sum is 8 more than 10. Who am I?

Exercise 1.2

1 Compare the numbers and put the appropriate symbol (>/</=).

(a) 45,251 ____ 6,81,320   (b) 10,024 ____ 10,204

(c) 8,00,756 ____ 7,84,245   (d) 92,475 ____ 85,784

(e) 6,87,999 ____ 1000   (f) 34,251 ____ 34,208

2 State whether the following are true (T) or false (F).

(a) 2,00,812 > Two lakh eight hundred two ☐

(b) 10,000 + 4000 + 20 + 1 < 10,000 + 400 + 90 + 8 ☐

(c) 4,00,000 + 50,000 + 3000 + 3 > 4,00,000 + 80,000 + 3000 + 30 + 3 ☐

(d) 6,00,000 + 600 + 30 + 7 < 6,00,000 + 6000 + 30 + 4 ☐

(e) 20,000 + 2000 + 1 > 20,000 + 200 + 10 ☐

ASCENDING AND DESCENDING ORDER

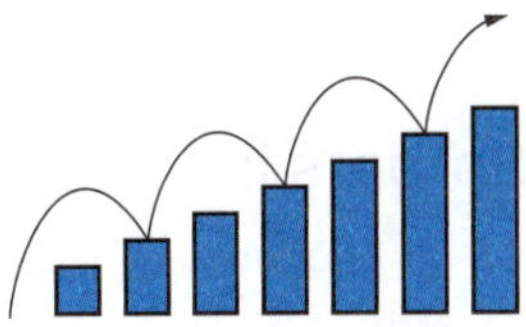

Ascending Order

→ Numbers when arranged from the smallest to the greatest are said to be in the ascending order.

Numbers when arranged from the greatest to the smallest are said to be in the descending order. ←

Descending Order

For example;

Ascending order – 10,245 17,405 17,845 38,712 72,125 72,807

Descending order – 8,14,545 6,54,747 4,05,751 4,05,324 2,09,007

GREATEST AND SMALLEST NUMBERS

How many 5-digit numbers are there?

How many 6-digit numbers are there?

There are a total of 90,000 5-digit numbers!

There are a total of 9,00,000 6-digit numbers!

Greatest and Smallest 5-digit Numbers

Arrange the digits in increasing order to get the smallest number. For example, by using the digits 1, 5, 7, 6 and 2 only once, the smallest number that can be formed is 12,567.

Arrange the digits in decreasing order to get the greatest number. For example, by using the digits 1, 5, 7, 6 and 2 only once, the greatest number that can be formed is 76,521.

Study the example given in the table. Also, fill in the empty boxes.

Digits	Smallest Number	Greatest Number
8, 3, 6, 7, 9	36,789	98,763
2, 1, 8, 4, 5		
9, 5, 8, 7, 4		

Note: If one of the digits is 0, then the smallest 5-digit number is obtained by first writing them in ascending order and then interchanging the digits at the ten thousands and thousands places.

Example: If the digits are 4, 8, 2, 0 and 3, then by arranging them in ascending order you get 02348. Interchange the positions of 0 and 2 such that the number we get is 20348. Therefore, 20,348 is the smallest 5-digit number that can be formed with the digits 4, 8, 2, 0 and 3.

The greatest 5-digit number can be obtained by writing the same numbers in descending order, that is, 84,320.

Greatest and Smallest 6-digit numbers

The steps to form the smallest 6-digit number from the given digits are the same as that of 5-digits numbers, that is, write the digits in ascending order. For example, the smallest 6-digit number that can be formed using the digits 5, 8, 9, 2, 4 and 1 is 1,24,589.

The greatest number is obtained by writing the digits in descending order, that is, 9,85,421.

Note: If one of the digits is 0, then the smallest 6-digit number is obtained by first writing them in ascending order and then interchanging the digits in lakhs and ten thousands places.

Example: If the digits are 7, 4, 8, 2, 0 and 3, then by arranging them in ascending order, you get 023478. Interchange the positions of 0 and 2 such that the number becomes 203478. Therefore, 2,03,478 is the smallest 6-digit number that can be formed with the digits 7, 4, 8, 2, 0 and 3.

The greatest 6-digit number can be obtained by writing the same numbers in descending order, that is, 8,74,320.

SUCCESSORS AND PREDECESSORS

The successor of a number is the number we get by adding 1 to the given number.

For example, if the number is 8,74,320, then the successor of the number will be 8,74,320 + 1 = 8,74,321.

The predecessor of a number is the number we get by subtracting 1 from the number.

For example, if the number is 8,74,320, then the predecessor of the number will be 8,74,320 – 1 = 8,74,319.

Exercise 1.3

1 Arrange the following numbers in ascending order.

(a) 12,054, 30,458, 20,105, 40,306 ____________

(b) 4,30,490, 2,41,475, 4,13,281, 4,30,087 ____________

(c) 75,802, 7,50,806, 7,50,608, 75,871 ____________

2 Tick (✓) the group of numbers in descending order.

(a) 8,51,407, 62,405, 30,112, 1845, 1001 ☐

(b) 72,924, 72,356, 89,425, 10,658, 10,012 ☐

(c) 6,75,852, 5,67,514, 4,06,489, 4,02,257, 2,56,200 ☐

3 Write the greatest and the smallest numbers that can be formed using all the digits only once.

	Digits	Smallest Number	Greatest Number
(a)	4, 5, 2, 3, 0, 8		
(b)	6, 9, 4, 7, 2, 8		
(c)	7, 4, 8, 0, 5, 6		
(d)	6, 1, 9, 2, 0, 3		
(e)	8, 1, 5, 2, 7		
(f)	0, 6, 4, 3, 8		

4 Write the successors and the predecessors of the following numbers.

(a) ________, 59768, ________ (b) ________, 23875, ________

(c) ________, 65793, ________ (d) ________, 35987, ________

5 Fill in the missing numerals to continue the pattern.

(a) 4,56,778; 4,56,779, ________, ________, ________.

(b) 1,23,244; 1,33,244, ________, ________, ________.

(c) 65,855; 65,955; ________, ________, ________.

(d) 5,36,400; 6,36,400; ________, ________, ________.

(e) 67,877; 77,878; ________, ________, ________.

ROUNDING OFF NUMBERS

Rounding off numbers to the nearest 10

Recall the method of rounding off numbers to the nearest 10. Consider the numbers as marked on a number line and find the nearest multiple of 10 on both sides of the number.

If the ones digit of a number is less than five, then it is rounded off to the ten to its left on the number line. If the ones digit is greater than or equal to 5, then it is rounded off to the ten to its right on the number line.

Example: The number 17 is rounded off to 20, whereas the number 12 will be rounded off to 10.

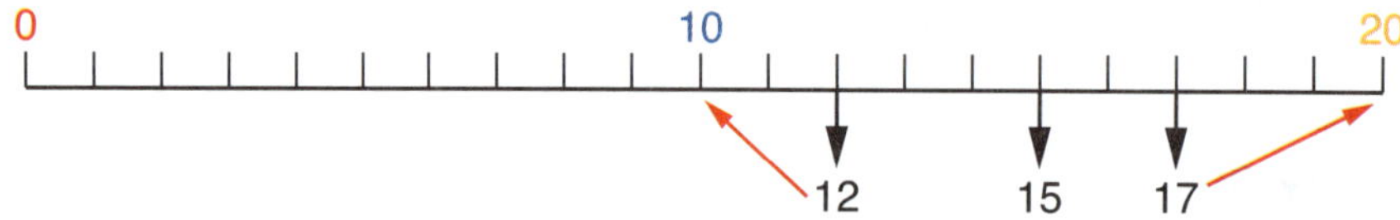

Consider some more examples.

Number	352	1028	95,789	42,135	1,35,245	5,19,022
Rounded off to 10	350	1030	95,790	42,140	1,35,250	5,19,020

Rounding off numbers to the nearest 100

Rule: If the last two digits of a number read together is less than 50, then round it off to the hundred to its left. If the last two digits of a number read together is greater than or equal to 50, then round it off to the hundred to its right.

Consider the example 365. Note that 65 is greater than 50. Therefore, 365 will be rounded off to 400. Similarly, 321 will be rounded off to 300 since 21 is less than 50.

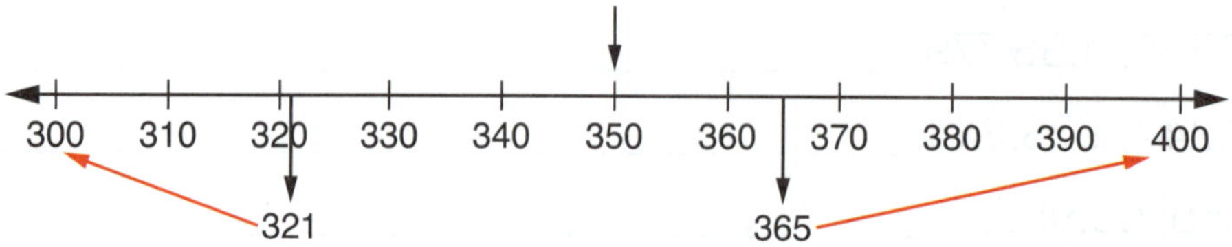

Consider some more examples.

Number	850	1028	95,789	42,135	1,35,245	5,19,028
Rounded off to 100	900	1000	95,800	42,100	1,35,200	5,19,000

Rounding off numbers to the nearest 1000

Rule: If the last three digits of a number read together is less than 500, then round it off to the thousand to its left. If the last three digits of a number read together is greater than or equal to 500, then round it off to the thousand to its right.

Consider the example 5198. Note that 198 is less than 500. Therefore, it will be rounded off to 5000, whereas 5712 will be rounded off to 6000 since 712 is greater than 500.

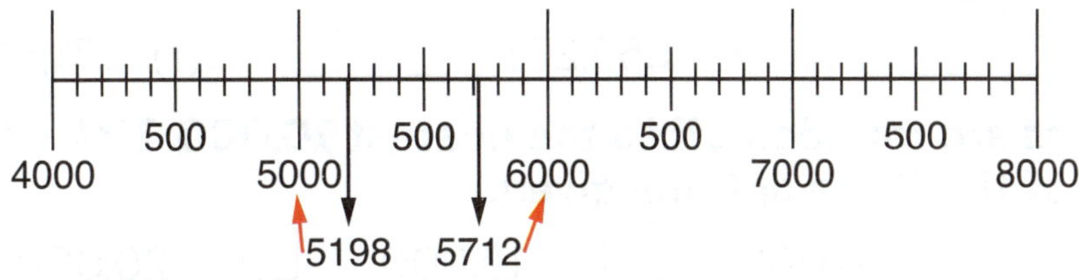

Consider some more examples.

Number	1850	7028	95,789	42,135	1,35,245	5,18,528
Rounded off to 1000	2000	7000	96,000	42,000	1,35,000	5,19,000

Rounding off numbers to the nearest 10,000

Rule: If the last four digits of a number read together is less than 5000, then round it off to the ten thousand to its left. If the last four digits of a number read together is greater than or equal to 5000, then round it off to the ten thousand to its right.

Example: 15,821 will be rounded off to 20,000 as 5821 is greater than 5000. 71,540 will be rounded off to 70,000 as 1540 is less than 5000.

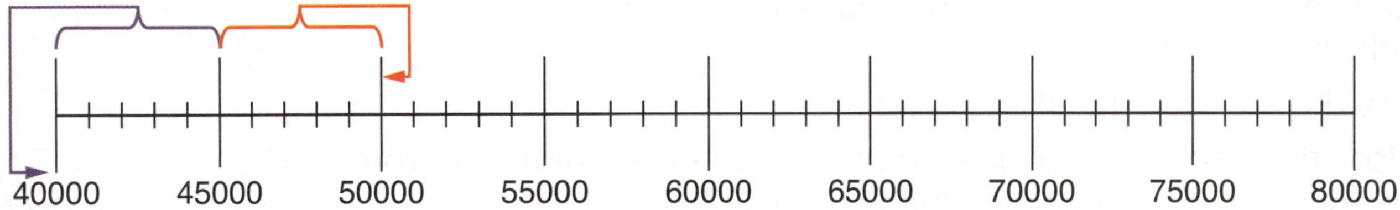

Consider some more examples.

Number	18,500	70,028	55,789	22,135	4,85,245	9,37,500
Rounded off to 10000	20,000	70,000	60,000	20,000	4,90,000	9,40,000

Exercise 1.4

1 **Round off the numbers to the nearest 100.**

(a) 51,202 ________ (b) 4,60,150 ________ (c) 82,500 ________

(d) 1,94,878 ________ (e) 6,71,012 ________ (f) 2,47,109 ________

2 **Round off the following numbers to the nearest 1000.**

(a) 78,124 ________ (b) 8,12,874 ________ (c) 80,945 ________

(d) 30,540 ________ (e) 1,55,201 ________ (f) 1,71,500 ________

3 **The numbers are rounded off to the nearest 10,000. Tick (✓) the correct option out of the three options given.**

(a) 18,136	–	10,000	☐	19,000	☐	20,000	☐
(b) 5,47,801	–	5,40,000	☐	5,50,000	☐	5,00,000	☐
(c) 53,851	–	53,000	☐	50,000	☐	60,000	☐
(d) 3,64,999	–	3,60,000	☐	3,80,000	☐	3,70,000	☐

4 **Round off the numbers in the following sentences to the nearest 10,000 and rewrite the sentences. The first one has been done for you.**

(a) In a stadium, there are 43,512 spectators.
In a stadium, there are about 40,000 spectators.

(b) The population of a city is 4,24,540.

(c) The distance from the planet Earth to Moon is 3,84,400 km.

ROMAN NUMERALS

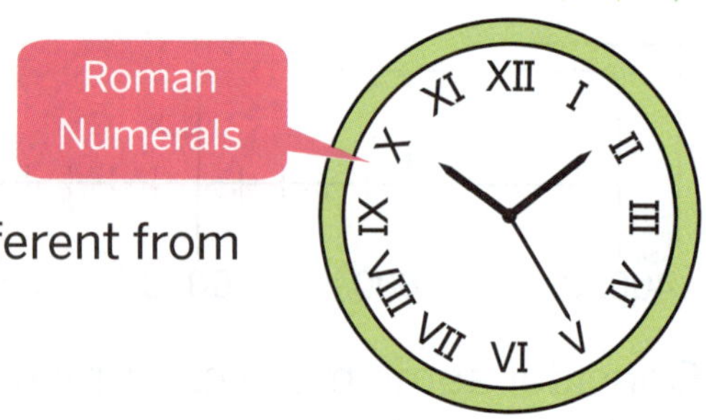

Look at the wall clock. How do you read time in this wall clock?

Are the numbers familiar to you?

Note that the numbers used in the wall clock are different from the numbers that we use, which are, 0, 1, 2, 3, 4 ...

The numbers used in the clock are given below.

I, II, III, IV, V, VI, VII, VIII, IX, X, XI, XII

These numbers are known as **Roman Numerals**. This way of writing numbers was used during the ancient Roman period.

The basic numerals are I, V, X, L, C, D and M.

Note*:* The Roman numeral system does not have 0.

Conversions between Roman numerals and Hindu-Arabic numbers

Roman numerals can be written in Hindu-Arabic numbers. The following table gives the basic symbols of Roman numerals and their value in Hindu-Arabic numbers.

There are certain rules to be followed in order to write different numbers using the basic symbols of Roman numerals.

Symbol	I	V	X	L	C	D	M
Value in Hindu-Arabic Number System	1	5	10	50	100	500	1000

Rules:

1

If a symbol is repeated, then its value is added as many times as it occurs.

Examples

III = 1 + 1 + 1 = 3

XX = 10 + 10 = 20

✗ IIII = 1 + 1 + 1 + 1 = 4 **Wrong!**

Explanation: If a smaller number is written to the left of a bigger number, then it has to be subtracted from the bigger number.

For example: IV = 5 – 1 = 4

IX = 10 – 1 = 9

Note: However, a symbol is not repeated more than three times.

Explanation: If a smaller number is written to the right of a bigger number, then it has to be added to the bigger number. For example: VI = 5 + 1 = 6

✗ VX = 10 – 5 = 5 **Wrong!**

Note: The symbol V is never written to the left of a bigger number.

2

Symbol of Smaller Value

I to the left of a number	I to the right of a number
Subtracted from the Number	Added to the Number
IV = 5 – 1 = 4	VI = 5 + 1 = 6
IX = 10 – 1 = 9	VIII = 5 + 1 + 1 + 1 = 8

XI = 10 + 1 = 11 XV = 10 + 5 = 15 XVI = 10 + 5 + 1 = 16

Forming Roman numbers from Hindu-Arabic Numbers

Expand the given number into tens and ones, and then form its Roman numeral by following the above rules.

Remember: The number should be expanded such that it can be written using the basic symbols of Roman numerals.

Examples:

14 = 10 + 4 = X + IV = XIV

19 = 10 + 9 = X + IX = XIX

37 = 10 + 10 + 10 + 7 = X + X + X + VII = XXXVII

Forming Hindu-Arabic numbers from Roman Numbers

Examples:

XXI = X + X + I = 10 + 10 + 1 = 21

XXXIV = X + X + X + IV = 10 + 10 + 10 + 4 = 34

XVI = X + V + I = 10 + 5 + 1 = 16

XXIII = X + X + I + I + I = 10 + 10 + 1 + 1 + 1 = 23

Exercise 1.5

Write the missing Roman numerals in the following table representing Roman numerals from 1 to 39.

Number System Table				
1 – I	9 – IX	17 – XVII	25 – XXV	33 – ______
2 – II	10 – X	18 – XVIII	26 – XXVI	34 – ______
3 – III	11 – XI	19 – ______	27 – ______	35 – ______
4 – IV	12 – ______	20 – XX	28 – XXVIII	36 – ______
5 – V	13 – XIII	21 – XXI	29 – ______	37 – ______
6 – VI	14 – ______	22 – ______	30 – XXX	38 – ______
7 – VII	15 – XV	23 – XXIII	31 – XXXI	39 – ______
8 – VIII	16 – XVI	24 – ______	32 – ______	

Revision Exercise

1 Write the numbers corresponding to the number names. Also, write the expanded forms.

(a) Forty-three thousand two hundred fifty-seven = ________

Expanded form: ____________________________

(b) Six lakh seventy-four thousand six hundred thirty-five = ________

Expanded form: ____________________________

(c) Ninety nine thousand twenty-nine = ________

Expanded form: ____________________________

(d) One lakh five thousand sixty-one = ________

Expanded form: ____________________________

(e) Eight lakh forty thousand four hundred ninety-nine = ________

Expanded form: ____________________________

(f) Twenty-two thousand nine = ________

Expanded form: ____________________________

2 Write the numbers in expanded form and also write the number names.

(a) 84,852 = ______________

Number name: ______________

(b) 52,901 = ______________

Number name: ______________

(c) 61,509 = ______________

Number name: ______________

(d) 3,17,656 = ______________

Number name: ______________

(e) 7,01,025 = ______________

Number name: ______________

(f) 9,93,100 = ______________

Number name: ______________

3 Write the place value of the underlined digits in the numbers.

(a) 5**6**,253 = ______________

(b) **4**5,069 = ______________

(c) 13,**7**07 = ______________

(d) 2,10,5**8**4 = ______________

(e) 9,**1**5,024 = ______________

(f) **2**,68,009 = ______________

4 **Write the smallest number and the greatest number that can be formed using the given digits only once.**

	Digits	Smallest Number	Greatest Number
(a)	3, 9, 1, 7, 8		
(b)	2, 8, 5, 4, 0, 6		
(c)	6, 1, 4, 2, 5, 3		

5 **Compare the numbers and place the appropriate symbols (</>/=).**

(a) 50,825 _____ 50,809
(b) 83,687 _____ 87,256
(c) 4,21,045 _____ 5,21,036
(d) 79,891 _____ 79,897
(e) 2,14,523 _____ 2,57,025
(f) 6012 _____ 76,009
(g) 40,000 _____ 4,00,000
(h) 6,75,036 _____ 6,75,031

6 **Fill in the blanks.**

(a) Round off 10,593 to the nearest 100 = __________

(b) Round off 7,53,126 to the nearest 10,000 = __________

(c) Round off 21,846 to the nearest 1000 = __________

(d) Round off 4, 17,605 to the nearest 10 = __________

7 **Write the missing numbers.**

(a) 18 = __________
(b) 12 = __________
(c) XXVI = __________
(d) 23 = __________
(e) 39 = __________
(f) IX = __________
(g) 30 = __________
(h) XXXIV = __________
(i) XV = __________

HOTS (Higher Order Thinking Skills)

Identify the wrong notations of Roman numerals. Also, correct them.

IIII = 4
XIX = 19
VX = 5
XXXIIIV = 38
XX = 20
XI = 11
XXXVIV = 39
VII = 7
IIX = 8
IX = 9
XIIIX = 17
XXIX = 29
XIXI = 22
VI = 6

2 Adding and Subtracting Large Numbers

Learning Objectives

- To add 5-digit and 6-digit numbers
- To subtract 5-digit and 6-digit numbers
- To solve word problems on addition and subtraction

Let's Get Started

Addition of two or more numbers can be carried out by adding the digits at different places and carrying them forward, if required. Add the ones first, then the tens, then the hundreds and then the thousands.

Example: Find out the total weight of the two bags of rice weighing 1255 kg and 3785 kg respectively.

Total weight = 1255 + 3785

Therefore, the total weight of the two bags of rice is 5040 kg.

	Th	H	T	O
	1	1	1	
	1	2	5	5
+	3	7	8	5
	5	0	4	0

ADDITION OF 5-DIGIT NUMBERS

Steps to add 5-digit numbers:

1. Add ones. Regroup the ones to tens, if required, and carry it forward to the tens place.
2. Add tens. Regroup the tens to hundreds, if required, and carry it forward to the hundreds place.

NUMBER FACTS

1 ten = 10 ones
1 hundred = 10 tens = 100 ones
1 thousand = 10 hundreds
1 ten thousand = 10 thousands
1 lakh = 10 ten thousands

3. Add hundreds. Regroup the hundreds to thousands, if required, and carry it forward to the thousands place.
4. Add thousands. Regroup the thousands to ten thousands, if required, and carry it forward to the ten thousands place.

Example: Look at some more examples. Complete the last one.

The cost of a television is ₹12,750 and that of a refrigerator is ₹14,999. Find out the total cost.

Total cost = 12,750 + 14,999

$$\begin{array}{r} 1\ {}^{1}2\ {}^{1}7\ 5\ 0 \\ +\ 1\ 4\ 9\ 9\ 9 \\ \hline 2\ 7\ 7\ 4\ 9 \\ \hline \end{array}$$

Solution: *Therefore, the total cost is ₹27,749.*

Examples: Look at some more examples. Complete the last one.

$$\begin{array}{r} {}^{1}4\ 9\ 1\ 4\ 3 \\ +\ 3\ 4\ 2\ 5\ 4 \\ \hline 8\ 3\ 3\ 9\ 7 \\ \hline \end{array} \qquad \begin{array}{r} 1\ 2\ {}^{1}1\ {}^{1}3\ 6 \\ +\ 3\ 4\ 2\ 9\ 4 \\ \hline 4\ 6\ 4\ 3\ 0 \\ \hline \end{array} \qquad \begin{array}{r} 2\ 9\ 9\ 9\ 9 \\ +\ 6\ 0\ 2\ 0\ 1 \\ \hline \\ \hline \end{array}$$

Note: Sometimes you may have to regroup the ten thousands into lakhs and write the answer in lakhs. For example, addition of the smallest 5-digit number and the greatest 5-digit number, that is, 10,000 + 99,999. The answer is 1,09,999.

L	TTh	Th	H	T	O
	1	0	0	0	0
+	9	9	9	9	9
1	0	9	9	9	9

ADDITION OF 6-DIGIT NUMBERS

The same procedure of adding 5-digit numbers can be extended to 6-digit numbers too. Here, you have digits in lakhs position also.

NUMBER FACTS

1 lakh = 10 ten thousands
1 ten lakh = 10 lakhs

Example: A farmer borrowed money from a bank worth ₹1,78,975 and ₹1,56,306 from another bank. Find out the total amount borrowed by him.

Total amount = 1,78,975 + 1,56,306

$$\begin{array}{rrrrrrr} & {}^{1}1 & {}^{1}7 & {}^{1}8 & 9 & {}^{1}7 & 5 \\ + & 1 & 5 & 6 & 3 & 0 & 6 \\ \hline & 3 & 3 & 5 & 2 & 8 & 1 \\ \hline \end{array}$$

Therefore, the total loan amount is ₹3,35,281.

Consider some more examples on the addition of 6-digit numbers. Complete the last one.

$$\begin{array}{rrrrrrr} & {}^{1}4 & 3 & {}^{1}6 & {}^{1}2 & {}^{1}8 & 6 \\ + & 3 & 9 & 1 & 9 & 5 & 7 \\ \hline & 8 & 2 & 8 & 2 & 4 & 3 \\ \hline \end{array} \qquad \begin{array}{rrrrrrr} & 5 & {}^{1}0 & {}^{1}8 & {}^{1}9 & {}^{1}9 & 9 \\ + & 1 & 5 & 9 & 8 & 0 & 4 \\ \hline & 6 & 6 & 8 & 8 & 0 & 3 \\ \hline \end{array} \qquad \begin{array}{rrrrrrr} & 3 & 7 & 8 & 3 & 4 & 2 \\ + & 1 & 6 & 5 & 6 & 7 & 5 \\ \hline & & & & & & \\ \hline \end{array}$$

Exercise 2.1

1 Add the following numbers and write the answers.

(a) 15,245 + 22,829 = ____________ (b) 54,826 + 18,194 = ____________

(c) 1,54,826 + 6,18,194 = ____________ (d) 5,22,584 + 3,48,452 = ____________

2 Find the sum of the following.

(a) 4,30,789 + 23,118 + 7803 + 4500 = ____________

(b) 8991 + 4660 + 1,12,332 + 10,004 = ____________

(c) 90,000 + 23,678 + 66,554 + 1,54,678 = ____________

(d) 2,23,456 + 12,345 + 45 + 6 = ____________

3 Add the numbers and write the missing digits.

(a) 15,750 + 1,21,825 = 1__7__7__ (b) 99,999 + 1,99,999 = __999__ __

(c) 87,486 + 98,254 = __857__ __ (d) 10,000 + 1,00,000 = 1__00__0

WORD PROBLEMS ON ADDITION

Example 1: The savings of Preeti for two years are ₹58,750 and ₹69,950 respectively. Find her total savings.

Amount saved in the first year = ₹58,750

Amount saved in the second year = ₹69,950

Total amount saved by Preeti = 58750 + 69950

$$\begin{array}{r} {}^{1}5\ {}^{1}8\ {}^{1}7\ 5\ 0 \\ +\ 6\ 9\ 9\ 5\ 0 \\ \hline 1\ 2\ 8\ 7\ 0\ 0 \\ \hline \end{array}$$

Therefore, the total amount saved by Preeti is ₹1,28,700.

Example 2: A small water reservoir had 1,62,915 litres of water. If 2,47,624 litres of water was added into the reservoir due to heavy rain, find the total quantity of water in the reservoir.

Total quantity of water
= 1,62,915 + 2,47,624

$$\begin{array}{r} {}^{1}1\ {}^{1}6\ {}^{1}2\ 9\ 1\ 5 \\ +\ 2\ 4\ 7\ 6\ 2\ 4 \\ \hline 4\ 1\ 0\ 5\ 3\ 9 \\ \hline \end{array}$$

Therefore, the total quantity of water is 4,10,539 litres.

Exercise 2.2

Solve the following word problems.

1. A bicycle company sold 75,890 bicycles in May and 63,458 bicycles in June. Find out the total number of bicycles sold in the two months.
2. A man sold his two houses for ₹4,58,000 and ₹3,75,000 respectively. Find out the total amount of money he got.
3. One water tank has the capacity of 42,812 litres and the other water tank has the capacity of 2,14,560 litres. Find out the total capacity of the two tanks.

4. The weight of one truck is 15,450 kg and the weight of another truck is 38,658 kg. Find the weight of the two trucks.

SUBTRACTION

Subtraction of two numbers involves finding the difference between them. In order to subtract two numbers, follow the steps given below.

1. Write the smaller number below the bigger number and subtract the ones. Borrow a ten from the tens place if there are not sufficient ones to subtract.
2. Subtract tens. Borrow a hundred from the hundreds place if there are not sufficient tens to subtract.
3. Subtract hundreds. Borrow a thousand from the thousands place if there are not sufficient hundreds to subtract.
4. Subtract thousands.

Example: There are 1584 students in a school, out of which 695 are boys. Find out the number of girls.

Total number of students = 1584

Number of boys = 695

Therefore, number of girls = 1584 – 695

Therefore, there are 889 girls in the school.

		14	17	
	0	4	7	14
	~~1~~	~~5~~	~~8~~	~~4~~
–		6	9	5
		8	8	9

SUBTRACTION OF 5-DIGIT NUMBERS

Two 5-digit numbers can be subtracted by the same method as we followed for subtracting 4-digit numbers. The steps are:

1. Subtract ones. Borrow a ten from the tens place, if required.
2. Subtract tens. Borrow a hundred from the hundreds place, if required.
3. Subtract hundreds. Borrow a thousand from the thousands place, if required.
4. Subtract thousands. Borrow a ten thousand from the ten thousands place, if required.
5. Subtract ten thousands.

	8	7	3	5	7
–	4	5	2	0	5
	4	2	1	5	2

Example: In a stadium, there are 27,587 people out of which 12,478 are men. Find out the number of women in the stadium.

Total number of people = 27,587

Number of men = 12,478

Therefore, number of women
= 27,587 – 12,478

$$\begin{array}{r} 2\ 7\ 5\ \overset{7}{\cancel{8}}\ \overset{17}{\cancel{7}} \\ -\ 1\ 2\ 4\ 7\ 8 \\ \hline 1\ 5\ 1\ 0\ 9 \\ \hline \end{array}$$

Borrow one ten as there are not sufficient ones

Therefore, there are 15,109 women in the stadium.

Verification: The answer can be checked by adding the total number of men and women, and verifying whether the sum gives the total number of people or not.

$$\begin{array}{r} 1\ 5\ 1\ \overset{1}{0}\ 9 \\ +\ 1\ 2\ 4\ 7\ 8 \\ \hline 2\ 7\ 5\ 8\ 7 \\ \hline \end{array}$$

Consider some more examples. Observe that the numbers are borrowed from different places.

$$\begin{array}{r} \overset{3}{\cancel{4}}\ \overset{12}{\cancel{2}}\ \overset{6}{\cancel{7}}\ \overset{14}{\cancel{4}}\ 5 \\ -\ 2\ 7\ 0\ 6\ 1 \\ \hline 1\ 5\ 6\ 8\ 4 \\ \hline \end{array} \qquad \begin{array}{r} 4\ 7\ \overset{4}{\cancel{5}}\ \overset{9}{\cancel{10}}\ \overset{10}{\cancel{0}} \\ -\ 2\ 4\ 3\ 5\ 1 \\ \hline 2\ 3\ 1\ 4\ 9 \\ \hline \end{array} \qquad \begin{array}{r} 7\ \overset{4}{\cancel{5}}\ \overset{11}{\overset{1}{\cancel{2}}}\ \overset{10}{\overset{0}{\cancel{1}}}\ \overset{17}{\cancel{7}} \\ -\ 4\ 1\ 5\ 6\ 9 \\ \hline 3\ 3\ 6\ 4\ 8 \\ \hline \end{array}$$

SUBTRACTION OF 6-DIGIT NUMBERS

In order to subtract two 6-digit numbers, subtract the ones, tens, hundreds, thousands, ten thousands and lakhs digits of both the numbers respectively. Borrow the numbers, if required.

Example: If ₹4,75,356 is withdrawn from a savings bank account having ₹7,96,487, then find the balance amount in the account.

Total amount in the account =

Amount withdrawn =

Therefore, the balance amount =

$$\begin{array}{r} 7\ 9\ 6\ 4\ 8\ 7 \\ -\ 4\ 7\ 5\ 3\ 5\ 6 \\ \hline 3\ 2\ 1\ 1\ 3\ 1 \\ \hline \end{array}$$

Therefore, the balance in the account in the bank is ₹3,21,131.

Verification:

$$\begin{array}{r} 3\ 2\ 1\ 1\ 3\ 1 \\ +\ 4\ 7\ 5\ 3\ 5\ 6 \\ \hline 7\ 9\ 6\ 4\ 8\ 7 \\ \hline \end{array}$$

Verification: The amount withdrawn and the balance amount together should be equal to the total amount.

Consider some more examples. Observe the borrowing of numbers from different places while subtracting.

$$\begin{array}{r} 3\,\overset{3}{\cancel{4}}\,\overset{12}{\cancel{2}}\,7\,\overset{4}{\cancel{5}}\,\overset{14}{\cancel{4}} \\ -\,1\,2\,9\,6\,3\,5 \\ \hline 2\,1\,3\,1\,1\,9 \\ \hline \end{array} \qquad \begin{array}{r} \overset{8}{\cancel{9}}\,\overset{\overset{17}{\cancel{7}}}{\cancel{8}}\,\overset{14}{\cancel{4}}\,\overset{5}{\cancel{6}}\,\overset{18}{\cancel{8}}\,7 \\ -\,5\,9\,6\,2\,9\,1 \\ \hline 3\,8\,8\,3\,9\,6 \\ \hline \end{array}$$

Subtraction of Numbers with Zeroes

If the population of a town is 5,75,000 and out of them 3,42,321 are females, then find out the number of males.

Carry out the subtraction.

$$\begin{array}{r} 5\,7\,\overset{4}{\cancel{5}}\,\overset{10}{\cancel{0}}\,0\,0 \\ -\,3\,4\,2\,3\,2\,1 \\ \hline \\ \hline \end{array} \rightarrow \begin{array}{r} 5\,7\,\overset{4}{\cancel{5}}\,\overset{\overset{9}{\cancel{10}}}{\cancel{0}}\,\overset{10}{\cancel{0}}\,0 \\ -\,3\,4\,2\,3\,2\,1 \\ \hline \\ \hline \end{array} \rightarrow \begin{array}{r} 5\,7\,\overset{4}{\cancel{5}}\,\overset{\overset{9}{\cancel{10}}}{\cancel{0}}\,\overset{\overset{9}{\cancel{10}}}{\cancel{0}}\,\overset{10}{\cancel{0}} \\ -\,3\,4\,2\,3\,2\,1 \\ \hline \\ \hline \end{array} \rightarrow \begin{array}{r} 5\,7\,\overset{4}{\cancel{5}}\,\overset{\overset{9}{\cancel{10}}}{\cancel{0}}\,\overset{\overset{9}{\cancel{10}}}{\cancel{0}}\,\overset{10}{\cancel{0}} \\ -\,3\,4\,2\,3\,2\,1 \\ \hline 2\,3\,2\,6\,7\,9 \\ \hline \end{array}$$

Therefore, there are 2,32,679 males in the city.

Exercise 2.3

1 Subtract the following and write the missing digits.

(a) 28,786 – 14,547 = 14__3__

(b) 2,80,560 – 1,76,410 = 1__4__5__

(c) 4,05,009 – 3,09,007 = 96__ __ __

(d) 94,312 – 76,400 = 1__9__2

(e) 7,19,876 – 4,45,948 = __7__9__ __

(f) 45,280 – 17,571 = 2__7__9

2 Subtract the following.

(a) $\begin{array}{r} 3\,3\,8\,1\,0 \\ -\,1\,9\,8\,2\,4 \\ \hline \\ \hline \end{array}$ (b) $\begin{array}{r} 7\,5\,6\,2\,4\,3 \\ -\,4\,1\,8\,5\,7\,8 \\ \hline \\ \hline \end{array}$ (c) $\begin{array}{r} 4\,2\,3\,5\,3\,1 \\ -\,1\,3\,7\,8\,4\,5 \\ \hline \\ \hline \end{array}$

WORD PROBLEMS ON SUBTRACTION

Example 1: The capacity of a water tank is 88,245 litres. If 42,983 litres of water is taken out, then how much water will be left in the tank?

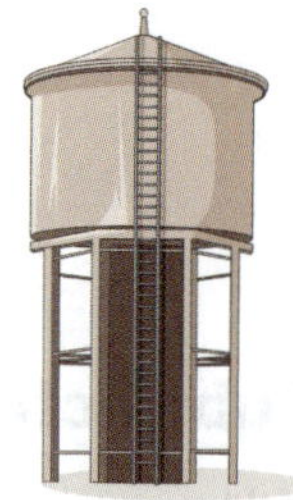

Capacity of the water tank =	8 8 2 4 5 (borrowing: 7, 11, 14)
Amount of water taken out =	− 4 2 9 8 3
Remaining water = 88,245 − 42,983	4 5 2 6 2

Therefore, 45,262 litres of water will be left in the tank.

Example 2: If the total weight of two loads is 1,87,416 kg and one of them weighs 84,568 kg, then find out the weight of the other load.

Weight of two loads =	1 8 7 4 1 6 (borrowing: 6, 13, 10, 16)
Weight of one of them =	− 8 4 5 6 8
Weight of the other =	1 0 2 8 4 8

Therefore, the weight of the other load is 1,02,848 kg.

Exercise 2.4

Solve the following word problems.

1. In an election, Candidate A secured 58,625 votes and Candidate B secured 34,970 votes. Find out by how many votes Candidate A won the election.
2. If the sum of two numbers is 1,67,410 and one of the numbers is 90,980, then find the other number.
3. A car manufacturing company produced 8,75,134 cars during a month and sold 7,89,052 cars. Find out the number of cars left unsold.

4. The odometer readings in two passenger cars are 75,862 km and 62,994 km. Find out the difference in the readings.

Revision Exercise

1 Solve the given addition and subtraction problems.

(a) 20,900 + 1029 + 7896 + 121 + 80 = ________

(b) The difference between 45,673 and 90,800 is = ________

(c) 89,021 + 1,23,786 – 56,783 = ________

2 Choose the appropriate operation symbols (+/–) to get the given answers.

(a) 47,890 ____ 21,850 = 26,040

(b) 4,05,312 ____ 3,15,874 = 7,21,186

(c) 15,987 ____ 32,205 = 48,192

(d) 9,36,478 ____ 7,85,912 = 1,50,566

3 Solve the following word problems.

(a) A person withdrew ₹51,280 and ₹1,18,750 from his account. How much amount has he withdrawn in all?

(b) An auto driver had to pay an amount of ₹1,50,875 to a bank. He has already paid ₹34,680 to the bank. How much does he still have to pay?

(c) Two tanks are filled with water. One tank has the capacity of 35,879 litres while the other tank has the capacity of 42,008 litres. Find out the total capacity of the two tanks.

(d) In an election, a candidate got 3,75,421 votes and his opponent won by 28,328 votes. Find out the number of votes secured by the opponent.

(e) The weights of two containers are 4,56,789 kg and 3,05,314 kg respectively. Find out their total weight.

(f) The population of a town is 6,28,347. If 4,87,264 are females, find the number of males.

3 Multiplication of Numbers

Learning Objectives

- To multiply a 3-digit number by a 3-digit number
- To solve word problems on the multiplication of numbers

Let's Get Started

In multiplication, two numbers are multiplied to get a product.

$$18 \times 12 = 216$$

18 → ***Multiplier*** 12 → ***Multiplicand*** 216 → ***Product***

For example, in $18 \times 12 = 216$, 18 and 12 are known as factors.

$$\begin{array}{r} 6\ 5 \\ \times\ 3\ 4 \\ \hline \square\square\square \\ +\ \square\square\square\square \\ \hline \square\square\square\square \end{array}$$

PROPERTIES OF MULTIPLICATION

(1) The product remains the same even if the order of the numbers multiplied is same.

Example: $9 \times 12 = 108$; $12 \times 9 = 108$

(2) The product of any number with one is the number itself.

Example: $19 \times 1 = 19$; $1 \times 243 = 243$

(3) The product of any number and zero is zero.

Example: $34 \times 0 = 0$; $987 \times 0 = 0$

(4) The product remains the same even when the grouping of numbers is changed.

$(5 \times 2) \times 6 = 60$ $5 \times (2 \times 6) = 60$ $6 \times (5 \times 2) = 60$

Exercise 3.1

Fill in the blanks:

(1) $6543 \times$ ________ $= 0$

(2) ________ $\times 879 = 879$

(3) $65 \times 34 = 34 \times$ ________

(4) $23 \times 15 \times 56 = 56 \times 23 \times$ ________

(5) $7890 \times 0 =$ ________

(6) $300 \times 222 = 222 \times$ ________

(7) $564 \times 321 \times$ ________ $= 321 \times 250 \times 564$

(8) $134 \times 0 =$ ________

(9) ________ $\times 1 = 475$

(10) $15{,}322 \times$ ________ $= 0$

MULTIPLICATION BY 10, 100 AND 1000

To multiply a number by 10, write a zero to the right of the number.

For example, $45 \times 10 = 450$; $16 \times 10 = 160$; $306 \times 10 = 3060$

Similarly, when you multiply a number by 100, write two zeros to the right of the number.

For example, $32 \times 100 = 3200$; $675 \times 100 = 67{,}500$; $560 \times 100 = 56{,}000$

Continuing the same pattern how many zeros will you add to the number when you multiply by 1000?

Write the following products.

$18 \times 1000 =$ ____; $49 \times 1000 =$ ____; $524 \times 1000 =$ ____

To multiply a number by 30, 300 or 3000

First multiply the given number by 3 and add the corresponding number of zeros.

Example: Find the products: $34 \times 30 =$ ___; $34 \times 300 =$ ___; $34 \times 3000 =$ ___

Let us first find the product 34×3, which is 102.

Now add the corresponding number of zeros after 102, we get,

$34 \times 30 = 1020$; $34 \times 300 = 10{,}200$; $34 \times 3000 = 1{,}02{,}000$

Exercise 3.2

Fill in the blanks:

(1) $3 \times 400 =$ ________

(2) $32 \times 60 =$ ________

(3) $181 \times 1000 =$ ________

(4) $5 \times 300 =$ ________

(5) $355 \times 20 =$ ________

(6) $75 \times$ ________ $= 750$

(7) $16 \times 4000 =$ ________

(8) $35 \times$ ________ $= 35,000$

(9) $100 \times$ ________ $= 10,000$

(10) $590 \times 500 =$ ________

MULTIPLICATION OF A 3-DIGIT NUMBER BY A 3-DIGIT NUMBER

Recall the steps followed to multiply a 3-digit number by a 2-digit number.

The same steps can be followed for the multiplication of a 3-digit number by a 3-digit number. Consider the example 245×124.

Step 1: Multiply by ones.

$245 \times 4 = 980$

		1	2	
		2	4	5
	×	1	2	④
		9	8	0
	□	□	□	□
+ □	□	□	□	□
□	□	□	□	□

Step 2: Multiply by tens.

$245 \times 20 = 4,900$

			1	
		2	4	5
	×	1	②	4
		9	8	0
	4	9	0	0
+ □	□	□	□	□
□	□	□	□	□

Step 3: Multiply by hundreds.

245 × 100 = 24,500

```
      2  4  5
   ×  ①  2  4
      9  8  0
   4  9  0  0
+ 2  4  5  0  0
  _  _  _  _  _
```

Step 4: Add the products.

```
        2  4  5
     ×  1  2  4
        9  8  0
   ²4  9  0  0
+ ¹2  4  5  0  0
   3  0  3  8  0
```

Therefore, $245 \times 124 = 30{,}380$

Note: During the multiplication process of 245×124, we got three numbers: 980, 4900 and 24,500. These numbers are known as **partial products**. Their sum will give the product of the numbers 245 and 124.

Multiplication of Numbers with One of the Digits as Zero

If one of the digits of a factor being multiplied is 0, that is, either in the ones or in the tens place, then the multiplication with that number can be avoided, as any number multiplied by zero is always 0. Consider the examples given below.

The ones digit is 0.

```
        5  4  8
     ×  1  2  0
        0  0  0    → This step can be skipped.
  1  0  9  6  0
+ 5  4  8  0  0
  6  5  7  6  0
```

The tens digit is 0.

```
           4  5  3
        ×  8  0  5
        2  2  6  5
     0  0  0  0  0    → This step can be skipped.
+ 3  6  2  4  0  0
  3  6  4  6  6  5
```

The ones digit and the tens digit are 0.

$$
\begin{array}{r}
845 \\
\times\ 400 \\
\hline
0000 \\
00000 \\
+\ 338000 \\
\hline
338000
\end{array}
$$

Both these steps can be skipped. (the rows 0000 and 00000)

Exercise 3.3

Multiply the following numbers using the standard multiplication method and write their products.

1. 135 × 281 = ______ 2. 424 × 356 = ______ 3. 485 × 278 = ______
4. 815 × 600 = ______ 5. 414 × 612 = ______ 6. 386 × 254 = ______
7. 232 × 304 = ______ 8. 198 × 110 = ______ 9. 214 × 546 = ______
10. 727 × 508 = ______

MULTIPLICATION – EXPANDED FORM OF A NUMBER

Consider the multiplication methods given below for each multiplication fact.

$$
\begin{array}{r}
42 \\
\times\ 14 \\
\hline
168 \\
+\ 420 \\
\hline
588
\end{array}
$$

In this method, one of the numbers is split up into tens and ones. Here, 14 is written as 10 + 4. The number 10 is multiplied by 42 and the number 4 is multiplied by 42. Their partial products are added to get the answer. 42 × 14 = (42 × 10) + (42 × 4)

×	10	4
42	420	168

→

$$
\begin{array}{r}
420 \\
+168 \\
\hline
588
\end{array}
$$

Note that in both the methods, the product is the same, that is,
42 × 14 = (42 × 10) + (42 × 4) = 588.

ESTIMATION OF PRODUCTS

Estimation is the method of finding an approximate value but not the exact value. It can be done by rounding off the digits to either the nearest tens or the hundreds.

(a) *If a box has 145 apples, then find out roughly how many apples will be there in 12 boxes.*

Total number of apples in 12 boxes = 145×12

145 can be rounded off to the ones place, which will make it 150.
Therefore, $150 \times 12 = 1800$.

Therefore, there are roughly 1800 apples in 12 boxes.

(b) *If a ticket costs ₹389, then estimate the cost of 17 tickets.*

Round off 389 to the hundreds place, which will be ₹400. Estimate the cost of 17 tickets, which will make it ₹400 × 17 = ₹6800.

Therefore, 17 tickets will cost roughly ₹6800.

NUMBER PATTERNS - MULTIPLICATION

Consider the following number patterns.

(a) 2, 4, 6, 8, 10, 12, 14, 16

Rule: Products of multiplication table of 2, starting with $2 \times 1 = 2$

(b) 6, 18, 30, 42, 54, 66, 78

Rule: Multiplication factors of 6 alternatively starting from 6

(c) 50, 100, 150, 200, 250

Rule: Multiplication of the number 10 by 5, 10, 15, 20, 25 and so on

(d) 1, 4, 9, 16, 25, 36

Rule: Multiplication of a number by itself, that is, $1 \times 1 = 1$, $2 \times 2 = 4$, $3 \times 3 = 9$, $4 \times 4 = 16$ and so on

PROBLEM SOLVING

In real life, we come across many problems for which we need to find solutions. In order to solve problems, we need to understand the problem and try to find out ways to solve it. So, it is important to develop problem-solving skills by being systematic.

Example 1: A train ticket from Bangalore to Mysore costs ₹120. If there are 315 passengers, then find out the total fare collected from them.

$$\begin{array}{r} 3\ 1\ 5 \\ \times\ 1\ 2\ 0 \\ \hline 0\ 0\ 0 \\ 6\ 3\ 0\ 0 \\ +\ 3\ 1\ 5\ 0\ 0 \\ \hline 3\ 7\ 8\ 0\ 0 \end{array}$$

Cost of one ticket from Bangalore to Chennai = ₹120

Total number of passengers on the train = 315

Total amount collected = ₹120 × 315

Therefore, the total fare collected is ₹37,800.

Example 2: A rice packet of company A costs ₹850 and a rice packet of company B costs ₹750. Arjun buys 150 rice packets of company A and 120 rice packets of company B. Find the total amount spent by Arjun.

$$\begin{array}{r} 8\ 5\ 0 \\ \times\ 1\ 5\ 0 \\ \hline 4\ 2\ 5\ 0\ 0 \\ 8\ 5\ 0\ 0\ 0 \\ \hline 1\ 2\ 7\ 5\ 0\ 0 \end{array}$$

Cost of one rice packet of company A = ₹850

Cost of 150 such packets = ₹850 × 150

Therefore, the total cost of 150 rice packets of company A is ₹1,27,500.

$$\begin{array}{r} 7\ 5\ 0 \\ \times\ 1\ 2\ 0 \\ \hline 1\ 5\ 0\ 0\ 0 \\ 7\ 5\ 0\ 0\ 0 \\ \hline 9\ 0\ 0\ 0\ 0 \end{array}$$

Cost of one rice packet of company B = ₹750

Cost of 120 such rice packets = ₹750 × 120

Therefore, the total cost of 120 rice packets of company B is ₹90,000.

Hence, the total amount spent by Arjun = ₹1,27,500 + 90,000 = ₹2,17,500

Exercise 3.4

1. Ramesh sells electrical appliances. He purchased 135 iron boxes at the rate of ₹780 each. Find the amount he spent to purchase the iron boxes for his shop.
2. A 250 ml pack of juice contains 165 calories. How many calories are there in 103 such juice packs?

3. A store in a mall ordered 493 mugs each worth ₹216. What is the amount to be paid by the store for the mugs?
4. Find the weight of 568 rice bags if each bag weighs 143 kg.
5. A bus can accommodate 106 people. How many people can be accommodated in 348 such buses?
6. A news article contains 652 words. The editorial section of a newspaper received 447 such articles. Find the total number of the words in all the articles.
7. A hotel charges ₹575 for a meal on weekdays and ₹650 during weekends. Find the amount paid by the customers if 318 people visited the hotel during weekdays and 724 visited during weekends.
8. Manu sold 384 movie tickets of different classes. He sold 284 tickets at ₹315 and the remaining at ₹405. Find the total amount collected by him.

Revision Exercise

1. **Fill in the missing digits.**

(a) $898 \times 214 = 1\_\_\_2\_\_\_72$ (b) $124 \times 151 = 1\_\_\_\_\_\_\_\_\_\_\_\_$

(c) $614 \times 257 = 15\_\_\_\_\_\_\_\_\_8$ (d) $18\_\_\_ \times 612 = 1{,}12{,}608$

2. **Tick (✓) the best estimate.**

(a) 291×19	7000	6000	3000
(b) 605×308	2,00,000	1,80,000	3,00,000

3. **Solve the following word problems.**

(a) In a town, there are 145 elderly people. The government gives ₹500 per month as pension to each one of them. Find out the total amount of money received as pension by these elderly people in a month.

(b) If a school charges ₹1285 as bus fees for 1 month, then find out the amount for 3 months, 6 months and 9 months.

4 Division

Learning Objectives

- Divide up-to 4 digit numbers by 1- or 2- digit numbers
- Identify the patterns in dividing by 10, 100, 1000
- To solve word problems on division of numbers

Let's Get Started

Division is equal sharing or equal grouping.

Terms used in division
Dividend: The number that is being divided
Divisor: The number which divides the dividend
Quotient: The number of times the divisor will go into the dividend
Remainder: The leftover number after long division, which is less than the divisor

Dividend = (Divisor × Quotient) + Remainder

Quotient → 154

Divisor ← 3) 464 → Dividend

```
      154
   ┌─────
 3 │ 464
   - 3
   ───
     16
   - 15
   ────
      14
      12
   ────
       2
```

2 → Remainder

MULTIPLICATION TABLES

11 Table	12 Table	13 Table	14 Table	15 Table	16 Table
1 × 11 = 11	1 × 12 = 12	1 × 13 = 13	1 × 14 = 14	1 × 15 = 15	1 × 16 = 16
2 × 11 = 22	2 × 12 = 24	2 × 13 = 26	2 × 14 = 28	2 × 15 = 30	2 × 16 = 32
3 × 11 = 33	3 × 12 = 36	3 × 13 = 39	3 × 14 = 42	3 × 15 = 45	3 × 16 = 48
4 × 11 = 44	4 × 12 = 48	4 × 13 = 52	4 × 14 = 56	4 × 15 = 60	4 × 16 = 64
5 × 11 = 55	5 × 12 = 60	5 × 13 = 65	5 × 14 = 70	5 × 15 = 75	5 × 16 = 80
6 × 11 = 66	6 × 12 = 72	6 × 13 = 78	6 × 14 = 84	6 × 15 = 90	6 × 16 = 96
7 × 11 = 77	7 × 12 = 84	7 × 13 = 91	7 × 14 = 98	7 × 15 = 105	7 × 16 = 112
8 × 11 = 88	8 × 12 = 96	8 × 13 = 104	8 × 14 = 112	8 × 15 = 102	8 × 16 = 128
9 × 11 = 99	9 × 12 = 108	9 × 13 = 117	9 × 14 = 126	9 × 15 = 135	9 × 16 = 144
10 × 11 = 110	10 × 12 = 120	10 × 13 = 130	10 × 14 = 140	10 × 15 = 150	10 × 16 = 160
11 × 11 = 121	11 × 12 = 132	11 × 13 = 143	11 × 14 = 154	11 × 15 = 165	11 × 16 = 176
12 × 11 = 132	12 × 12 = 144	12 × 13 = 156	12 × 14 = 168	12 × 15 = 180	12 × 16 = 192

Properties of Division

1) Any number divided by 1 is the number itself. Example: 587 ÷ 1 = 587
2) Any number divided by the same number is always 1. Example: 3456 ÷ 3456 = 1
3) Zero divided by any number is always zero. Example: 0 ÷ 152 = 0

Exercise 4.1

Fill in the blanks.

1. 265 ÷ 1 = _______
2. 579 ÷ 579 = _______
3. 315 ÷ 315 = _______
4. 0 ÷ 2010 = _______
5. 3618 ÷ 1 = _______
6. 0 ÷ 32514 = _______

Division by Short Method

(a) Consider 248 ÷ 2
248 = 2 hundreds + 4 tens + 8 ones
2 hundreds divided by 2 = 1 hundred
4 tens divided by 2 = 2 tens
8 ones divided by 2 = 4 ones
Therefore, 248 ÷ 2 = 1 hundred + 2 tens + 4 ones = 124

$$2 \overline{)248} \quad 124$$

Q = 124; R = 0

(b) Consider 76 ÷ 2
76 = 7 tens + 6 ones
7 tens divided by 2 = 3 tens with 1 ten remaining
We know that 1 ten = 10 ones
Therefore the total number of ones = 10 ones + 6 ones = 16 ones
16 ones divided by 2 = 8 ones
Therefore, 76 ÷ 2 = 3 tens + 8 ones = 38

$$2 \overline{)76} \quad 38$$

Q = 38; R = 0

Exercise 4.2

Divide the following using short method.

1. 33 ÷ 3 = _______
2. 404 ÷ 4 = _______
3. 963 ÷ 3 = _______
4. 95 ÷ 5 = _______
5. 72 ÷ 4 = _______
6. 75 ÷ 3 = _______
7. 96 ÷ 6 = _______
8. 52 ÷ 2 = _______
9. 64 ÷ 2 = _______

LONG DIVISION

Division of 3-digit number by a single digit number When the Remainder is Zero

Consider 648 ÷ 4

Step 1: Divide hundreds digit i.e, 6 by 4. It gives 1 as quotient leaving 2 as remainder.
Write 1 in the hundreds place of the quotient. Write 4 under the hundreds place of the dividend and subtract that is,

$$\begin{array}{r} 1 \\ 4\overline{)648} \\ -4 \\ \hline 2 \end{array}$$

6 – 4 = 2. Write 2 as shown.

Step 2: Bring down 4 from tens place of the dividend. Now divide 24 by 4. It gives 6 as the quotient with remainder 0. Write 6 in the tens place of the quotient.

$$\begin{array}{r} 16 \\ 4\overline{)648} \\ -4 \\ \hline 24 \\ -24 \\ \hline 0 \end{array}$$

Step 3: Now bring down 8 from the ones place of the dividend. Divide 8 by 4, we get 2 as the quotient with remainder 0. Write 2 in the ones place of the quotient.

$$\begin{array}{r} 162 \\ 4\overline{)648} \\ -4 \\ \hline 24 \\ -24 \\ \hline 08 \\ -8 \\ \hline 0 \end{array}$$

∴ 648 ÷ 4 = 162. Here, Divisor = 4, Dividend = 648, Quotient = 162, Remainder = 0

(Divisor × Quotient) + Remainder = Dividend

(4 × 162) + 0 = 648

When the Remainder is Other Than Zero

Here are some examples where the remainder is not zero.

$$\begin{array}{r} 426 \\ 2\overline{)853} \\ -8 \\ \hline 05 \\ -4 \\ \hline 13 \\ -12 \\ \hline 1 \end{array}$$

Quotient = 426;
Remainder = 1
(426 × 2) + 1 = 853

$$\begin{array}{r} 98 \\ 5\overline{)493} \\ -45 \\ \hline 43 \\ -40 \\ \hline 3 \end{array}$$

Quotient = 98;
Remainder = 3
(98 × 5) + 3 = 493

Division of 4-digit number by a single digit number

Follow the same steps of dividing a 3-digit number by a single digit number and extend it to 4-digit numbers. Few examples are given below.

```
   509
  ____
3)1527
 -15↓↓
  ----
   027
 - 027
  ----
     0
```

We have placed 0 in the tens place as we have borrowed 2 digits at a time.

Quotient = 509;
Remainder = 0
(509 × 3) + 0 = 1527

```
  1231
  ____
4)4925
 -4↓
  ----
  09
 -  8
  ----
    12
 -  12
  ----
    05
 -   4
  ----
     1
```

Quotient = 1231;
Remainder = 1
(1231 × 4) + 1 = 4925

Exercise 4.3

Divide the following by long division method.

1. 575 ÷ 5 = ______
2. 345 ÷ 3 = ______
3. 128 ÷ 2 = ______
4. 4456 ÷ 4 = ______
5. 2198 ÷ 7 = ______
6. 6515 ÷ 5 = ______
7. 3232 ÷ 8 = ______
8. 5760 ÷ 8 = ______
9. 7128 ÷ 6 = ______

DIVISION BY 10, 100 AND 1000

Division by 10

Observe the quotients and the remainders of numbers when divided by 10. Can you see a relation between the digits at different places of the given number and its quotient and remainder?

Number	Quotient	Remainder
35	3	5
370	37	0
547	54	7
7009	700	9

Note that when we divide a number by 10, the remainder is the digit at the ones place of the number. The rest of the digits form the quotient. For example, in 124 ÷ 10, 4 is the remainder and 12 is the quotient.

Division by 100

Can you extend the above method while dividing a number by 100?
The digit at the ones and the tens places form the remainder, while the rest of the digits form the quotient. For example, in 718 ÷ 100, 18 is the remainder and 7 is the quotient.

Number	Quotient	Remainder
135	1	35
718	7	18
1182	11	82

Division by 1000

If we divide a number by 1000, then the digits at the ones, tens and hundreds places form the remainder while the rest of the digits form the quotient.

Number	Quotient	Remainder
1835	1	835
9718	9	718
10182	10	182

Exercise 4.4

1. **Find the quotient and remainder on division by 10 for the following:**

   (a) 2 (b) 999 (c) 1074

2. **Find the quotient and remainder on division by 100 for the following:**

   (a) 759 (b) 624 (c) 3738

3. **Find the quotient and remainder on division by 1000 for the following:**

   (a) 2277 (b) 6520 (c) 71,085

DIVISION OF A 2-DIGIT NUMBER BY A 2-DIGIT NUMBER

When the Remainder is Zero

A crayon box can contain only 12 crayons. If there are 84 crayons, then find out the number of boxes required to pack them.

In a box, 12 crayons can be packed.

So, the number of boxes required to pack 84 crayons = 84 ÷ 12

Find how many times the divisor 12 can go into the dividend 84.

$$\begin{array}{r} 7 \\ 12\overline{)84} \\ -84 \\ \hline 0 \end{array}$$

Therefore, the number of boxes required to pack 84 crayons is 7.

12 times table
1 × 12 = 12
2 × 12 = 24
3 × 12 = 36
4 × 12 = 48
5 × 12 = 60
6 × 12 = 72
7 × 12 = 84
8 × 12 = 96
9 × 12 = 108
10 × 12 = 120

When the Remainder is Other Than Zero

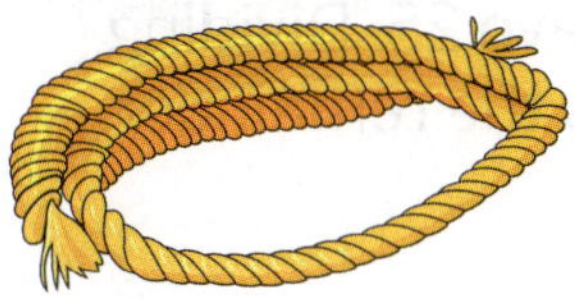

If a rope of length 94 metres is cut into 13 equal parts, then find the length of each part. Will there be some extra piece of rope left?

$13 \times 6 = 78$

$13 \times 7 = 91$

$13 \times 8 = 104$

A rope of length 94 metres is cut into 13 equal parts.
So, the length of each part is 94 ÷ 13.

Note: List the multiplication facts of 13 until the product crosses 94. Then, choose the one immediately before 94. Here, it is $13 \times 7 = 91$.

$$\begin{array}{r} 7 \\ 13\overline{)94} \\ -91 \\ \hline 3 \end{array}$$

Therefore, the length of each part is 7 metres and 3 metres of rope is left.

Common Error!

$$\begin{array}{r} 61 \\ 13\overline{)94} \\ -78 \\ \hline 16 \\ -13 \\ \hline 3 \end{array}$$

Exercise 4.5

Divide the following in your notebook and write the quotient and the remainder in each case.

1. 75 ÷ 16 2. 90 ÷ 15 3. 96 ÷ 32 4. 45 ÷ 18 5. 63 ÷ 19 6. 88 ÷ 36

DIVISION OF A 3-DIGIT NUMBER BY A 2-DIGIT NUMBER

When the Remainder is Zero

If a sack of rice weighs 25 kg, then how many such sacks can be made from 525 kg of rice?

Quantity of rice in one sack = 25 kg

So, the number of sacks that can be made from 525 kg of rice = 525 ÷ 25

Step 1: As the digit 5 at the hundreds place of the dividend is less than 25, take the hundreds and the tens digits together, that is, 52. 2 times 25 gives 50, leaving 2 as the remainder.

```
      2
25)525
  -50
    2
```

Step 2: Now, 2 is smaller than 25. So, bring down the digit 5. Now, you have 25. Dividing 25 by 25 gives 1, leaving 0 as the remainder.

```
      21
25)525
  -50↓
    25
  - 25
     0
```

Therefore, 21 sacks can be made out of 525 kg of rice such that each sack has 25 kg of rice.

Consider some more examples. Complete the last example.

```
     34           48
14)476       15)720       36)648
  -42↓         -60↓
    56          120
  - 56         -120
     0            0
```

When the Remainder is Other Than Zero

In the long division method, if the remainder is less than the divisor, then further division can't be carried out. For example, let us see what happens when 876 is divided by 35.

Step 1: As the digit 8 at the hundreds place is less than 35. Take the hundreds and tens digits together, that is, 87. 2 times 35 gives 70, leaving 17 as the remainder. Note that $35 \times 3 = 105$, which is more than 87.

$$\begin{array}{r} 2 \\ 35\overline{)876} \\ -70 \\ \hline 17 \end{array}$$

Step 2: The number 17 is smaller than 35. So, bring down the number 6. Now, you have 176. 5 times 35 gives 175, leaving 1 as the remainder. Here, 1 is smaller than the divisor.

$$\begin{array}{r} 25 \\ 35\overline{)876} \\ -70\downarrow \\ \hline 176 \\ -\ 175 \\ \hline 1 \end{array}$$

Therefore, the quotient of this division is 25 and the remainder is 1.

Some more examples are given below. Complete the last example.

$$\begin{array}{r} 31 \\ 12\overline{)376} \\ -36\downarrow \\ \hline 16 \\ -\ 12 \\ \hline 4 \end{array} \qquad \begin{array}{r} 26 \\ 27\overline{)720} \\ -54\downarrow \\ \hline 180 \\ -162 \\ \hline 18 \end{array} \qquad \begin{array}{r} \\ 43\overline{)896} \end{array}$$

Exercise 4.6

Divide the following in your notebook. Write the quotient and the remainder in each case.

1. $875 \div 24$
2. $741 \div 54$
3. $925 \div 37$
4. $832 \div 64$
5. $276 \div 16$
6. $563 \div 12$

DIVISION OF A 4-DIGIT NUMBER BY A 2-DIGIT NUMBER

When the Remainder is Zero

If an amount of ₹4410 is to be distributed equally among 15 workers, then find out the amount each worker would get.

Total amount to be distributed among the workers = ₹4410

Number of workers = 15

So, the amount of money that each one would get = ₹4410 ÷ 15

Step 1: As the thousands digit, that is, 4 is less than 15, take the thousands and the hundreds digits together, that is, 44. 2 times 15 gives 30, leaving 14 as the remainder.

```
        2
   ______
15 ) 4410
    - 30
    ----
     14
```

Step 2: Bring down 1 from the tens place. The new dividend is 141. 9 times 15 gives 135, leaving 6 as the remainder.

```
        29
   _______
15 ) 4410
    - 30↓
    -----
     141
   - 135
    -----
       6
```

Step 3: Now, bring down 0 from the ones place. The new dividend is 60. 4 times 15 gives 60, leaving 0 as the remainder.

```
        294
   ________
15 ) 4410
    - 30↓
    -----
     141
    -135↓
    -----
       60
   -   60
    -----
        0
```

Therefore, each worker would get ₹294.

Note: If the thousands and the hundreds digits taken together is less than the divisor, then consider the tens digit also.

When the Remainder is Other Than Zero

Consider some examples where the remainder is not 0.

```
        154
   ________
17 ) 2627
    - 17↓
    -----
       92
    -  85↓
    -----
       77
    -  68
    -----
        9
```

```
        94
   _______
32 ) 3020
    -288↓
    -----
      140
    - 128
    -----
       12
```

Common Errors!

```
          41                 401
     ________           ________
✗ 15 ) 6019         15 ) 6019      ✓
      - 60↓↓             - 60↓↓
      ------             ------
          19                 19
      -   15             -   15
      ------             ------
           4                  4
```

Here, digits 1 and 9 are brought down one after the other. If two digits are brought down simultaneously, then you should place 0 in the quotient before dividing further.

Note that (15 × 41) + 4 = 619 which is not equal to the dividend, whereas (15 × 401) + 4 = 6019 which is equal to the dividend.

Exercise 4.7

Divide the following in your notebook. Write the quotient and remainder in each case.

1. $2487 \div 42$
2. $8916 \div 73$
3. $5608 \div 24$
4. $8075 \div 19$
5. $7490 \div 35$
6. $8382 \div 64$

DIVISION FACTS FOR A GIVEN MULTIPLICATION FACT

Recall that you can write two division facts for a given multiplication fact. Consider the following example.

Multiplication fact: $12 \times 5 = 60$

Division facts: $60 \div 12 = 5$ and $60 \div 5 = 12$

The division concept can be used to find missing factors in a multiplication fact.

Example:

$12 \times$ ______ $= 552$

Here, the other factor can be found by dividing 552 by 12.

Therefore, the other factor is 46, that is, $12 \times 46 = 552$.

$$\begin{array}{r} 46 \\ 12\overline{)552} \\ -48\downarrow \\ \hline 72 \\ -\ \ 72 \\ \hline 0 \end{array}$$

Exercise 4.8

Calculate and fill in the missing numbers.

1. ____ $\times 11 = 858$
2. $25 \times$ ____ $= 2000$
3. ____ $\times 26 = 8970$
4. $49 \times$ ____ $= 7448$
5. $14 \times$ ____ $= 1414$
6. ____ $\times 99 = 6237$
7. ____ $\times 64 = 2368$
8. ____ $\times 74 = 6068$
9. $39 \times$ ____ $= 4641$

ESTIMATION OF QUOTIENTS

In some cases, you may have to roughly estimate the quotient in order to get an idea of the quantity.

If for a birthday party you are charged ₹5934 for 23 people, then by estimating the quotient, you can get to know the cost of food for one person.

Estimation can be done by rounding off the dividend and the divisor. For example, in

5934 ÷ 23, 5934 can be rounded off to 6000 and 23 can be rounded off to 20.

6000 ÷ 20 gives the estimated quotient, that is, 300. So, the food for one person roughly costs ₹300.

Example: If 18 T-shirts cost ₹2810, then estimate the cost of each T-shirt.

2810 can be rounded off to 3000 and 18 can be rounded off to 20.

In 3000 ÷ 20, the quotient is 150.

So, a T-shirt will roughly cost ₹150 each.

WORD PROBLEMS

1. A class of 27 students went for a picnic, and the total expenditure of the trip came out to be ₹4968. Find out the amount to be paid by each student.

```
      184
   ______
27 ) 4968
   - 27
   ------
     226
   - 216
   ------
      108
   -  108
   ------
        0
```

Number of students that went for the picnic = 27

Total expenditure = ₹4968

Amount to be paid by each student = ₹4968 ÷ 27

Therefore, each student would have to pay ₹184.

2. What is the least number that should be subtracted from 5974 to make it exactly divisible by 71?

```
       84
   ______
71 ) 5974
   - 568
   ------
      294
   -  284
   ------
       10
```

In order to find the answer, first divide 5974 by 71.

The remainder is 10. In order to make 5974 completely divisible by 71, you need to subtract 10 from 5974.

So, 5964 ÷ 71 = 84.

Exercise 4.9

Solve the following word problems.

1. A person sold 18 balloons for ₹90. What is the cost of 1 balloon?
2. Anu donated 98 items equally to 14 social service centers. Find the number of items donated by her to each center.
3. There are 893 sweets in 47 boxes. How many sweets are there in each box?
4. Find the number of books on each row if 83 rows can hold 4482 books.
5. An educational trip was announced and ₹9765 was collected from 63 students. How much did each student pay?
6. A typist types 957 words in 33 minutes. How many words can the typist type in a single minute?
7. What is the weight of a rack if 117 racks weigh 5967 kg?

PROBLEM SOLVING USING MULTIPLE OPERATIONS

In order to solve word problems, you first need to read the given information and identify the unknown values. Then, you need to identify the operation to be used in order to find the unknown values. Finally, you need to verify your answer. The four basic operations are addition (+), subtraction (−), multiplication (×) and division (÷).

Sometimes you may have to use more than one operation in order to solve a given problem. In such cases, identify both the operations and solve the problem.

Consider the following example.

Rahul bought 8 eggs, 6 bananas and 5 kg of rice from a shop. He gave ₹300 to the shopkeeper. Find out the bill amount and also find out the balance amount that Rahul should get back.

Item	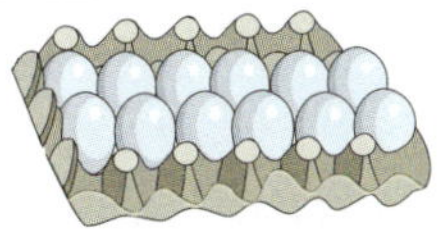		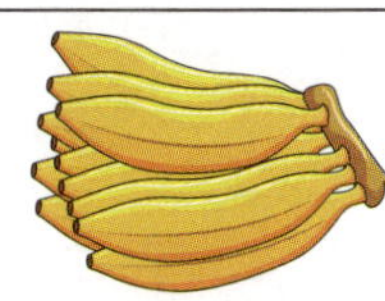
Price (₹)	1 dozen eggs (12 eggs) = ₹48	1 kg of rice = ₹35	1 dozen bananas = ₹36

Price per unit (₹)	₹48 ÷ 12 = ₹4	₹35	₹36 ÷ 12 = ₹3

The cost of 8 eggs = 8 × 4 = ₹32

The cost of 6 bananas = 6 × 3 = ₹18

The cost of 5 kg of rice = 35 × 5 = ₹175

Therefore, the total cost of all the items = 32 + 18 + 175 = ₹225

Item	Price (₹)
8 eggs	32
6 bananas	18
5 kg of rice	175

Rahul paid ₹300 and the bill amounted to ₹225.

Therefore, the amount that Rahul should get back is 300 – 225 = ₹75.

Exercise 4.10

1. **Use the data given in the example on the previous page and solve the following problem.**

   Reeta purchased 4 eggs, 9 bananas and 10 kg of rice. She gave ₹400 to the shopkeeper. Find out the amount that she should get back.

2. Kunal has to wrap 250 gifts to distribute to the guests in her daughter's birthday party. In the first hour he wraps 50 gifts, in the second hour he wraps 75 gifts and in the third hour he wraps 100 gifts. Now he has only few minutes left to finish this task. How many more gifts he has to wrap in the remaining time?

3. Shashank has ₹500. He went to the market and bought 2 kg of potatoes at ₹40 per kg. Then he went to a grocery shop and bought 5 kg of sugar at ₹35 per kg. From there he went to a toy shop and wanted to buy a toy of worth ₹250. Is the amount left with him sufficient to buy the toy? If not, how much more money does he need?

Revision Exercise

1 Divide the numbers by long division method and find out the quotient and the remainder.

(a) divisor = 14; dividend = 364; remainder = ______; quotient = ______

(b) divisor = 31; dividend = 2697; remainder = ______; quotient = ______

(c) divisor = 19; dividend = 6560; remainder = ______; quotient = ______

2 Calculate and write the missing numbers.

(a) ________ × 12 = 216

(b) 61 × ________ = 5185

(c) 93 × ________ = 2232

(d) ________ × 34 = 3434

3 Tick (✓) the problems wherein the remainder is not 0.

(a) 265 ÷ 25

(b) 3750 ÷ 50

(c) 1249 ÷ 15

(d) 896 ÷ 10

(e) 5602 ÷ 100

(f) 4970 ÷ 10

4 Estimate the quotients.

(a) 7170 ÷ 15 (b) 8124 ÷ 22 (c) 3645 ÷ 81 (d) 9089 ÷ 89 (e) 415 ÷ 12

5 Solve the following word problems.

(a) A gift coupon of ₹ 9250 was given to all the 37 employees of a company to be shared equally. Calculate how much amount each employee got.

(b) The product of the age of two persons is 2438 years. If one of them is 46 years old, then find out the age of the other person.

(c) What number should be subtracted from 3700 in order to make it exactly divisible by 24?

(d) If 25 kg of rice cost ₹1125, then find the cost of 14 kg of rice.

(e) A train covers a distance of 2340 km in 36 hours. Find out the distance covered by the train in the first 15 hours. Assume that the train runs with the same speed.

(f) Find the cost of fencing 50 m if fencing 72 m costs ₹9000.

ASSESSMENTS

ASSESSMENT 1

Chapters 1–4

A Choose the correct option for each of the following.

1. The digit 3 in the sum of 14,789 and 20,652 stands for ______________.

   (a) 30 (b) 300 (c) 3000 (d) 30,000

2. 24 thousands 2 hundreds and 10 ones when written in numeral is ______________.

   (a) 24,201 (b) 24,210 (c) 24,300 (d) 24,301

3. 35,876 ______________ 35,786

   (a) > (b) = (c) < (d) None of these

4. 25,698 – 19,586 = ______________

   (a) 6002 (b) 6112 (c) 6102 (d) 6012

5. 3,25,684 + 1,32,915 = ______________

   (a) 4,58,599 (b) 4,58,959 (c) 1,92,769 (d) 1,97,269

6. ______________ × 59 = 2950

   (a) 15 (b) 10 (c) 50 (d) 20

7. A factory can manufacture 132 pairs of boots in a day. In 14 days, how many pairs of boots can it manufacture?

   (a) 1848 (b) 1488 (c) 1884 (d) 1448

8. ______________ ÷ 4 = 64

   (a) 16 (b) 24 (c) 256 (d) 246

9. When a number is divided by 9, the quotient is 63 and the remainder is 8. What is the number?

   (a) 504 (b) 513 (c) 567 (d) 575

10. What is the difference between the quotient and the remainder of 4986 ÷ 17?

    (a) 288 (b) 298 (c) 293 (d) 297

B Fill in the blanks.

1. The difference between the place values of the digit 2 and the digit 7 in 82,371 is ______________.

2. 10 hundreds more than 69,000 is ______________.

3. Fill in the blanks with appropriate operational symbols (+/–).

   25,689 __________ 4,58,265 __________ 3,62,859 = 1,21,095

4. 150 × _____ = (150 × 3) + (150 × 9)

5. __________ is a number which lies between 50 and 65. It is completely divisible by 3 and 4.

C State whether the following statements are True (T) or False (F).

1. 99 is expressed in Roman numeral as XCVIIII. ☐
2. There were 12,063 red buttons and 76,355 green buttons. Out of all the buttons, if 23 are damaged, then there would be 88,385 buttons in good condition. ☐
3. There will be 310 fruits altogether if we arrange 12 fruits in 25 boxes. ☐
4. If a shopkeeper packs 1080 sweets into 24 boxes, he can pack 45 sweets in each box. ☐

D Match the following.

1. Add or subtract the numbers and match them.

Column A	Column B
(a) 2,56,852 + 3,59,862	(i) 8,00,000 + 90,909
(b) 7,58,625 – 5,87,699	(ii) 7,14,804 – 98,090
(c) 9,89,898 – 98,989	(iii) 94,489 + 76,437

2. Mary baked some cookies. She sold 9 boxes of cookies. There were 12 cookies in each box. She had 3 boxes of 3 cookies in each box left. Match the numbers.

Column A	Column B
(a) Cookies baked	(i) 108
(b) Cookies left	(ii) 117
(c) Cookies sold	(iii) 9

5 Factors and Multiples

Learning Objectives

- To apply the tests of divisibility by 10, 5, 2, 3 and 9
- To find the common factors and the common multiples of given numbers
- To find the highest common factor (HCF) and the lowest common multiple (LCM) of the given pair of numbers
- To differentiate between prime and composite numbers
- To learn the prime factorisation of a given composite number

Let's Get Started

Solve and classify the following division problems into two categories, one where the remainder is 0 and the other where the remainder is not 0.

(a) 84 ÷ 3 = _____, quotient = _____, remainder = _____

(b) 72 ÷ 8 = _____, quotient = _____, remainder = _____

(c) 124 ÷ 4 = _____, quotient = _____, remainder = _____

(d) 145 ÷ 6 = _____, quotient = _____, remainder = _____

(e) 350 ÷ 5 = _____, quotient = _____, remainder = _____

Problems where remainder is 0	Problems where remainder is not 0

Note: In a division problem, the number to be divided is called the **dividend** and the number that divides is called the **divisor**. When a number is divided by another number and the remainder is 0, then the number is said to be *completely divisible* by the divisor.

Example: The number 84 is completely divisible by 12.

7 ← Quotient

Divisor → 12) 84 ← Dividend

−84

0 ← Remainder

DIVISIBILITY RULES

Is it possible for you to say whether a given number is divisible by another number without doing actual division?

Note: The process of checking whether a number is divisible by a given number or not without actual division is known as the **test of divisibility**.

Divisibility Rule by 10

Consider the examples of division by 10.

Divide the following numbers and fill in the table.

Division problem	Is It completely divisible?
20 ÷ 10	Yes
160 ÷ 10	
2050 ÷ 10	

Division problem	Is it completely divisible?
84 ÷ 10	No
191 ÷ 10	
5036 ÷ 10	

Observe that the numbers which are divisible by 10 have 0 in their ones place. Also, if the digit is not 0, then the number is not completely divisible by 10.

Divisibility Rule by 10: A number is divisible by 10 only if it has 0 in its ones place.

Divisibility Rule by 5

Activity: Take some numbers and divide them by 5. Write the numbers which are divisible by 5 and observe the digits in the ones place.

Note that the digit in the ones place of the numbers divisible by 5 is either 0 or 5.

Divisibility Rule by 5: A number is divisible by 5 only if it has 5 or 0 in its ones place.

Divisibility Rule by 2

Activity: Take some numbers and divide them by 2. Write the numbers which are divisible by 2 and observe the digits in their ones place.

Note that the numbers which are divisible by 2 have 0, 2, 4, 6 or 8 in their ones place. Numbers with 1, 3, 5, 7 or 9 in their ones place are not divisible by 2.

Divisibility Rule by 2: A number is divisible by 2 only if the digit in its ones place is 0, 2, 4, 6, or 8.

Divisibility Rule by 3

Activity: Take some numbers and divide them by 3. Write the numbers which are divisible by 3 and observe the sum of the digits.

Divisibility Rule by 3: If the sum of the digits of a number is divisible by 3, then the number is also divisible by 3, otherwise it is not.

Divisibility Rule by 9

Activity: Take some numbers and divide them by 9. Write the numbers which are divisible by 9 and observe the sum of the digits.

Divisibility Rule by 9: If the sum of the digits of a number is divisible by 9, then the number is also divisible by 9, otherwise it is not.

CHALLENGE

Can we say that a number divisible by 10 is also divisible by 2 and 5? Justify.

Exercise 5.1

1 **Write 'yes' or 'no' under the divisibility of each number.**

Number	Divisible by 2	Divisible by 5	Divisible by 10	Divisible by 3	Divisible by 9
24					
40					
876					
7800					
1000					

2 **Write two examples each of the numbers which are not divisible by 5, 2, 10, 3 and 9 in your notebook.**

FACTORS

Raj has 6 potted plants. He wants to arrange the flower pots in a rectangular flower bed with the same number of plants in each row. Help Raj to find the different possibilities.

Let us discuss the different possibilities.

Arrangement 1: All the six flower pots in one row, that is, $1 \times 6 = 6$

Arrangement 2: Three flower pots each in two rows, that is, $2 \times 3 = 6$

Arrangement 3: Two flower pots each in three rows, that is, $3 \times 2 = 6$

Arrangement 4: Six rows and one flower pot in each row, that is, $6 \times 1 = 6$

Multiplication facts representing the four arrangements are:

$1 \times 6 = 6$ $\quad$ $2 \times 3 = 6$ $\quad$ $3 \times 2 = 6$ $\quad$ $6 \times 1 = 6$

In each multiplication fact, there are two multiplicands and they divide their product exactly. For example, in $2 \times 3 = 6$, both 2 and 3 divide 6 exactly. The numbers which divide a number exactly are known as **factors**. Here, 2 and 3 are factors of 6. Similarly, 1 and 6 are factors of 6.

Therefore, the factors of 6 are 1, 2, 3 and 6.

A number is said to be a factor of another number if one number divides the other number completely.

6 is not a factor of 10 since it does not divide it completely.

Similarly, 5 is not a factor of 21.
$18 = 1 \times 18$; $18 = 2 \times 9$; $18 = 3 \times 6$
So, the factors of 18 are 1, 2, 3, 6, 9 and 18.

$$\begin{array}{r|l} & 1 \\ 6 & 10 \\ & -6 \\ \hline & 4 \end{array} \qquad \begin{array}{r|l} & 4 \\ 5 & 21 \\ & -20 \\ \hline & 1 \end{array}$$

Method of finding the factors of a given number: Write all the possible multiplication facts for the given number and then list the factors of a given number.

Example: Find the factors of 30.

The factors of 30 are 1, 2, 3, 5, 6, 10, 15 and 30.

Find out the factors of 12 and 24.

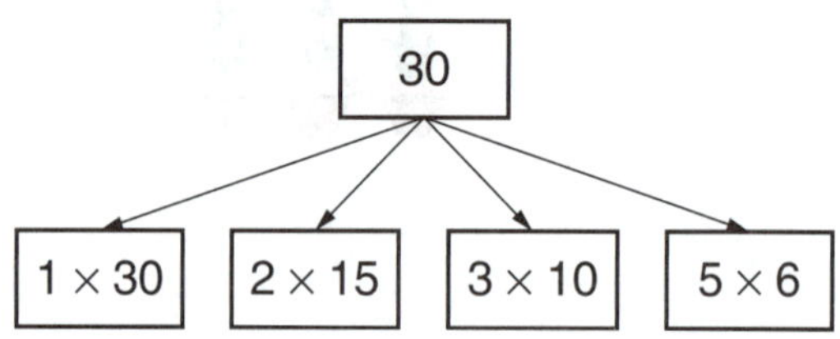

PROPERTIES OF FACTORS

Write the factors of the following numbers and answer the questions.

Number	Factors
6	
16	
20	
24	
36	

1. Is 1 a factor of every number?
2. Is every number a factor of itself?
3. Count the number of factors of each number. Are they countable?
4. Is every factor less than or equal to the given number?
5. Is every factor an exact divisor of the given number?

Fact 1: 1 is a factor of every number since it divides the number exactly.

For example: 10 ÷ 1 = 10   14 ÷ 1 = 14   27 ÷ 1 = 27

$$\begin{array}{r} 1 \\ 10\overline{)\,10} \\ -10 \\ \hline 0 \end{array}$$

Fact 2: Every number is a factor of itself since the number divides itself exactly. For example: 10 ÷ 10 = 1   14 ÷ 14 = 1   27 ÷ 27 = 1

Fact 3: The number of factors of a number is countable. For example, the factors of 6 are 1, 2, 3 and 6, that is, 6 has four factors.

Fact 4: Every factor of a number is less than or equal to the given number. For example, the factors of 6 are 1, 2, 3 and 6. Note that the factors are either less than or equal to 6.

Fact 5: Every factor is an exact divisor of the given number. For example, the factors of 6 are 1, 2, 3 and 6. Note that each one divides 6 completely.

CHALLENGE

Can a number have odd number of factors? Why or why not?

MULTIPLES

Read the sentences given below and find the meaning of the word 'multiple'.

- A juice company sells its products in quantities of 250 ml, 500 ml, 750 ml, 1 litre and in multiples of 2 litres.

The word 'multiples' means a mathematical product. It is obtained by multiplying two numbers. For example, in 6 × 2 = 12, 12 is a multiple of 6 and also a multiple of 2.

6	×	2	=	12
↓		↓		↓
Factor		Factor		Multiple

The numbers 6 and 2 are known as **factors**, and the number 12 is known as **multiple**.

Note that 12 is a multiple of 6 since 6 divides 12 completely. Similarly, 12 is a multiple of 2 since 2 divides 12 completely.

12 is not a multiple of 5 since 5 does not divide 12 completely.

$$\begin{array}{r} 2 \\ 5\overline{)\,12} \\ -10 \\ \hline 2 \end{array}$$

A number is said to be a multiple of another number if it is divided by the other number completely.

FINDING THE MULTIPLES OF A NUMBER

Let us study the method of writing the multiples of a number, say 2. Multiply the number 2 by 1, 2, 3, 4, 5, 6 and so on to get different multiples of number 2.

Therefore, the multiples of 2 are 2, 4, 6, 8, 10, 12, 14, 16, 18, 20, 22, 24, 26, 28 and so on.

In order to write the multiples of a number, multiply the number by 1, 2, 3, 4 and so on. The products are the multiples of a given number.

(a) Write the first 7 multiples of 5. (b) Write the first 6 multiples of 9.

PROPERTIES OF MULTIPLES

Observe the table with multiples of different numbers.

Number	Multiples
3	3, 6, 9, 12, 15, 18, 21, 24, 27, 30, 33, 36, 39, 42, 45 ...
4	4, 8, 12, 16, 20, 24, 28, 32, 36, 40, 44, 48, 52, 56, 60 ...
6	6, 12, 18, 24, 30, 36, 42, 48, 54, 60, 66, 72, 78, 84, 90 ...
7	7, 14, 21, 28, 35, 42, 49, 56, 63, 70, 77, 84, 91, 98, 105 ...
8	8, 16, 24, 32, 40, 48, 56, 64, 72, 80, 88, 96, 104, 112, 120 ...

Note that 3 is a multiple of 3; 4 is a multiple of 4; 6 is a multiple of 6.

Fact 1: Every number is a multiple of itself.
Also, note from the table that the multiples of 3 start with 3 and the rest of the numbers are greater than 3. Similarly, the multiples of 4 start with 4 and the rest of the numbers are greater than 4.

Fact 2: Every multiple of a number is greater than or equal to that number.

Note that you can write as many multiples as you can think of. There is no end to the list of multiples of a number.

Fact 3: The number of multiples of a given number is infinite.

Cross-curricular Link: Find the meaning of the word 'infinite' and make some sentences with it.

Write first 5 multiples of 9 starting with 9.

__________, __________, __________, __________, __________

Exercise 5.2

1 Write all the factors of the following numbers:

(a) 27 (b) 45 (c) 9 (d) 19 (e) 30

2 Write the first five multiples of the following numbers.

(a) 7 (b) 8 (c) 3 (d) 12 (e) 10

3 Tick (✓) the factor(s) of the given numbers.

(a) **42** 4 7 8 10 (b) **16** 5 2 8 15 (c) **55** 5 10 4 11

(d) **24** 8 5 6 13 (e) **19** 6 4 8 19 (f) **13** 1 15 10 13

4 Tick (✓) the multiple(s) of the given numbers.

(a) **7** 56 77 18 24 (b) **11** 11 12 88 48 (c) **8** 14 80 26 32

(d) **3** 81 18 22 13 (e) **10** 5 100 150 200 (f) **9** 72 63 21 27

5 State whether the following statements are true (T) or false (F).

(a) The multiple of a number is less than the given number. ☐

(b) The number of factors of a number is infinite. ☐

(c) 1 is multiple of all numbers. ☐

(d) The factor of a number is less than or equal to the number itself. ☐

COMMON FACTORS

The factors which are common to two or more numbers are known as **common factors**. Let us take an example of two numbers 12 and 15.

Look at the factors which are common to both the numbers as shown.

Factors of 12	1, 2, 3, 4, 6, 12
Factors of 15	1, 3, 5, 15

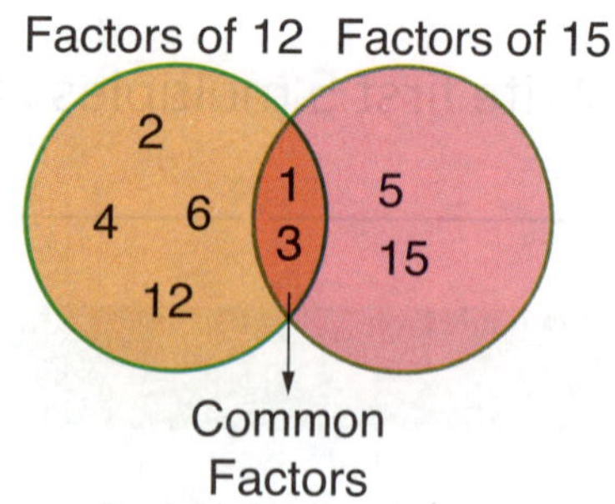

Therefore, the common factors of 12 and 15 are 1 and 3.

The same can be represented using a different representation.

Write the common factors in the intersection area of both the circles and the rest in their respective circles.

Note: (a) 1 is always a common factor of any two given numbers. Hence, it is sufficient to write the common factors other than 1. For example, the common factors of 24 and 18 are 2, 3 and 6.

(b) Sometimes, two numbers may not have common factors. For example, 12 and 17 do not have any common factors other than 1.

Highest Common Factor (HCF)

As the name suggests, the highest common factor of two or more given numbers is the greatest number which exactly divides each of the numbers.

In the above example, we observed that the common factors of 12 and 15 are 1 and 3. That is, 1 and 3 divide 12 and 15 exactly. Also, 3 is the greater of the two. Hence, 3 is the highest common factor of 12 and 15.

Exercise 5.3

1. **Find the common factors of the following pairs of numbers.**

   (a) 15, 20 (b) 16, 32 (c) 7, 22 (d) 24, 18 (e) 36, 40 (f) 12, 10

2. **Find the HCF of the following numbers by finding all the common factors.**

   (a) 9, 15 (b) 35, 42 (c) 10, 50 (d) 49, 21 (e) 40, 64

COMMON MULTIPLES

The multiples which are common to two or more numbers are known as **common multiples**. Let us take an example of two numbers 3 and 5.

Look at the multiples which are common to both the numbers as shown.

Multiples of 3	3, 6, 9, 12, 15, 18, 21, 24, 27, 30
Multiples of 5	5, 10, 15, 20, 25, 30, 35, 40, 45, 50

Therefore, in the first ten common multiples of 3 and 5, two common multiples are 15 and 30. If you write the next ten multiples, you will get some more common multiples.

Least Common Multiple (LCM)

As the name suggests, the least common multiple of two or more given numbers is the smallest of their common multiples.

In the above example, we observed that the common multiples of 3 and 5 are 15, 30... The number 15 is the smallest among the common multiples. Hence, 15 is the least common multiple (LCM) of 3 and 5.

To Check Whether a Given Number is a Common Multiple or Not

To find out whether a given number is a common multiple of two numbers, divide the given number by both the numbers separately. If both the numbers divide it completely, then the given number is a common multiple of the two numbers, otherwise it is not.

Example 1: Check whether 120 is a common multiple of 2 and 3.

Step 1: 120 ÷ 2 = 60 **Step 2**: 120 ÷ 3 = 40

Therefore, 120 is a common multiple of 2 and 3.

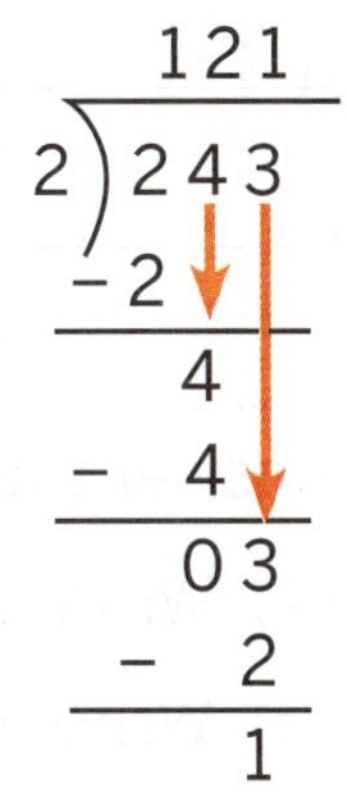

Example 2: Check whether 243 is a common multiple of 2 and 3.

Step 1: 243 ÷ 3 = 81 **Step 2**: 243 ÷ 2 = ? We find that 243 is not completely divisible by 2.

Therefore, 243 is not a common multiple of 2 and 3.

Note: You can also divide the given number by the product of the two numbers. If it divides completely, then it is a common multiple, otherwise it is not. This is applicable if two numbers have no common factors. For example, 16 is a common multiple of 4 and 8, but 16 is not divisible by 4 × 8 = 32 as 4 and 8 have common factors.

Exercise 5.4

1. **Write the first two common multiples of the following pair of numbers.**

   (a) 4, 5 (b) 10, 20 (c) 5, 3 (d) 8, 12 (e) 10, 15 (f) 7, 21

2. **Find the LCM of the following pairs of numbers.**

   (a) 6 and 8 (b) 10 and 30 (c) 9 and 27 (d) 12 and 18

3. Check whether 225 is common multiple of 3 and 5.

4. Check whether 178 is common multiple of 6 and 2.

PRIME AND COMPOSITE NUMBERS

Write the factors of the following numbers and count them. The first two have been done for you.

Number	Factors	Number of Factors
14	1, 2, 7, 14	4
23	1, 23	2
45		
41		

Answer the following questions.

(a) Write the numbers that have only two factors. _______________

(b) Write the numbers that have more than two factors. _______________

You will notice that some numbers have only two factors, that is, 1 and the number itself. Such numbers are known as *prime numbers*.

For example, 2 is a prime number since its factors are 1 and 2. Some more examples of prime numbers are 3, 5, 7, 11, 13, 17, 23, 29, 31 and so on.

Prime Numbers: The numbers which only have 1 and the number itself as their factors are known as prime numbers.

You will also find numbers which have more than two factors. Such numbers are known as composite numbers. For example, the number 4 has three factors, namely 1, 2 and 4. So, 4 is a composite number. Some more examples of composite numbers are 6, 8, 9, 10, 12, 14, 15, 16, 18 and so on.

Composite Numbers: The numbers which have more than two factors are known as composite numbers.

Note: 1 is neither a prime nor a composite number.

TWIN PRIMES

Consider the following pairs of prime numbers. Find out the difference between them.

Pair of Prime Numbers	Difference
3, 5	5 – 3 = 2
5, 7	
11, 13	
17, 19	
41, 43	

You will notice that the difference between the primes is 2. Such pairs of numbers are known as twin prime numbers.

If the difference between two prime numbers is 2, then they are said to be twin primes.

For example, the numbers 37 and 39 are twin primes since 39 – 37 = 2. 11 and 17 are not twin primes as their difference is not 2, that is, 17 – 11 = 6.

CO-PRIMES

Consider any two numbers and write their factors. Also, find out their common factors. If their common factor is only 1, then such numbers are said to be co-prime numbers.

Example: Factors of 6: 1, 2, 3, 6

Factors of 35: 1, 5, 7 and 35

The common factor of 6 and 35 is 1.

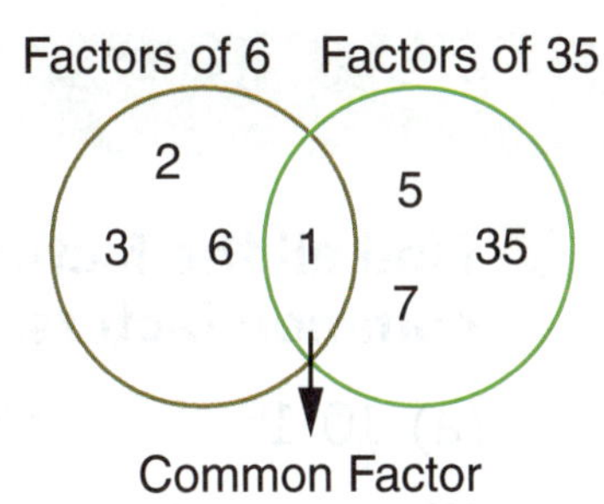

If the common factor of the two given numbers is 1, then such numbers are called co-prime numbers.

Note: Co-prime numbers need not be prime numbers.

PRIME FACTORISATION

Prime Factors: The factors of a number which are prime are known as prime factors.

Consider a composite number and let us write it as a product of numbers. For example, take 24.

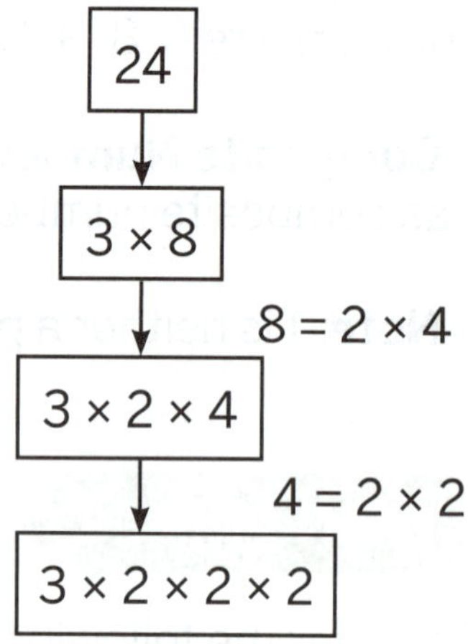

24 is expressed as a product of the numbers 2 and 3. So, $24 = 3 \times 2 \times 2 \times 2$, where all the factors are prime.

Prime factorisation refers to the method of expressing a number as a product of its prime factors.

Consider some more examples given below.

$9 = 3 \times 3$ $18 = 3 \times 3 \times 2$ $40 = 5 \times 2 \times 2 \times 2$ $34 = 2 \times 17$

Exercise 5.5

1. Write down all the prime numbers between 10 and 40.
2. List the composite numbers between 60 and 80.
3. **Tick the prime numbers from the given numbers.**
   2 9 10 31 56 78
   43 61 7 29 88
4. **State whether the following are True (T) or False (F).**
   (a) 13 and 15 are twin primes
   (b) 7 and 18 are co-prime numbers
5. **Prime factorise the following numbers.**
   (a) 10 (b) 18 (c) 16 (d) 28 (e) 27 (f) 90 (g) 81 (h) 100 (i) 98

Revision Exercise

1. **Find all the factors of the following pairs of numbers. Also, find their common factors.**
   (a) 10, 15 (b) 12, 16 (c) 18, 24 (d) 16, 18 (e) 14, 35
2. **Write the first ten multiples of the following numbers. Also, find their common multiples.**
   (a) 3, 7 (b) 2, 6 (c) 8, 3 (d) 5, 2 (e) 4, 3

3 **Tick (✓) the common factor(s) of the given numbers.**

(a) 18, 10 8 2 9 3 (b) 9, 18 2 6 3 9

(c) 15, 30 5 2 6 3 (d) 12, 14 5 7 6 2

4 **Tick (✓) the common multiple(s) of the given numbers.**

(a) 2, 7 56 77 14 24 (b) 6, 2 6 12 18 26

(c) 4, 2 90 16 48 25 (d) 3, 4 20 12 18 36

5 **Write 'yes' or 'no' under the divisibility of each number.**

Number	Divisible by 2	Divisible by 5	Divisible by 10
120			
35			
5872			

6 **Match the following.**

LCM of 4 and 5 28

HCF of 9 and 12 1

LCM of 7 and 28 20

HCF of 5 and 9 3

7 **Find the factors by prime factorisation of the following numbers.**

(a) 21 (b) 35 (c) 45

HOTS (Higher Order Thinking Skills)

1. Are all the factors of a number a multiple of it? Justify your answer.
2. If Q is divisible by P, then which of the following is correct? Tick the right answer(s).

(a) P is a factor of Q. ☐ (b) Q is a factor of P. ☐

(c) P is a multiple of Q. ☐ (d) Q is a multiple of P ☐

6 Fractions

Learning Objectives

- To understand the concept of equivalent fractions
- To understand the types of fractions and compare fractions
- To convert mixed fraction into improper fraction and improper fraction into mixed fraction
- To add and subtract like fractions, unlike fractions and mixed fractions

Let's Get Started

The word 'fraction' means a part of the whole object.

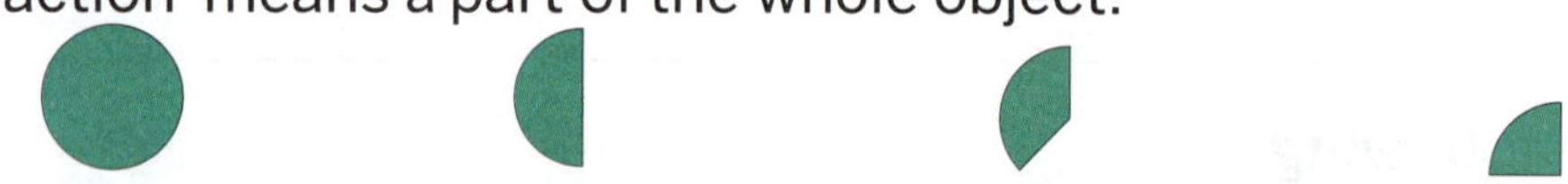

One whole $\frac{1}{2}$ (One-half) $\frac{1}{3}$ (One-third) $\frac{1}{4}$ (One-fourth)

Fraction = $\frac{\text{Numerator}}{\text{Denominator}}$

Numerator: It tells you the required number of equal parts.

Denominator: It tells you the number of equal parts into which the whole has been divided.

Fractions with the same denominator are called **like fractions**.

Example $\frac{1}{4}, \frac{2}{4}$ and $\frac{3}{4}$ are like fractions.

Fractions which have different denominators are called **unlike fractions**.

Example $\frac{2}{7}, \frac{5}{11}$ and $\frac{13}{19}$ are unlike fractions.

Fractions in which the numerator is a smaller number than the denominator are called proper fractions.

Example $\frac{1}{6}, \frac{2}{10}, \frac{3}{5}, \frac{4}{12}$ are proper fractions.

Fractions in which the numerator is a greater number than the denominator are called **improper fractions**.

Example: $\frac{16}{6}, \frac{12}{5}, \frac{23}{15}, \frac{24}{12}$ are **improper fractions**.

Fractions with one as numerator are known as **unit fractions**.

Example: $\frac{1}{2}, \frac{1}{12}, \frac{1}{6}, \frac{1}{14}$ are unit fractions.

EQUIVALENT FRACTIONS

Look at all these representations of fractions.

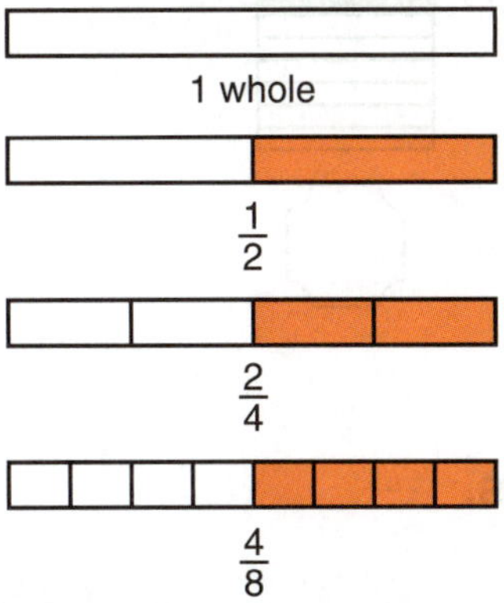

These fractions are $\frac{1}{2}, \frac{2}{4}, \frac{4}{8}$ and they represent the parts taken from the total number of parts. If you compare the pictorial representation of these fractions when placed one over the other, you will find them to be equal. These are called equivalent fractions.

Therefore, these are written as $\frac{1}{2} = \frac{2}{4} = \frac{4}{8}$.

Equivalent fractions are two or more fractions which have the same value.

Finding Equivalent Fractions

To find an equivalent fraction, you need to multiply the numerator and the denominator by the same number.

Example 1:

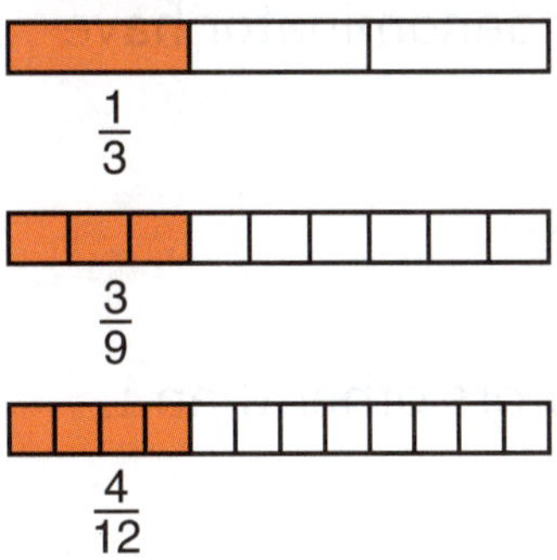

Write two equivalent fractions of $\frac{1}{3}$.

Multiply the numerator and denominator by 3.

$$\frac{1}{3} = \frac{1 \times 3}{3 \times 3} = \frac{3}{9}$$

Multiply both numerator and denominator by 4.

$$\frac{1}{3} = \frac{1 \times 4}{3 \times 4} = \frac{4}{12}$$

That is, $\frac{1}{3} = \frac{3}{9} = \frac{4}{12}$

Exercise 6.1

1 Write the fraction and then match the equivalent fractions.

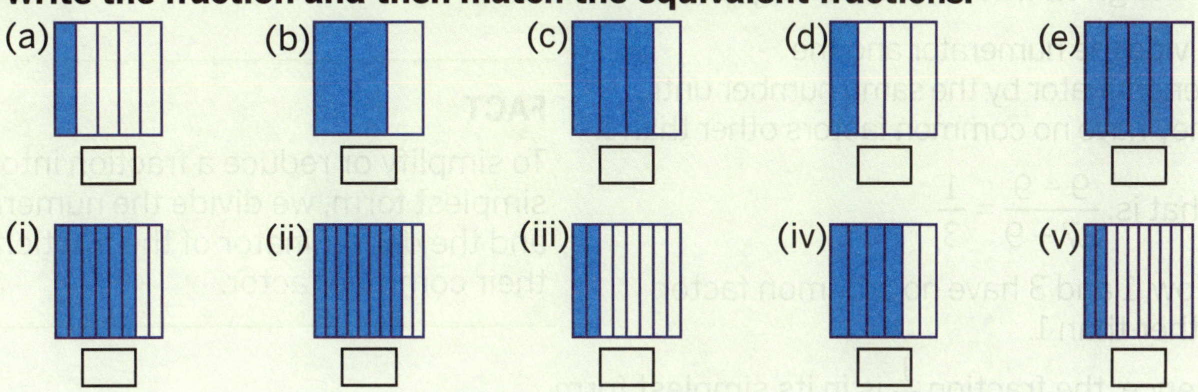

2 **Write the fractions and identify the pairs of equivalent fractions.**

(a)  (b) 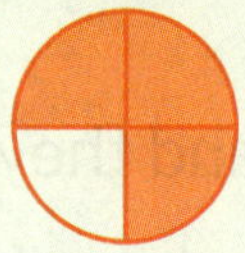 (c) 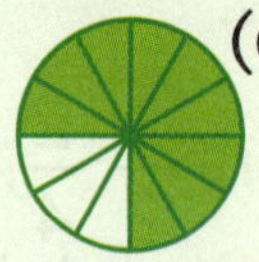 (d)  (e)  (f) 

Pairs of equivalent fractions: ____________

3 **Fill in the boxes for the given set of equivalent fractions.**

(a) $\frac{2}{3} = \frac{4}{\square} = \frac{6}{\square} = \frac{\square}{12} = \frac{\square}{\square}$ (b) $\frac{1}{7} = \frac{2}{\square} = \frac{\square}{21} = \frac{4}{\square} = \frac{\square}{\square}$

(c) $\frac{3}{5} = \frac{6}{\square} = \frac{\square}{15} = \frac{12}{\square} = \frac{\square}{\square}$ (d) $\frac{1}{4} = \frac{3}{\square} = \frac{\square}{16} = \frac{6}{\square} = \frac{\square}{\square}$

The Simplest Form of a Fraction

A fraction is said to be in the simplest form if its numerator and denominator have no common factor other than 1.

Example 1:

Consider the fraction $\frac{1}{2}$.

Factors of 1: 1
Factors of 2: 1 and 2

Here, the numerator and the denominator have no common factors other than 1.

Therefore, the fraction $\frac{1}{2}$ is in its simplest form.

Example 2:

Consider the fraction $\frac{9}{27}$.

How do you convert it into its simplest form?

Is the given fraction in the simplest form? No.

Divide the numerator and the denominator by the same number until they have no common factors other than 1.

That is, $\frac{9 \div 9}{27 \div 9} = \frac{1}{3}$

Now, 1 and 3 have no common factor other than 1.

Hence, the fraction $\frac{1}{3}$ is in its simplest form.

FACT

To simplify or reduce a fraction into its simplest form, we divide the numerator and the denominator of the fraction by their common factor.

Exercise 6.2

Reduce the following fractions into their simplest forms.

1. $\frac{64}{72}$ 2. $\frac{27}{81}$ 3. $\frac{28}{56}$ 4. $\frac{110}{550}$

5. $\frac{48}{96}$ 6. $\frac{75}{225}$ 7. $\frac{9}{63}$ 8. $\frac{64}{216}$

Checking the Equivalence of Two Fractions

To check whether the given two fractions are equivalent or not, you need to find the simplest form of the given fractions. If the simplest form of both the fractions is same, then they are equivalent fractions.

Example 1:

Check if $\frac{3}{4}$ and $\frac{6}{8}$ are equivalent fractions.

The simplest form of $\frac{3}{4}$ is $\frac{3}{4}$.

The simplest form of $\frac{6}{8}$ is $\frac{\cancel{6}^{3}}{\cancel{8}_{4}} = \frac{3}{4}$.

Therefore, $\frac{3}{4}$ and $\frac{6}{8}$ are equivalent fractions.

Did You Know?

We can check whether the two fractions are equivalent or not by the method of cross-multiplying.

Example: Are $\frac{1}{3}$ and $\frac{3}{9}$ equivalent fractions?

We cross multiply them. $\frac{1}{3} \times \frac{3}{9}$

That is, $3 \times 3 = 1 \times 9$

$9 = 9$

Hence, we can say that the two fractions are equivalent.

Exercise 6.3

Check whether the given fractions are equivalent or not.

1. $\frac{4}{5}$ and $\frac{8}{10}$ 2. $\frac{1}{3}$ and $\frac{8}{24}$ 3. $\frac{1}{7}$ and $\frac{2}{14}$ 4. $\frac{3}{7}$ and $\frac{9}{14}$

5. $\frac{5}{6}$ and $\frac{10}{12}$ 6. $\frac{3}{5}$ and $\frac{2}{3}$ 7. $\frac{4}{9}$ and $\frac{16}{38}$ 8. $\frac{1}{4}$ and $\frac{6}{7}$

IMPROPER FRACTIONS AND MIXED FRACTIONS

An improper fraction is the fraction where the numerator is greater than the denominator. **Example:** $\frac{13}{7}, \frac{17}{8}, \frac{29}{18}, \frac{34}{23}$ are improper fractions.

A **mixed fraction** is a combination of one whole number and one proper fraction. **Example**: $2\frac{3}{4}, 3\frac{2}{5}, 9\frac{3}{4}$ are mixed fractions.

Conversion of Mixed Fractions to Improper Fractions

You can convert mixed fractions to improper fractions by multiplying the whole number with the denominator and adding the numerator to it, and keep the denominator as it is.

Convert $2\frac{1}{2}$ into an improper fraction.

Multiply the whole number with the denominator and add the answer to the numerator.

In general, to convert mixed fractions to improper fractions

$$\text{Improper fraction} = \frac{(\text{whole number} \times \text{denominator}) + \text{numerator}}{\text{denominator}}$$

That is, $2\frac{1}{2} = \frac{(2 \times 2) + 1}{2} = \frac{4+1}{2} = \frac{5}{2}$. Therefore, $2\frac{1}{2} = \frac{5}{2}$

Conversion of Improper Fractions to Mixed Fractions

You can convert an improper fraction into a mixed fraction by dividing the numerator by denominator to get the whole number. The remainder divided by the divisor is the fraction and quotient is the whole number.

Convert $\frac{3}{2}$ into a mixed fraction.

Divide the numerator by the denominator.

$$\begin{array}{r|l} & 1 \rightarrow \textbf{Quotient} \\ 2 & 3 \\ & -2 \\ \hline & 1 \rightarrow \textbf{Remainder} \end{array}$$

Write the quotient as the whole number. Write the remainder divided by the divisor as a fraction. That is, $1\frac{1}{2}$.

In general, to convert improper fractions to mixed fractions

$$\text{Mixed fraction} = \text{Quotient}\,\frac{\text{Remainder}}{\text{Divisor}}$$

Exercise 6.4

1 Convert the following mixed fractions to improper fractions.

(a) $3\frac{1}{5}$ (b) $4\frac{2}{5}$ (c) $6\frac{6}{7}$ (d) $10\frac{5}{10}$ (e) $14\frac{2}{3}$

2 Convert the following improper fractions to mixed fractions.

(a) $\frac{9}{7}$ (b) $\frac{11}{6}$ (c) $\frac{15}{8}$ (d) $\frac{12}{5}$ (e) $\frac{22}{17}$

COMPARING FRACTIONS

We will first compare like fractions and then unlike fractions.

Comparison of Like Fractions

We have learnt to compare like fractions in class 3.

In general, while comparing two like fractions, the fraction having a greater value in the numerator is greater than the other fraction. Let us see one more example:

Example: Compare $\frac{5}{13}$ and $\frac{11}{13}$.

The given fractions are like fractions. Therefore, the fraction having a greater value in numerator is greater than the other fraction.

We observe that 11 is greater than 5. Hence, $\frac{11}{13} > \frac{5}{13}$.

Comparison of Unlike Fractions

To compare unlike fractions, convert them into like fractions using the **LCM** of their denominators.

Consider $\frac{2}{3}$ and $\frac{1}{4}$. Which fraction is bigger?

Step 1: Find the LCM of the denominators.

That is, the LCM of 3 and 4 is 12.

Multiples of 3: 3, 6, 9, 12...
Multiples of 4: 4, 8, 12, 16...

Step 2: Write the given fractions with denominator as LCM obtained in Step 1, that is, 12.

$$\frac{2}{3} = \frac{2 \times 4}{3 \times 4} = \frac{8}{12}; \frac{1}{4} = \frac{1 \times 3}{4 \times 3} = \frac{3}{12}$$

Step 3: Compare the like fractions obtained in Step 2.

$\frac{8}{12} > \frac{3}{12}$ since 8 > 3.

Therefore, $\frac{2}{3} > \frac{1}{4}$.

Did You Know?

Two fractions can also be compared by using the cross-multiplication method. In general, if $\frac{p}{q}$ and $\frac{r}{s}$ are any two fractions, then their cross products are $p \times s$ and $q \times r$.

Example: Which is greater: $\frac{9}{4}$ or $\frac{6}{3}$?

The cross products are: $9 \times 3 = 27$ and $4 \times 6 = 24$.

27 > 24, so $\frac{9}{4} > \frac{6}{3}$.

Exercise 6.5

1 **Compare the fractions and put appropriate signs (=/ >/<) in brackets.**

(a) $\frac{10}{15}$ ( ) $\frac{8}{15}$ (b) $\frac{13}{46}$ ( ) $\frac{32}{46}$ (c) $\frac{3}{9}$ ( ) $\frac{5}{9}$

(d) $\frac{9}{31}$ ( ) $\frac{4}{31}$ (e) $\frac{12}{24}$ ( ) $\frac{11}{24}$ (f) $\frac{10}{19}$ ( ) $\frac{9}{19}$

2 **Compare the fractions and put an appropriate sign (>/</=) in the brackets.**

(a) $\frac{4}{9}$ ( ) $\frac{4}{6}$ (b) $\frac{5}{8}$ ( ) $\frac{7}{10}$ (c) $\frac{2}{7}$ ( ) $\frac{2}{9}$ (d) $\frac{5}{6}$ ( ) $\frac{3}{4}$ (e) $\frac{1}{2}$ ( ) $\frac{2}{4}$

3 **Arrange the following in ascending order.**

(a) $\frac{1}{10}, \frac{3}{5}, \frac{4}{15}$ (b) $\frac{3}{5}, \frac{7}{10}, \frac{3}{4}$ (c) $\frac{3}{8}, \frac{2}{5}, \frac{1}{10}$

4 **Arrange the following in descending order.**

(a) $\frac{7}{8}, \frac{5}{6}, \frac{1}{4}$ (b) $\frac{3}{4}, \frac{1}{12}, \frac{5}{6}$ (c) $\frac{1}{4}, \frac{1}{3}, \frac{1}{5}$

ADDITION AND SUBTRACTION OF LIKE FRACTIONS

Addition of Like Fractions

To add two like fractions, follow the steps given below:

Step 1: Add the numerators. **Step 2**: Retain the (common) denominator.

Step 3: Write the fraction as: $\frac{\text{Sum of the numerators}}{\text{Common denominator}}$

Example: Add $\frac{13}{19}$ and $\frac{11}{19}$

Step1: Adding the numerators, we get, 3 + 11 = 24

Step 2: Retain the (common) denominator that is 19

Step 3: The fraction after adding the given fractions is $\frac{24}{19}$

$\frac{24}{19}$, written as mixed fraction is $1\frac{5}{19}$

Example: Swati gave $\frac{2}{5}$ of the cake to her sister and $\frac{1}{5}$ of the cake to her brother. What fraction of the cake did she give give in all?

Fraction of the cake Swati gave to her sister = $\frac{2}{5}$

Fraction of cake Swati gave to her brother = $\frac{1}{5}$

Fraction of cake she gave in all = $\frac{2}{5} + \frac{1}{5} = \frac{3}{5}$ (Adding the numerator and retaining the common denominator)

Subtraction of Like Fractions

To subtract two like fractions, follow the steps given below:

Step 1: Subtract the smaller numerator from the bigger numerator.

Step 2: Retain the (common) denominator.

Step 3: Write the fraction as: $\frac{\text{Difference of the numerators}}{\text{Common denominator}}$

Example: Subtract $\frac{4}{15}$ from $\frac{14}{15}$

Step 1: Subtracting smaller numerator from bigger numerator, we get, 14 – 4 = 10.

Step 2: Retain the (common) denominator, that is, 15.

Step 3: The fraction after subtracting the given fraction is $\frac{10}{15}$.

$\frac{10}{15}$, written in its simplest form is $\frac{2}{3}$

Example: Out of $\frac{6}{7}$ of the pizza, Ali gave $\frac{3}{7}$ of it to his mother. What fraction of pizza is left with Ali?

Fraction of the pizza Ali had = $\frac{6}{7}$

Fraction of the pizza he gave to his mother = $\frac{3}{7}$

Fraction of pizza he is left with = $\frac{6}{7} - \frac{3}{7} = \frac{3}{7}$

Exercise 6.6

1 **Add the following fractions and write the results in the simplest form.**

(a) $\frac{2}{7}+\frac{3}{7}$ (b) $\frac{5}{9}+\frac{4}{9}$ (c) $\frac{1}{12}+\frac{3}{12}$ (d) $\frac{7}{15}+\frac{5}{15}$ (e) $\frac{9}{18}+\frac{2}{18}$

2 **Subtract the following fractions and write the results in the simplest form.**

(a) $\frac{17}{23}-\frac{11}{23}$ (b) $\frac{7}{21}-\frac{2}{21}$ (c) $\frac{10}{22}-\frac{1}{22}$ (d) $\frac{6}{14}-\frac{2}{14}$ (e) $\frac{12}{17}-\frac{5}{17}$

3 **Solve the following in your notebook.**

(a) Class 4 students were taken for a picnic. $\frac{2}{11}$ of the boys wore blue and $\frac{1}{11}$ of the girls wore blue. What fraction of boys and girls wore blue?

(b) Sameer read $\frac{6}{14}$ of a story book on Monday. He read $\frac{7}{14}$ of the book on Tuesday. What fraction of the story book did he read on Monday and Tuesday?

(c) Mihir had $\frac{9}{15}$ of the cake with him. He ate $\frac{3}{15}$ of the cake. What fraction of the cake is left with him now?

(d) Heena had $\frac{5}{19}$ of pizza. She gave $\frac{1}{19}$ to her friend. What fraction of the pizza is left with her?

ADDITION AND SUBTRACTION OF UNLIKE FRACTIONS

Addition of Unlike Fractions

Raghav completed $\frac{1}{5}$ th of his homework on Wednesday and $\frac{1}{6}$ th on Thursday. How much did he complete in two days?

Homework completed on Wednesday = $\frac{1}{5}$

Homework completed on Thursday = $\frac{1}{6}$

Total homework done in two days = $\frac{1}{5} + \frac{1}{6}$

Step 1: Convert the two unlike fractions to like fractions by finding the LCM of the denominators.

LCM of 5 and 6 is 30.

$\frac{1}{5} = \frac{1 \times 6}{5 \times 6} = \frac{6}{30}; \frac{1}{6} = \frac{1 \times 5}{6 \times 5} = \frac{5}{30}$

Step 2: Add the like fractions obtained.

That is, $\frac{1}{5} + \frac{1}{6} = \frac{6}{30} + \frac{5}{30} = \frac{11}{30}$

Steps to Add Unlike Fractions

1. Convert unlike fractions to like fractions.
2. Add the like fractions.
3. Keep the sum in the simplest form.

Step 3: Keep the sum in the simplest form. That is, $\frac{1}{5} + \frac{1}{6} = \frac{11}{30}$

Therefore, Raghav completed $\frac{11}{30}$ of his homework in two days.

Exercise 6.7

1 **Add the following fractions.**

(a) $\frac{1}{4} + \frac{1}{5}$ (b) $\frac{2}{5} + \frac{3}{10}$ (c) $\frac{4}{5} + \frac{5}{6}$ (d) $\frac{3}{4} + \frac{5}{6}$

(e) $\frac{3}{8} + \frac{7}{12}$ (f) $\frac{7}{10} + \frac{3}{8}$ (g) $\frac{8}{9} + \frac{5}{12}$ (h) $\frac{6}{11} + \frac{10}{33}$

(i) $\frac{4}{7} + \frac{3}{10}$ (j) $\frac{2}{5} + \frac{5}{7}$ (k) $\frac{5}{9} + \frac{1}{6}$ (l) $\frac{11}{20} + \frac{7}{10}$

2 **Solve the following in your notebook.**

(a) Ruhi had a piece of ribbon with her. He gave $\frac{2}{5}$ of the ribbon to her mother and $\frac{4}{15}$ to her sister. What fraction of the ribbon did she give in total?

(b) In a birthday party, Juby ate $\frac{1}{15}$ of the cake and Zoya ate $\frac{2}{3}$ of the cake. What fraction of the cake did they eat in all ?

(c) Suhani read $\frac{4}{13}$ of a story book on Monday. She read $\frac{7}{26}$ of the same book on Tuesday. What fraction of the pages did she read in all on both the days?

(d) Raman sold $\frac{1}{7}$ of the total mangoes in the morning and $\frac{5}{12}$ in the evening. What fraction of the total mangoes did he sell in the entire day?

(e) Sana got $\frac{4}{7}$ of the cake from her mother and $\frac{5}{14}$ of the cake from her father. What fraction of the cake does she have now?

Subtraction of Unlike Fractions

Anita spent $\frac{3}{4}$ of an hour in the school library and Sunil spent $\frac{1}{2}$ an hour in the library reading books. Who spent more time and how much?

Time spent by Anita in the library = $\frac{3}{4}$;

Time spent by Sunil in the library = $\frac{1}{2}$

Therefore, the difference in the time spent = $\frac{3}{4} - \frac{1}{2}$

Step 1: Convert the two unlike fractions to like fractions by finding the LCM of the denominators.

LCM of 4 and 2 is 4.

$\frac{3}{4} = \frac{3 \times 1}{4 \times 1} = \frac{3}{4}; \frac{1}{2} = \frac{1 \times 2}{2 \times 2} = \frac{2}{4}$

Step 2: Subtract the like fractions obtained.

$\frac{3}{4} - \frac{1}{2} = \frac{3}{4} - \frac{2}{4} = \frac{3-2}{4} = \frac{1}{4}$

Step 3: Keep the difference in the simplest form, which is $\frac{1}{4}$.

Therefore, Anita spent $\frac{1}{4}$ of an hour more in the library than Sunil.

Steps to Subtract Unlike Fractions

1. Convert the two unlike fractions to like fractions by taking the LCM of the denominators.
2. Subtract the like fractions.
3. Keep the difference in the simplest form.

Exercise 6.8

1 Subtract the following fractions.

(a) $\frac{2}{4}-\frac{2}{5}$ (b) $\frac{6}{10}-\frac{5}{12}$ (c) $\frac{8}{13}-\frac{7}{26}$ (d) $\frac{3}{7}-\frac{4}{49}$

(e) $\frac{3}{16}-\frac{1}{10}$ (f) $\frac{3}{4}-\frac{5}{9}$ (g) $\frac{17}{21}-\frac{9}{14}$ (h) $\frac{9}{11}-\frac{7}{10}$

(i) $\frac{4}{7}-\frac{4}{9}$ (j) $\frac{7}{10}-\frac{2}{15}$ (k) $\frac{7}{13}-\frac{1}{7}$ (l) $\frac{8}{9}-\frac{6}{11}$

2 Solve the following in your notebook.

(a) Shruti spent $\frac{4}{5}$ of an hour in the library. Sunil spent $\frac{1}{4}$ of an hour in the library. Who spent more time in the library and by how much?

(b) Rohit had $\frac{9}{14}$ of a piece of cloth. He used $\frac{2}{7}$ of the cloth in making a shirt. What fraction of the cloth is left with him?

(c) Diya was given $\frac{9}{11}$ of a cake. She gave away $\frac{3}{22}$ of the cake to her sister. How much cake is left with her?

(d) Sanskriti bought ribbon which measures $\frac{6}{15}$ m. She gave $\frac{1}{5}$ m ribbon to her best friend. Find the length of the ribbon left with her.

Addition of Mixed Fractions

Add $2\frac{1}{5}$ and $3\frac{1}{2}$

Method 1: Adding the whole numbers and fractions separately we get,

$= 2\frac{1}{5} + 3\frac{1}{2} = (2 + 3) + \left(\frac{1}{5} + \frac{1}{2}\right)$

$= 5 + \left(\frac{1}{5} + \frac{1}{2}\right)$

Now, to add $\frac{1}{5} + \frac{1}{2}$ we need to convert them into like fractions by finding the LCM of the denominators.

So, $2 + 3 + \left(\frac{2}{10} + \frac{5}{10}\right) = 5 + \frac{7}{10}$

So, we get $5\frac{7}{10}$.

Method 2: We can convert the mixed numbers to improper fractions and add them.

So, $2\frac{1}{5} + 3\frac{1}{2} = \frac{11}{5} + \frac{7}{2}$

LCM of 5 and 2 is 10.

Therefore, we get $\frac{22}{10} + \frac{35}{10} = \frac{57}{10}$.

The answer should always be in the simplest form.

So we get $5\frac{7}{10}$.

Subtraction of Mixed Fractions

Example 1: $5\frac{3}{4} - 1\frac{2}{3}$

Converting both into improper fractions, we get

$\frac{23}{4} - \frac{5}{3}$

LCM = 12

$\frac{23}{4} = \frac{23 \times 3}{4 \times 3} = \frac{69}{12}$; $\frac{5}{3} = \frac{5 \times 4}{3 \times 4} = \frac{20}{12}$

Therefore, $5\frac{3}{4} - 1\frac{2}{3} = \frac{69}{12} - \frac{20}{12} = \frac{49}{12}$

Converting the improper fraction into mixed number, $\frac{49}{12} = 4\frac{1}{12}$

Example 2: Subtract $1\frac{3}{7}$ from 5.

That is, $5 - 1\frac{3}{7}$

Since 5 is a whole number, we write 5 as $\frac{5}{1}$. Convert $1\frac{3}{7}$ into improper fraction.

So, we get $\frac{5}{1} - \frac{10}{7}$.

LCM = 7

$= \frac{5 \times 7}{1 \times 7} - \frac{10}{7}$

$= \frac{35}{7} - \frac{10}{7} = \frac{25}{7} = 3\frac{4}{7}$

Exercise 6.9

Solve the following.

1. $15\frac{3}{4} + 2\frac{1}{5}$
2. $4 + 1\frac{1}{8}$
3. $3\frac{3}{4} - \frac{1}{5}$
4. $7\frac{3}{10} - 2\frac{1}{5}$
5. $10 - \frac{7}{8}$
6. $4\frac{2}{3} + 2\frac{1}{15}$
7. $9 + 4\frac{2}{7}$
8. $11\frac{3}{4} - 6\frac{2}{3}$
9. $5\frac{7}{6} - 3\frac{11}{18}$
10. $12 - \frac{8}{13}$
11. $7\frac{1}{3} - 3\frac{5}{9}$
12. $9\frac{7}{10} - 7\frac{2}{3}$

Revision Exercise

1 **Write the possible equivalent fractions.**

(a) $\frac{[\ ]}{[\ ]}, \frac{6}{20}, \frac{[\ ]}{[\ ]}, \frac{12}{40}, \frac{[\ ]}{[\ ]}$ (b) $\frac{2}{16}, \frac{4}{32}, \frac{[\ ]}{[\ ]}, \frac{[\ ]}{[\ ]}, \frac{[\ ]}{[\ ]}$

2 **Write the following fractions in their lowest forms.**

(a) $\frac{16}{40}$ (b) $\frac{63}{18}$ (c) $\frac{36}{72}$ (d) $\frac{69}{90}$

3 **Express the following improper fractions as mixed fractions.**

(a) $\frac{19}{5}$ (b) $\frac{11}{6}$ (c) $\frac{17}{2}$ (d) $\frac{25}{7}$

4 **Express the following mixed fractions as improper fractions.**

(a) $3\frac{5}{7}$ (b) $1\frac{2}{4}$ (c) $4\frac{2}{3}$ (d) $1\frac{3}{5}$

5 **Add or subtract the following fractions as given.**

(a) $\frac{2}{3}+\frac{1}{3}=\frac{2+1}{3}=\frac{3}{3}$ ☐ (b) $\frac{3}{4}-\frac{1}{4}=\frac{3-1}{4}=\frac{2}{4}$ ☐ (c) $\frac{4}{5}+\frac{2}{5}$ ☐

(d) $\frac{4}{6}-\frac{1}{6}$ ☐ (e) $\frac{4}{7}+\frac{1}{7}$ ☐

6 **Add or subtract the following as given.**

(a) $\frac{1}{6}+\frac{1}{2}$ (b) $\frac{3}{8}-\frac{1}{4}$ (c) $\frac{5}{18}-\frac{2}{9}$ (d) $\frac{9}{11}-\frac{3}{22}$ (e) $\frac{13}{16}-\frac{3}{8}$

7 **Add or subtract the following as given.**

(a) $3\frac{1}{2}+4\frac{4}{5}$ (b) $3\frac{3}{4}-2\frac{1}{2}$ (c) $5\frac{1}{2}-1\frac{1}{4}$

(d) $4\frac{1}{3}+2\frac{1}{6}$ (e) $2\frac{2}{7}-1\frac{1}{14}$

8 **Solve the following word problems.**

(a) Radha has a tape of $\frac{2}{4}$ metre in length. Suma gives her a tape of $\frac{2}{8}$ metre in length. How much length of tape does Radha have now?

(b) Rahul bought $\frac{1}{6}$ litres of milk on Monday and $\frac{4}{6}$ litres of milk on Tuesday. Which day did he buy more milk and how much more?

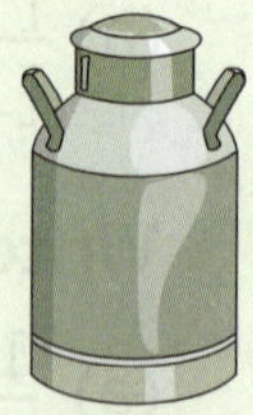

(c) Mrs Gupta bought $\frac{5}{10}$ kg of sugar and used $\frac{2}{5}$ kg of sugar to prepare sweets. How much sugar is Mrs Gupta left with?

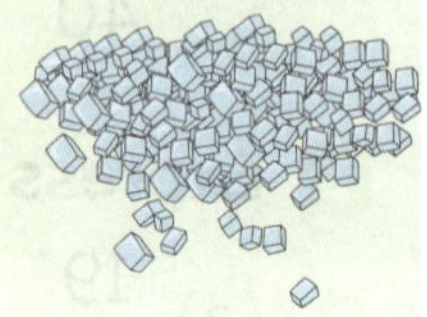

HOTS (Higher Order Thinking Skills)

How many numbers of improper fractions can be formed using numbers from 1 to 10? Answer this question without listing them.

Maths Lab Activity

Aim: To identify equivalent fractions

Materials required: Paper cut-outs of shapes in circles with even number of divisions

Procedure: Ask the students to represent $\frac{1}{2}, \frac{2}{4}, \frac{3}{6}, \frac{4}{8}$ and $\frac{5}{10}$ on different circles.

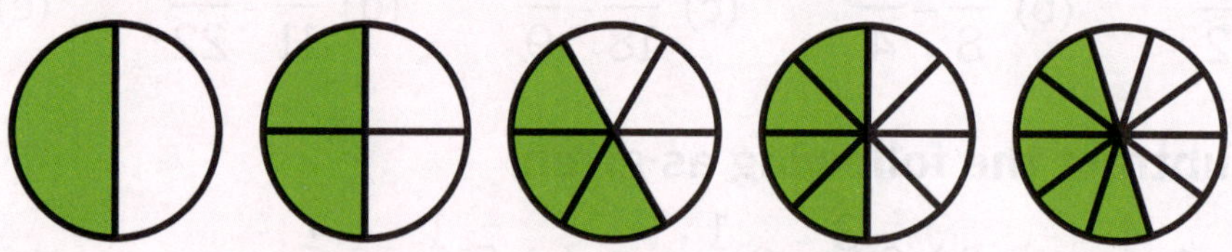

Ask them not to shade the parts randomly, instead shade the parts in a proper order from one side. Now, place all the circular cut-outs one above the other. Then, ask the students to compare the shaded parts in all the figures.

Conclusion: Equivalent fractions are two or more fractions which have the same value.

7 Money

Learning Objectives

- To convert rupees into paise and paise into rupees
- To add and subtract money
- To use basic operations for solving real-life problems on money

CONVERSION OF UNITS OF MONEY

Remember the following rules to convert money from one unit to another unit:

(a) Multiply to convert a bigger unit into a smaller unit.

(b) Divide to convert a smaller unit into a bigger unit.

₹1 = 100 paise

(a) Divyanshi bought balloons for ₹5.00. How many paise does that amount to?

₹1 = 100 paise

Multiply by 100 to convert rupees into paise.

₹5 = 5 × 100 paise = 500 paise

₹5 = 500 paise

(b) Arun has 900 paise. How many rupees does that amount to?

100 paise make a rupee.

Divide by 100 to convert paise into rupees.

900 ÷ 100 = 9

900 paise = ________

$$\begin{array}{r} 9 \\ 100\overline{)900} \\ -900 \\ \hline 000 \end{array}$$

Some more conversions

Rupees to Paise

₹4 = 4 × 100 = 400 paise

₹7 = 7 × ________ = ________ paise

₹13 = ________ × ________ = ________ paise

₹10.50 = 10 × 100 + 50

= 1000 + 50 = 1050 paise

Paise to Rupees

10,000 paise = 10,000 ÷ 100 = ₹100

50 paise = 50 ÷ 100 = $\frac{1}{2}$ rupee

75 paise = 75 ÷ 100 = $\frac{3}{4}$ rupee

25 paise = 25 ÷ ________ = ________ rupee

ADDITION AND SUBTRACTION OF MONEY

When you add or subtract money, remember to place the dots one below the other, before adding or subtracting the numbers. Place the dot to separate rupees from paise. The dot should be before two places from the right. In your answer also, put the dot at the same place.

Look at the examples given.

(a) ₹45.50 + ₹63.50 + ₹230.25 = ₹________

```
     1
   4 5 . 5 0
   6 3 . 5 0
 1
+2 3 0 . 2 5
------------
 3 3 9 . 2 5
```

(b) ₹200 − ₹175.75 = ₹________

```
   9  9    9
 1 10 10   10 10
   2  0  0 . 0  0
 − 1  7  5 . 7  5
 -----------------
   0  2  4 . 2  5
```

(c) Read this bill from a restaurant.

Bill		
Items	**Cost per item**	**₹ . P**
2 Rava dosa	70.00	140.00
1 Apple milkshake	35.00	35.00
1 Coffee	15.00	15.00
	Total	190.00
	Amount paid = ₹200.00	
	Change returned = ₹10.00	

Paid

Exercise 7.1

1 **Convert the following amounts into paise.**

(a) ₹6.50 (b) ₹17 (c) ₹8 (d) ₹20
(e) ₹82.09 (f) ₹191.32 (g) ₹40 and 5 paise (h) ₹23 and 6 paise

2 **Convert the following amounts into rupees.**

(a) 786 paise (b) 23 paise (c) 2556 paise (d) 30,000 paise

3 **Compare the amounts on either side of the box and put the correct symbol [< / > / =] in the boxes.**

(a)

(b)

4 Mr Banerjee buys 1 kg sugar for ₹25, 1 kg rice for ₹32 and 1 kg flour for ₹27. He has one note of ₹50, two notes of ₹10 and one coin of ₹5. Does he have enough money to pay the bill? If not, how much more money does he need to pay the bill?

5 **Complete the following bills.**

(a)

Bill		
Items	**Cost per item**	**₹ . P**
1 Chess 2 Chinese checkers 1 Ludo	89.00 ______ 45.00	______ 124.00 ______
	Total	
	Amount paid = ₹______ Change returned = ₹______	

Paid

(b)

Bill		
Items	**Cost per item**	**₹ . P**
1 can of mango juice 2 cans of grape juice 1 glass of fresh lime	12.00 10.50 ____	____ ____ 14.50
	Total	
	Amount paid = ₹________ Change returned = ₹________	

Paid

6 **You have four ₹1 coins, four ₹2 coins, one ₹5 coin, five ₹10 notes, two ₹20 notes, five ₹50 notes, three ₹100 notes and two ₹500 notes.**

Which currency will you give to buy each of the following items? Write two possible ways for each item.

₹5

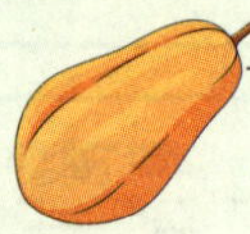
₹47

₹512

MULTIPLICATION OF MONEY

(a) The cost of 1 sweet is 25 paise. What will be the cost of 15 sweets?

$0.25 \times 15 =$ ₹________

Remove the dot and multiply the numbers.

$$\begin{array}{r} 15 \\ \times\ 25 \\ \hline 75 \\ +\ 300 \\ \hline 375 \end{array} \rightarrow 3.75$$

Now, place the dot before two digits from the right.

Therefore, 15 sweets will cost ₹3.75.

(b) 1 pen set costs ₹89.25. What will be the cost of two such sets?

The cost of 2 pen sets = ₹89.25 × 2 = ________

$$\begin{array}{r} 8925 \\ \times\ 2 \\ \hline 17850 \end{array} \rightarrow 178.50$$

Therefore, 2 pen sets will cost ₹178.50.

DIVISION OF MONEY

(a) Prem and Preet bought a gift for their friend for ₹62.50. How much did each contribute?

₹62.50 ÷ 2 = ₹________

```
     3 1.2 5
   ---------
2) 6 2.5 0
  -6
  ------
   0 2
  -  2
  ------
     0 5
  -    4
  ------
       1 0
  -    1 0
  ------
       0 0
```

Therefore, Prem and Preeti contributed ₹31.25 each.

(b) Shilpa bought two pencil boxes for ₹105.50. What is the cost of each pencil box?

₹105.50 ÷ 2 = ₹________

```
     5 2.7 5
   ----------
2) 1 0 5.5 0
  -1 0
  ---------
   0 0 5
    -  4
  ---------
     0 1 5
    -  1 4
  ---------
       0 1 0
    -    1 0
  ---------
           0
```

Therefore, the cost of each pencil box is ₹52.75.

Exercise 7.2

1 Multiply the following amounts.

(a) ₹25 × 4 (b) ₹33.25 × 9 (c) ₹74.50 × 10 (d) ₹96 × 5

(e) ₹17.38 × 7 (f) ₹60.04 × 6

2 Divide the following amounts.

(a) ₹44 ÷ 4 (b) ₹52.50 ÷ 2 (c) ₹84 ÷ 12 (d) ₹126 ÷ 3

(e) ₹45.75 ÷ 5 (f) ₹97.20 ÷ 6

Real-life Applications

1 Sajid's family of 6 members went to the zoo. If each ticket costs ₹10.50, how much did Sajid pay? If he pays ₹70, how much change does he get back?

2 The cost of a newspaper is ₹2.50. How much will Mr Singh pay for the month of November?

3 Nirmala sold 10 home-made chocolates at a fair and earned ₹150. What was the cost of each chocolate?

4 The students of Class 4 are going for a picnic. If there are 30 students in the class and the total cost of the trip is ₹1140, how much should each student pay?

PROBLEM SOLVING

(a) Mr Ravi earns ₹20,595 per month, and Mrs Ravi earns ₹20,785 per month. How much do they both earn together?

₹20,595 + ₹20,785 =

$$\begin{array}{r} 20595 \\ +\ 20785 \\ \hline 41380 \\ \hline \end{array}$$

Therefore, together they earn ₹41,380.

(b) Mrs Mathew bought a new washing machine in exchange for her old one. If the cost of the new washing machine is ₹8745 and she got ₹2299 for her old washing machine, how much did she pay for the new washing machine?

₹8745 – ₹2299 = ?

$$\begin{array}{r} 8745 \\ -\ 2299 \\ \hline 6446 \\ \hline \end{array}$$

Therefore, Mrs Mathew paid ₹6446 for the new washing machine.

When amounts are divided, the quotient and the remainder mean different things in different situations.

Look at the following examples.

(c) Five people have collected ₹550 to buy storybooks for an orphanage. Each story book costs ₹27. How many books can they buy? What amount will be left over?

The amount collected = ₹550

The cost of each book = ₹27

The number of books that can be bought = ₹550 ÷ 27

$$\begin{array}{r} 20 \\ 27\overline{)550} \\ -54 \\ \hline 10 \\ \hline \end{array}$$

Quotient = 20

Remainder = 10

Here, the quotient is the number of books that can be bought and the remainder is the amount that will be leftover.

Therefore, they can buy 20 books and ₹10 will be left over.

Exercise 7.3

1. Sudheer bought an oven for ₹3367 and a mixer for ₹2750. How much did he spend on both?
2. Dipti has ₹290 with her and she wants to buy a dress for ₹575. How much more money does she need?
3. Vikki had ₹150. He bought 5 balls, each costing ₹12. How much money is left with him?
4. Anita and four of her friends shared an auto fare of ₹180 equally among themselves. How much did each pay?
5. The cost of an air conditioner is ₹24,284. Eight friends decide to buy it together. How much amount will each friend have to contribute?
6. The cost of one mat is ₹325. If Shraddha has ₹1000, how many mats can she buy? How much money will be left with her?
7. The amount required for buying an art kit is ₹235. Nandu and his three friends want to buy the kit. How much should each pay? How much more money do they need?
8. **Read the questions given below. Write what operation is needed to solve the question. The first one has been done for you.**

   (a) Seema buys an item for some amount and another item for a different amount. How much should she pay? *Operation:* addition

   (b) Jiten and his five friends went to the cinema. Jiten bought tickets for all of them. How much should each pay him? *Operation:* ________________

   (c) Vrinda paid some cash to the shopkeeper and is waiting for the change. How much money should she get back? *Operation:* ________________

   (d) Sudha studies every day for some time. How many hours would she have studied in a month? *Operation:* ________________

Revision Exercise

1 **Match the following piggy banks to the total amount and the amount required to make ₹500. One has been done for you.**

Total amount	Notes and coins	Amount needed to make ₹500
₹400	 ₹100 × 2, ₹50 × 1, ₹5 × 10, ₹2 × 5, ₹1 × 8	₹225
₹303	 ₹50 × 4, ₹20 × 2, ₹10 × 2, ₹5 × 2, ₹1 × 5	₹100
₹318	 ₹100 × 3, ₹50 × 1, ₹10 × 2, ₹5 × 5, ₹1 × 5	₹58
₹442	 ₹100 × 1, ₹50 × 2, ₹20 × 2, ₹10 × 2, ₹5 × 6, ₹2 × 4, ₹1 × 5	₹182
₹275	 ₹50 × 5, ₹20 × 4, ₹10 × 5, ₹5 × 7, ₹2 × 10, ₹1 × 7	₹197

2 Divya's mother deposits ₹100 into Divya's account every month. How much money will Divya have in her account after 15 months? If she withdraws ₹200, how much money will be left in her account?

3 On March 4, Mr Jai paid ₹5000 as house rent, ₹550 as electricity bill, ₹2000 for groceries and ₹250 to the cable operator. How much did he spend on that day?

4 Jim ate a pastry for ₹12, a samosa for ₹10 and bought some bananas for ₹26. After paying for these items, he had ₹8 left with him. How much money did he have?

5 Minu and her seven friends want to contribute ₹3800 to an orphanage. How much should each pay?

ASSESSMENT 2

Chapters 5-7

A Choose the correct option for each of the following.

1. 6, 12, 18, 24, ... These numbers are the common multiples of ________________.
   (a) 6 and 8 (b) 2 and 4 (c) 4 and 6 (d) 2 and 3
2. What is the sum of the first five multiples of 8?
   (a) 40 (b) 80 (c) 112 (d) 120
3. 5 and 10 are common factors of 30 and ________________.
   (a) 15 (b) 60 (c) 45 (d) 25
4. Identify the correct option.
   (a) $\frac{1}{2}<\frac{5}{2}<\frac{3}{2}<\frac{7}{2}$ (b) $\frac{1}{2}<\frac{7}{2}<\frac{5}{2}<\frac{3}{2}$ (c) $\frac{1}{2}<\frac{3}{2}<\frac{5}{2}<\frac{7}{2}$ (d) $\frac{1}{2}<\frac{7}{2}<\frac{3}{2}<\frac{5}{2}$
5. Identify the like fractions from the following set of fractions.
   (a) $\frac{1}{6}, \frac{6}{2}$ (b) $\frac{1}{4}, \frac{1}{2}$ (c) $\frac{9}{11}, \frac{2}{9}$ (d) $\frac{4}{9}, \frac{8}{9}$
6. In the given figure, what is the fraction form of the orange-shaded portion?
   (a) $\frac{3}{10}$ (b) $\frac{4}{10}$ (c) $\frac{2}{10}$ (d) $\frac{1}{10}$

7. Mrs Sinha went to a shop with ₹100. She bought two bowls each of ₹25.50 and a cup for ₹37.00. Which of the following statements is correct?
   (a) She will have a shortage of ₹22.00. (c) An amount of ₹22.00 will be remaining with her.
   (b) She will have a shortage of ₹12.00. (d) An amount of ₹12.00 will be remaining with her.

B Fill in the blanks.

1. The difference between the 8th multiple of 5 and the 6th multiple of 6 is ________________.
2. $\frac{1}{24}+\frac{11}{24}=$ ________________
3. 6000 paise = ₹ ________________

C State whether the following statements are True (T) or False (F).

1. 63 is a multiple of 9. ☐
2. 7 is a factor of 117. ☐
3. $\frac{2}{10}$ is an example of a unit fraction. ☐
4. There are eight 25-paise coins in ₹2.00. ☐
5. The cost of 1 chocolate is ₹8. Ram will have to pay ₹34 to buy 4 chocolates. ☐

D Match the following.

Column A	Column B
(a) Sum of all odd factors of 20	(i) $3\frac{6}{7}, 1\frac{5}{3}, 18\frac{4}{6}, 13\frac{2}{15}$
(b) Sum of all even factors of 20	(ii) $\frac{1}{6}, \frac{3}{10}, \frac{5}{15}, \frac{9}{11}$
(c) Proper fractions	(iii) 36
(d) Improper fractions	(iv) $\frac{12}{8}, \frac{13}{9}, \frac{5}{3}, \frac{7}{2}$
(e) Mixed fractions	(v) 6
(f) ₹1.50	(vi) $1\frac{1}{4}$ rupee
(e) ₹1.25	(vii) $1\frac{1}{2}$ rupee

COMPREHENSIVE ASSESSMENT

Chapters 1-7

A Choose the correct option for each of the following.

1. What is the smallest 5-digit even number that can be formed using the digits 3, 9, 2, 0 and 6 (without repeating the digits)?
   (a) 23,096 (b) 20,396 (c) 20,936 (d) 02,396
2. Which of the following does not have a remainder when divided by 14?
   (a) 12,988 (b) 42,920 (c) 51,712 (d) 53,788
3. $275 \times 20 =$ ____________ $\times 10$
   (a) 55 (b) 550 (c) 5500 (d) 5550
4. The factors of 35 are 1, 5 and ____________.
   (a) 2 (b) 3 (c) 6 (d) 7
5. Find the multiples of 6 which are between 30 and 60.
   (a) 36, 42, 48, 54 (b) 33, 39, 45, 54 (c) 32, 36, 40, 44 (d) 18, 24, 36, 42
6. $$\begin{array}{r} 1\ 5\ 8\ 2\ 3 \\ +\,7\ 8\ 2\ 0\ 5 \\ \hline 9\ 3\ 0\ 2\ 8 \end{array}$$
   Identify the wrong digit in the answer.
   (a) 9 (b) 3 (c) 2 (d) 8
7. Which of the following options is correct for $\frac{2}{7} = \frac{8}{[\ ]}$?
   (a) $\frac{2}{7} = \frac{8}{16}$ (b) $\frac{2}{7} = \frac{8}{13}$ (c) $\frac{2}{7} = \frac{8}{28}$ (d) $\frac{2}{7} = \frac{8}{35}$
8. The sum of the fractions $\frac{1}{18}$ and $\frac{1}{18}$ is given by
   (a) $\frac{2}{36}$ (b) $\frac{1}{9}$ (c) $\frac{36}{18}$ (d) None of these
9. Which of the following combinations make ₹125?

(a) 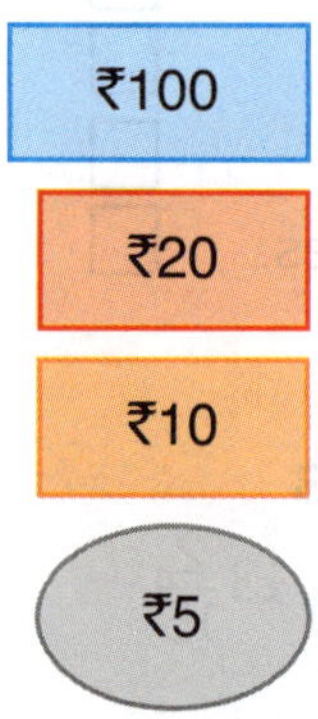

(b) 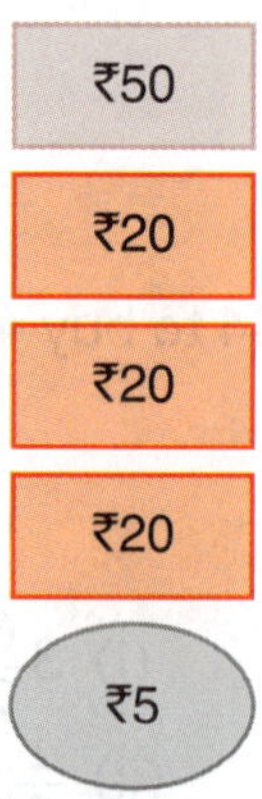

(c) 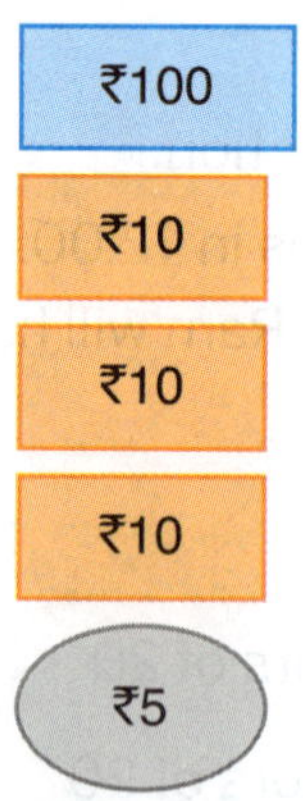

(d) 

10. Chhaya had ₹60 with her. She bought a pen for ₹15, a paint brush for ₹7 and an ice cream for ₹30. What amount did she spend and what amount is remaining with her?
    (a) ₹58, ₹2 (b) ₹50, ₹10 (c) ₹52, ₹8 (d) ₹45, ₹15

B Fill in the blanks.

1. 3420 ÷ ____________ = 342
2. Find the product of 128 and 6. When it is rounded off to the nearest 100, it would be ____________.
3. 400 books are arranged in 50 shelves equally. The possible combination of books in rows and columns are ____________ and ____________.
4. Difference between the smallest 6-digit number and the largest 5-digit number is ____________.

C Answer the following questions briefly.

1. If the number of people watching a performance to the nearest 1000 is 300000, what is the largest possible even number of people watching the performance?
2. Subtract 56725 from the sum of 42238 and 24278.
3. What is the product of 298 and 316?
4. Reduce the fraction $\frac{24}{60}$ to its simplest form.
5. 15 friends went on a trip. The trip costed ₹7500 in total. How much did each pay?

D Answer the following questions.

1. Lokesh, a fruit seller, has 22,150 fruits. 2525 of the fruits are apples. The number of oranges is twice the number of apples. The rest are pears. How many pears does Lokesh have?
2. There are 742 boxes in a storeroom. There are 38 half-sleeve shirts and 12 full-sleeve shirts in each box. Find the total number of half-sleeves shirts, full-sleeve shirts and both the types of shirts.
3. A sparrow knits $\frac{5}{7}$ part of its nest in 1 day. What part of nest remains to be knit after a day?
4. Which is less and by how much (₹115.50 + ₹75.75) or (₹315.25 – ₹102.00)?

E Answer the following.

1. There are 54 sweets which have to be distributed equally among students. List all the possible number of students and the number of sweets distributed to them in each case.
2. Mr Harish weighs between 60 kg and 80 kg. His actual weight is a multiple of 8 and also a multiple of 9. What is his actual weight?

ANSWERS

Chapter 1

Exercise 1.1

1. **(a)** 91,584 – Ninety one thousand five hundred eighty-four **(b)** 23,850 – Twenty three thousand eight hundred fifty
(c) 60,008 – Sixty thousand eight
2. **(a)** Number: 45,695; Expanded form: 40,000 + 5,000 + 600 + 90 + 5
(b) Number: 1,00,219; Number name: One lakh two hundred nineteen
(c) Number: 2,60,082; Expanded form: 2,00,000 + 60,000 + 80 + 2
(d) Number: 86,542; Number name: Eighty six thousand five hundred forty two
3. **(a)** 6 **(b)** 20,000 **(c)** 7,00,000 **(d)** 700 **(e)** 50 **(f)** 9000

Exercise 1.2

1. **(a)** < **(b)** < **(c)** > **(d)** > **(e)** > **(f)** >
2. **(a)** T **(b)** F **(c)** F **(d)** T **(e)** T

Exercise 1.3

1. **(a)** 12,054, 20,105, 30,458, 40,306 **(b)** 2,41,475, 4,13,281, 4,30,087, 4,30,490 **(c)** 75,802, 75,871, 7,50,608, 7,50,806
2. **(a), (c)**
3. **(a)** Smallest: 2,03,458 Greatest: 8,54,320 **(b)** Smallest: 2,46,789 Greatest: 9,87,642 **(c)** Smallest: 4,05,678 Greatest: 8,76,540
(d) Smallest: 1,02,369 Greatest: 9,63,210 **(e)** Smallest: 12,578 Greatest: 87,521 **(f)** Smallest: 30,468 Greatest: 86,430
4. **(a)** 59,767; 59,768; 59,769 **(b)** 23,874; 23,875; 23,876 **(c)** 65,792; 65,793; 65,794 **(d)** 35,986; 35,987; 35,988
5. **(a)** 4,56,780, 4,56,781, 4,56,782 **(b)** 1,43,244, 1,53, 244, 1,63,244 **(c)** 66,055, 66,155, 66,255
(d) 7,36,400; 8,36,400; 9,36,400 **(e)** 87,879; 97,880; 1,07,881

Exercise 1.4

1. **(a)** 51,200 **(b)** 4,60,200 **(c)** 82,500 **(d)** 1,94,900 **(e)** 6,71,000 **(f)** 2,47,100
2. **(a)** 78,000 **(b)** 8,13,000 **(c)** 81,000 **(d)** 31,000 **(e)** 1,55,000 **(f)** 1,72,000
3. **(a)** 20,000 **(b)** 5,50,000 **(c)** 50,000 **(d)** 3,60,000
4. **(b)** The population of a city is about 4,20,000. **(c)** The distance from the planet Earth to the Moon is about 3,80,000.

Exercise 1.5

12 – XII 14 – XIV 19 – XIX 22 – XXII 24 – XXIV
27 – XXVII 29 – XXIX 32 – XXXII 33 – XXXIII 34 – XXXIV
35 – XXXV 36 – XXXVI 37 – XXXVII 38 – XXXVIII 39 – XXXIX

Revision Exercise

1. **(a)** 43,257 = 40,000 + 3000 + 200 + 50 + 7 **(b)** 6,74,635 = 6,00,000 + 70,000 + 4000 + 600 + 30 + 5
(c) 99,029 = 90,000 + 9000 + 20 + 9 **(d)** 1,05,061 = 1,00,000 + 5000 + 60 + 1
(e) 8,40,499 = 8,00,000 + 40,000 + 400 + 90 + 9 **(f)** 22,009 = 20,000 + 2000 + 9
2. **(a)** 84,852 = 80,000 + 4000 + 800 + 50 + 2 Eighty-four thousand eight hundred fifty-two
(b) 52,901 = 50,000 + 2000 + 900 + 1 Fifty-two thousand nine hundred one
(c) 61,509 = 60,000 + 1000 + 500 + 9 Sixty-one thousand five hundred nine
(d) 3,17,656 = 3,00,000 + 10,000 + 7000 + 600 + 50 + 6 Three lakh seventeen thousand six hundred fifty-six
(e) 7,01,025 = 7,00,000 + 1000 + 20 + 5 Seven lakh one thousand twenty-five
(f) 9,93,100 = 9,00,000 + 90,000 + 3000 + 100 Nine lakh ninety-three thousand one hundred
3. **(a)** 6000 **(b)** 40,000 **(c)** 700 **(d)** 80 **(e)** 10,000 **(f)** 2,00,000
4. **(a)** Smallest number = 13,789 Greatest number = 98,731 **(b)** Smallest number = 2,04,568 Greatest number = 8,65,420
(c) Smallest number = 1,23,456 Greatest number = 6,54,321
5. **(a)** > **(b)** < **(c)** < **(d)** < **(e)** < **(f)** < **(g)** < **(h)** >
6. **(a)** 10,600 **(b)** 7,50,000 **(c)** 22,000 **(d)** 4,17,610
7. **(a)** XVIII **(b)** XII **(c)** 26 **(d)** XXIII **(e)** XXXIX **(f)** 9 **(g)** XXX **(h)** 34 **(i)** 15

HOTS (Higher Order Thinking Skills)

IV = 4 V = 5 XXXVIII = 38 XXXIX = 39 VIII = 8 XVII = 17 XXII = 22

Chapter 2

Exercise 2.1

1. **(a)** 38,074 **(b)** 73,020 **(c)** 7,73,020 **(d)** 8,71,036
2. **(a)** 4,66,210 **(b)** 1,35,987 **(c)** 3,34,910 **(d)** 2,35,852
3. **(a)** 137575 **(b)** 299998 **(c)** 185740 **(d)** 110000

Exercise 2.2

(1) 1,39,348 bicycles **(2)** ₹8,33,000 **(3)** 2,57,372 litres **(4)** 54,108 kg

Exercise 2.3

1. **(a)** 14239 **(b)** 104150 **(c)** 96002 **(d)** 17912 **(e)** 273928 **(f)** 27709
2. **(a)** 13,986 **(b)** 3,37,665 **(c)** 2,85,686

Exercise 2.4

(1) 23,655 votes **(2)** 76,430 **(3)** 86,082 cars **(4)** 12,868 km

Revision Exercise

1. **(a)** 30,026 **(b)** 45,127 **(c)** 1,56,024
2. **(a)** – **(b)** + **(c)** + **(d)** –
3. **(a)** ₹1,70,030 **(b)** ₹1,16,195 **(c)** 77,887 litres **(d)** 4,03,749 votes **(e)** 7,62,103 kg **(f)** 1,41,083

Chapter 3

Exercise 3.1

1. 0 **2.** 1 **3.** 65 **4.** 15 **5.** 0 **6.** 300 **7.** 250 **8.** 0 **9.** 475 **10.** 0

Exercise 3.2

1. 1200 **2.** 1920 **3.** 1,81,000 **4.** 1500 **5.** 7100 **6.** 10 **7.** 64,000 **8.** 1000 **9.** 100 **10.** 2,95,000

Exercise 3.3

1. 37,935 **2.** 1,50,944 **3.** 1,34,830 **4.** 4,89,000 **5.** 2,53,368
6. 98,044 **7.** 70,528 **8.** 21,780 **9.** 1,16,844 **10.** 3,69,316

Exercise 3.4

1. ₹1,05,300 **2.** 16,995 calories **3.** ₹1,06,488 **4.** ₹81,244 kg
5. 36,888 people **6.** 2,91,444 words **7.** ₹6,53,450 **8.** ₹1,29,960

Revision Exercise

1. **(a)** 192172 **(b)** 18724 **(c)** 157798 **(d)** 184 × 612 = 1,12,608

2. **(a)** 6000 **(b)** 1,80,000 **3.** **(a)** ₹72,500 **(b)** ₹3,855 ₹7710 ₹11,565

Chapter 4

Exercise 4.1

1. 265 **2.** 1 **3.** 1 **4.** 0 **5.** 3618 **6.** 0

Exercise 4.2

1. 11 **2.** 101 **3.** 321 **4.** 19 **5.** 18 **6.** 25 **7.** 16 **8.** 26 **9.** 32

Exercise 4.3

1. 115 **2.** 115 **3.** 64 **4.** 1114 **5.** 314 **6.** 1303 **7.** 404 **8.** 720 **9.** 1188

Exercise 4.4

1. **(a)** **Q** = 2 **R** = 4 **(b)** **Q** = 99 **R** = 9 **(c)** **Q** = 107 **R** = 4
2. **(a)** **Q** = 7 **R** = 59 **(b)** **Q** = 6 **R** = 24 **(c)** **Q** = 37 **R** = 38
3. **(a)** **Q** = 2 **R** = 277 **(b)** **Q** = 6 **R** = 520 **(c)** **Q** = 71 **R** = 85

Exercise 4.5

1. **Q** = 4 **R** = 11 **2.** **Q** = 6 **R** = 0 **3.** **Q** = 3 **R** = 0
4. **Q** = 2 **R** = 9 **5.** **Q** = 3 **R** = 6 **6.** **Q** = 2 **R** = 16

Exercise 4.6

1. **Q** = 36 **R** = 11 **2.** **Q** = 13 **R** = 39 **3.** **Q** = 25 **R** = 0 **4.** **Q** = 13 **R** = 0
5. **Q** = 17 **R** = 4 **6.** **Q** = 46 **R** = 11

Exercise 4.7

1. **Q** = 59 **R** = 9 **2.** **Q** = 122 **R** = 10 **3.** **Q** = 233 **R** = 16
4. **Q** = 425 **R** = 0 **5.** **Q** = 214 **R** = 0 **6.** **Q** = 130 **R** = 62

Exercise 4.8

1. 78 **2.** 80 **3.** 345 **4.** 152 **5.** 101 **6.** 63 **7.** 37 **8.** 82 **9.** 119

Exercise 4.9

1. ₹5 **2.** 7 items **3.** 19 sweets **4.** 54 books **5.** ₹155 **6.** 29 words **7.** 51 kg

Exercise 4.10

1. ₹7 **2.** Kunal has to wrap 25 more gifts. **3.** Shashank needs ₹5 more to buy the toy.

Revision Exercise

1. **(a)** Remainder = 0, Quotient = 26 **(b)** Remainder = 0, Quotient = 87 **(c)** Remainder = 5, Quotient = 345
2. **(a)** 18 **(b)** 85 **(c)** 24 **(d)** 101
3. **(a)**, **(c)**, **(d)**, **(e)**
4. **(a)** 350 (7000 ÷ 20) **(b)** 400 (8000 ÷ 20) **(c)** 50 (4000 ÷ 80) **(d)** 100 (9000 ÷ 90) **(e)** 40 (400 ÷ 10)
5. **(a)** ₹250 **(b)** 53 years **(c)** 4 **(d)** ₹630 **(e)** 975 km **(f)** ₹6250

Chapter 5

Exercise 5.1

1.

Number	Divisible by 2	Divisible by 5	Divisible by 10	Divisible by 3	Divisible by 9
24	yes	no	no	yes	no
40	yes	yes	yes	no	no
1025	no	yes	no	no	no
876	yes	no	no	yes	no
7800	yes	yes	yes	yes	no
1000	yes	yes	yes	no	no

2. Not Divisible by 5: 24, 876
Not Divisible by 2: 1025, 2005
Not Divisible by 10: 1025, 9122
Not Divisible by 3: 1000, 2012
Not Divisible by 9: 24, 40, 2010

Exercise 5.2

1. 27 – **1, 3, 9, 27**
   45 – **1, 3, 5, 9, 15, 45**
   9 – **1, 3, 9**
   19 – **1, 19**
   30 – **1, 2, 3, 5, 6, 10, 15, 30**
2. 7 – **7, 14, 21, 28, 35**
   8 – **8, 16, 24, 32, 40**
   3 – **3, 6, 9, 12, 15**
   12 – **12, 24, 36, 48, 60**
   10 – **10, 20, 30, 40, 50**
3. **(a)** 7 **(b)** 2 and 8 **(c)** 5 and 11 **(d)** 8 and 6 **(e)** 19 **(f)** 1 and 13
4. **(a)** 56 and 77 **(b)** 11 and 88 **(c)** 80 and 32 **(d)** 81 and 18 **(e)** 100, 150 and 200 **(f)** 72, 63 and 27
5. **(a)** False **(b)** False **(c)** False **(d)** True

Exercise 5.3

1. **(a)** 1 and 5 **(b)** 1, 2, 4, 8 and 16 **(c)** 1 **(d)** 1, 2, 3, 6 **(e)** 1, 2, 4 **(f)** 1, 2
2. **(a)** 3 **(b)** 7 **(c)** 10 **(d)** 7 **(e)** 8

Exercise 5.4

1. **(a)** 20, 40 **(b)** 20, 40 **(c)** 15, 30 **(d)** 24, 48 **(e)** 30, 60 **(f)** 21, 42
2. **(a)** 24 **(b)** 30 **(c)** 27 **(d)** 36 **3.** Yes **4.** No

Exercise 5.5

1. 11, 13, 17, 19, 23, 29, 31, 37
2. 62, 63, 64, 65, 66, 68, 69, 70, 72, 74, 75, 76, 77, 78
3. Prime numbers: 2, 31, 43, 61, 7, 29
4. **(a)** F **(b)** T
5. **(a)** 2×5 **(b)** $2 \times 3 \times 3$ **(c)** $2 \times 2 \times 2 \times 2$ **(d)** $2 \times 2 \times 7$ **(e)** $3 \times 3 \times 3$ **(f)** $2 \times 3 \times 3 \times 5$ **(g)** $3 \times 3 \times 3 \times 3$ **(h)** $2 \times 2 \times 5 \times 5$ **(i)** $2 \times 7 \times 7$

Revision Exercise

1. **(a)** The factors of 10 are 1, 2, 5 and 10. The factors of 15 are 1, 3, 5 and 15. The common factor = 5.
   (b) The factors of 12 are 1, 2, 3, 4, 6 and 12. The factors of 16 are 1, 2, 4, 8 and 16. The common factors = 2, 4.
   (c) The factors of 18 are 1, 2, 3, 6, 9 and 18. The factors of 24 are 1, 2, 3, 4, 6, 8, 12 and 24. The common factors = 2, 3 and 6
   (d) The factors of 16 are 1, 2, 4, 8 and 16. The factors of 18 are 1, 2, 3, 6, 9 and 18. The common factor = 2
   (e) The factors of 14 are 1, 2, 7 and 14. The factors of 35 are 1, 5, 7 and 35. The common factor = 7
2. **(a)** The first ten multiples of 3 are 3, 6, 9, 12, 15, 18, 21, 24, 27 and 30. The first ten multiples of 7 are 7, 14, 21, 28, 35, 42, 49, 56, 63 and 70. Common multiple = 21
   (b) The first ten multiples of 2 are 2, 4, 6, 8, 10, 12, 14, 16, 18 and 20. The first ten multiples of 6 are 6, 12, 18, 24, 30, 36, 42, 48, 54 and 60. Common multiples = 6, 12 and 18
   (c) The first ten multiples of 8 are 8, 16, 24, 32, 40, 48, 56, 64, 72 and 80. The first ten multiples of 3 are 3, 6, 9, 12, 15, 18, 21, 24, 27 and 30. Common multiple = 24
   (d) The first ten multiples of 2 are 2, 4, 6, 8, 10, 12, 14, 16, 18 and 20. The first ten multiples of 5 are 5, 10, 15, 20, 25, 30, 35, 40, 45 and 50. Common multiples = 10 and 20
   (e) The first ten multiples of 4 are 4, 8, 12, 16, 20, 24, 28, 32, 36 and 40. The first ten multiples of 3 are 3, 6, 9, 12, 15, 18, 21, 24, 27 and 30. Common multiples = 12 and 24
3. **(a)** 2 **(b)** 3, 9 **(c)** 5, 3 **(d)** 2
4. **(a)** 14, 56 **(b)** 6, 12, 18 **(c)** 16, 48 **(d)** 12, 36
5.

Number	Divisible by 2	Divisible by 5	Divisible by 10
120	yes	yes	yes
35	no	yes	no
5,872	yes	no	no

7. **(a)** 3, 7 (3×7) **(b)** 5, 7 (5×7) **(c)** 3, 5 $(3 \times 3 \times 5)$

HOTS (Higher Order Thinking Skills)

1. No, for example, 2 is a factor of 4 but it is no t a multiple of 4.
2. **(a), (d)**

Chapter 6

Exercise 6.1

1. **(a)** - (v) **(b)** - (iv) **(c)** - (i) **(d)** - (iii) **(e)** - (ii)
2.

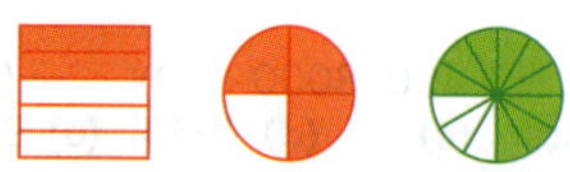

$\frac{2}{5}$ $\frac{3}{4}$ $\frac{9}{12}$

$\frac{4}{10}$ $\frac{1}{4}$ $\frac{2}{8}$

Pairs of equivalent fractions:

$\frac{2}{5} = \frac{4}{10}; \frac{3}{4} = \frac{9}{12}; \frac{1}{4} = \frac{2}{8}$

3. **(a)** $\frac{2}{3} = \frac{4}{6} = \frac{6}{9} = \frac{8}{12} = \frac{10}{15}$ **(b)** $\frac{1}{7} = \frac{2}{14} = \frac{3}{21} = \frac{4}{28} = \frac{5}{35}$
   (c) $\frac{3}{5} = \frac{6}{10} = \frac{9}{15} = \frac{12}{20} = \frac{15}{25}$ **(d)** $\frac{1}{4} = \frac{3}{12} = \frac{4}{16} = \frac{6}{24} = \frac{7}{28}$

Exercise 6.2

1. $\frac{8}{9}$ 2. $\frac{1}{3}$ 3. $\frac{1}{2}$ 4. $\frac{1}{5}$
5. $\frac{1}{2}$ 6. $\frac{1}{3}$ 7. $\frac{1}{7}$ 8. $\frac{8}{27}$

Exercise 6.3

1. Equivalent 2. Equivalent 3. Equivalent 4. Not equivalent 5. Equivalent 6. Not equivalent
7. Not equivalent 8. Not equivalent

ANSWERS

Exercise 6.4

1. (a) $\frac{16}{5}$ (b) $\frac{22}{5}$ (c) $\frac{48}{7}$ (d) $\frac{105}{10}$ (e) $\frac{44}{3}$ 2. (a) $1\frac{2}{7}$ (b) $1\frac{5}{6}$ (c) $1\frac{7}{8}$ (d) $2\frac{2}{5}$ (e) $1\frac{5}{17}$

Exercise 6.5

1. (a) > (b) < (c) < (d) > (e) > (f) >
2. (a) < (b) < (c) > (d) > (e) =
3. (a) $\frac{1}{10} < \frac{4}{15} < \frac{3}{5}$ (b) $\frac{3}{5} < \frac{7}{10} < \frac{3}{4}$ (c) $\frac{1}{10} < \frac{3}{8} < \frac{2}{5}$
4. (a) $\frac{7}{8} > \frac{5}{6} > \frac{1}{4}$ (b) $\frac{5}{6} > \frac{3}{4} > \frac{1}{12}$ (c) $\frac{1}{3} > \frac{1}{4} > \frac{1}{5}$

Exercise 6.6

1. (a) $\frac{5}{7}$ (b) $\frac{9}{9}=1$ (c) $\frac{1}{3}$ (d) $\frac{4}{5}$ (e) $\frac{11}{18}$
2. (a) $\frac{6}{23}$ (b) $\frac{5}{21}$ (c) $\frac{9}{22}$ (d) $\frac{2}{7}$ (e) $\frac{7}{17}$
3. (a) $\frac{3}{11}$ (b) $\frac{13}{14}$ (c) $\frac{2}{5}$ (d) $\frac{4}{19}$

Exercise 6.7

1. (a) $\frac{9}{20}$ (b) $\frac{7}{10}$ (c) $1\frac{19}{30}$ (d) $1\frac{7}{12}$ (e) $\frac{23}{24}$ (f) $1\frac{3}{40}$ (g) $1\frac{11}{36}$ (h) $\frac{28}{33}$ (i) $\frac{61}{70}$ (j) $1\frac{4}{35}$ (k) $\frac{13}{18}$ (l) $1\frac{1}{4}$
2. (a) $\frac{2}{3}$ of the ribbon (b) $\frac{11}{15}$ of the cake (c) $\frac{15}{26}$ of the story book (d) $\frac{47}{84}$ of the total mangoes (e) $\frac{13}{14}$ of the cake

Exercise 6.8

1. (a) $\frac{1}{10}$ (b) $\frac{11}{60}$ (c) $\frac{9}{26}$ (d) $\frac{17}{49}$ (e) $\frac{7}{80}$ (f) $\frac{7}{36}$ (g) $\frac{7}{42}=\frac{1}{6}$ (h) $\frac{13}{110}$ (i) $\frac{8}{63}$ (j) $\frac{17}{30}$ (k) $\frac{36}{91}$ (l) $\frac{34}{99}$
2. (a) Shruti spent more time in the library by $\frac{11}{20}$ of an hour (b) $\frac{5}{14}$ of the cloth (c) $\frac{15}{22}$ of the cake (d) $\frac{1}{5}$ m

Exercise 6.9

1. $17\frac{19}{20}$ 2. $5\frac{1}{8}$ 3. $\frac{71}{20}=3\frac{11}{20}$ 4. $\frac{51}{10}$ or $5\frac{1}{10}$ 5. $9\frac{1}{8}$ 6. $6\frac{11}{15}$ 7. $13\frac{2}{7}$ 8. $5\frac{1}{12}$ 9. $\frac{23}{9}$ or $2\frac{5}{9}$
10. $11\frac{5}{13}$ 11. $3\frac{7}{9}$ 12. $2\frac{1}{30}$

Revision Exercise

1. (a) $\frac{3}{10}, \frac{6}{20}, \frac{9}{30}, \frac{12}{40}, \frac{15}{50}$ (b) $\frac{2}{16}, \frac{4}{32}, \frac{6}{48}, \frac{8}{64}, \frac{10}{80}$ 2. (a) $\frac{2}{5}$ (b) $\frac{7}{2}$ (c) $\frac{1}{2}$ (d) $\frac{23}{30}$
3. (a) $3\frac{4}{5}$ (b) $1\frac{5}{6}$ (c) $8\frac{1}{2}$ (d) $3\frac{4}{7}$ 4. (a) $\frac{26}{7}$ (b) $\frac{6}{4}$ (c) $\frac{14}{3}$ (d) $\frac{8}{5}$
5. (a) $\frac{3}{3}=1$ (b) $\frac{1}{2}$ (c) $\frac{6}{5}$ or $1\frac{1}{5}$ (d) $\frac{3}{6}$ or $\frac{1}{2}$ (e) $\frac{5}{7}$ 6. (a) $\frac{2}{3}$ (b) $\frac{1}{8}$ (c) $\frac{1}{18}$ (d) $\frac{21}{22}$ (e) $\frac{7}{16}$
7. (a) $8\frac{3}{10}$ (b) $1\frac{1}{4}$ (c) $4\frac{1}{4}$ (d) $6\frac{1}{2}$ (e) $1\frac{3}{14}$ 8. (a) $\frac{6}{8}$ or $\frac{3}{4}$ m (b) Tuesday by $\frac{3}{6}$ or $\frac{1}{2}$ litres (c) $\frac{1}{10}$ kg

HOTS (Higher Order Thinking Skills)

We can form 42 numbers of improper fractions.

Explanation: Numbers: 1, 2, 3, 4, 5, 6, 7, 8, 9, 10

Fractions with denominator	Improper fractions	Total
1	$\frac{2}{1}, \frac{3}{1}, \frac{4}{1}, \frac{5}{1}, \frac{6}{1}, \frac{7}{1}, \frac{8}{1}, \frac{9}{1}, \frac{10}{1}$	9
2	$\frac{3}{2}, \frac{4}{2}, \frac{5}{2}, \frac{6}{2}, \frac{7}{2}, \frac{8}{2}, \frac{9}{2}, \frac{10}{2}$	8
3	$\frac{4}{3}, \frac{5}{3}, \frac{6}{3}, \frac{7}{3}, \frac{8}{3}, \frac{9}{3}, \frac{10}{3}$	7
4	$\frac{5}{4}, \frac{6}{4}, \frac{7}{4}, \frac{8}{4}, \frac{9}{4}, \frac{10}{4}$	6
5	$\frac{6}{5}, \frac{7}{5}, \frac{8}{5}, \frac{9}{5}, \frac{10}{5}$	5
6	$\frac{7}{6}, \frac{8}{6}, \frac{9}{6}, \frac{10}{6}$	4
7	$\frac{8}{7}, \frac{9}{7}, \frac{10}{7}$	3
8	$\frac{9}{8}, \frac{10}{8}$	2
9	$\frac{10}{9}$	1
Total number of improper fractions		45

Chapter 7

Exercise 7.1

1. **(a)** 650 paise **(b)** 1700 paise **(c)** 800 paise **(d)** 2000 paise **(e)** 8209 paise **(f)** 19,132 paise **(g)** 4005 paise **(h)** 2306 paise
2. **(a)** ₹ 7.86 **(b)** ₹ 25.56 **(c)** ₹10 **(d)** ₹300
3. **(a)**

(b)

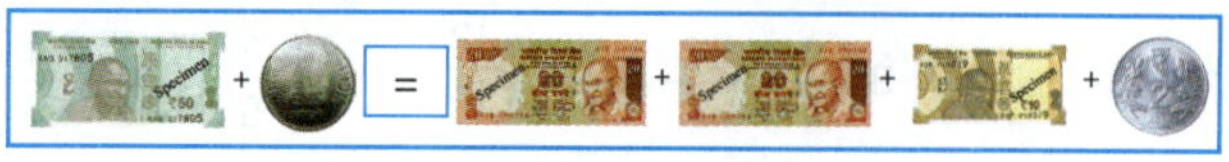

3. ₹ 9
5. **(a)**

Bill		
Items	**Cost per item**	**₹ . P**
1 Chess	89.00	89.00
2 Chinese checkers	62.00	124.00
1 Ludo	45.00	45.00
	Total	258.00
	Amount paid = ₹260.00 Change returned = ₹2.00	

(b)

Bill		
Items	**Cost per item**	**₹ . P**
1 can of mango juice	12.00	12.00
2 cans of grape juice	10.50	21.00
1 glass of fresh lime	14.50	14.50
	Total	47.50
	Amount paid = ₹50.00 Change returned = ₹2.50	

Exercise 7.2

1. **(a)** ₹100 **(b)** ₹299.25 **(c)** ₹745 **(d)** ₹480
   (e) ₹121.66 **(f)** ₹360.24
2. **(a)** ₹11 **(b)** ₹26.25 **(c)** ₹7 **(d)** ₹42
   (e) 9.15 **(f)** 16.2

Real-life Applications

1. ₹63 needed to pay and balance is ₹ 7
2. ₹75 **3.** ₹15 each **4.** ₹38

Revision Exercise

2. ₹1500, ₹1300 **3.** ₹7800 **4.** ₹56 **5.** ₹475

Exercise 7.3

1. ₹6.117 **2.** ₹285 more
3. ₹90 left with him **4.** ₹36 each
5. ₹3035.50 will be contributed by each friend.
6. Shraddha can buy 3 mats and the amount left with her will be ₹ 25.
7. ₹58, ₹3
7. **(b)** Division **(c)** Subtraction **(d)** Multiplication

SCIENCE

1 The Green Plants

Learning Checklist

- Leaf
- How do plants make their food?
- Interdependence of plants and animals

Let's Get Started

Leaves of different plants differ in shape, size and colour. Look at the pictures of leaves given below and fill in the blanks using the given words.

long needle-like coloured

The leaves are ____________

The leaves are ____________

The leaf is ____________

Let us learn more about leaves and their functions in this chapter.

LEAF

A leaf is a flat structure growing from the stem or branch of a plant. Most plants have green leaves. The green colour is due to the presence of a pigment[1] called **chlorophyll** in the leaves.

The flat part of the leaf is called the **leaf blade** or **lamina**. The part that attaches the leaf to the stem or branch, or supports the leaf is called the **petiole**. Leaf has a main vein called the **midrib** and many small veins branching off from it. These small veins transport water, minerals and nutrients to and from the leaves of a plant.

Word Web

[1]**Pigment**: coloured substance

The underside of every leaf has tiny openings called **stomata** (singular: stoma). Stomata are like the nostrils of a plant that help them to breathe. Two bean-shaped structures called **guard cells** surround the stomata. Guard cells control the opening and closing of stomata.

Parts of a leaf

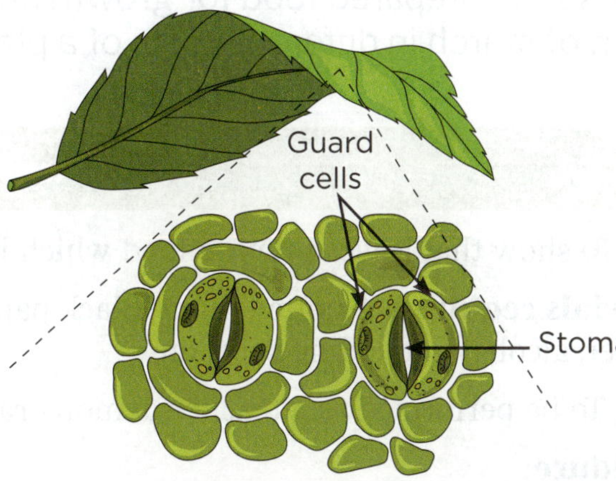

Leaf cells

HOW DO PLANTS MAKE THEIR FOOD?

Green plants make their own food by a process called **photosynthesis** (*photo* means light and *synthesis* means to put together). Photosynthesis takes place in the leaves; that is why leaves are called the food factory or the kitchen of a plant.

The following things are required by a plant to carry out photosynthesis:

(a) Carbon dioxide

(b) Light

(c) Water

(d) Chlorophyll

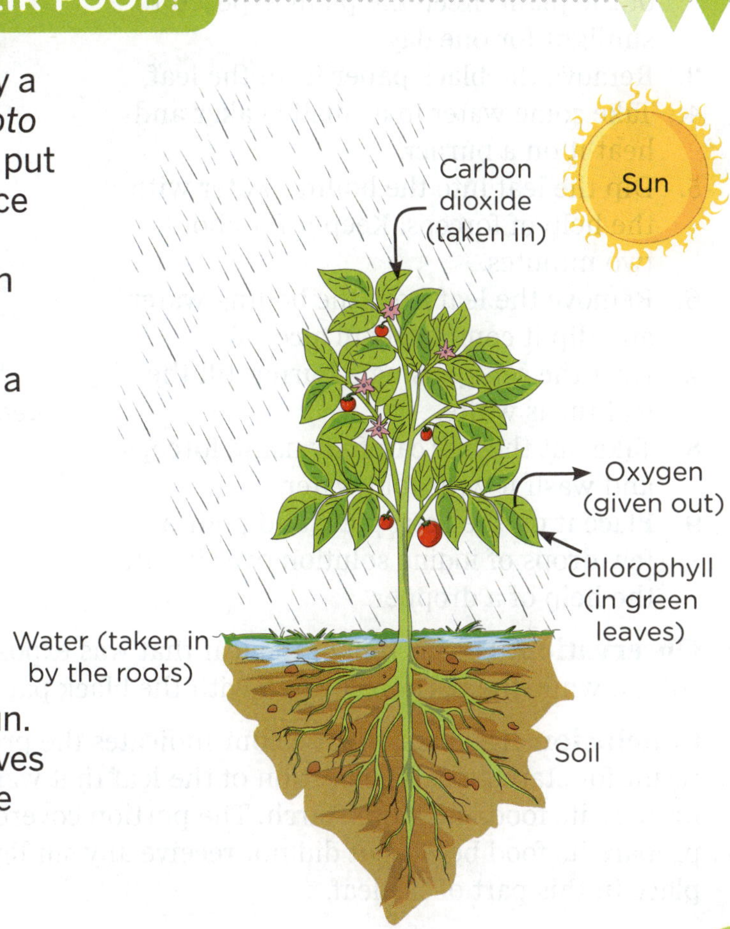

Light is mostly obtained from the sun. Chlorophyll present in the green leaves absorbs the sunlight. Carbon dioxide enters the leaves through stomata. Water is taken in by the roots and carried to the leaves by the stem. The products of photosynthesis are sugar and oxygen.

$$\text{Carbon dioxide} + \text{Water} \xrightarrow[\text{Chlorophyll}]{\text{Light}} \text{Sugar} + \text{Oxygen}$$

Plants use the prepared food for growth and other functions. Extra food is stored in the form of starch in different parts of a plant.

Activity

Aim: To show that leaves prepare food which is stored in the form of starch

Materials required: A potted plant, black paper, beaker, burner, water, forceps, Petri-plate, dropper, alcohol and iodine solution

Note: To be performed as a teacher demonstration

Procedure:

1. Keep the potted plant in a dark room for two or three days.
2. Clip some black paper to a green leaf of the plant. Keep the plant exposed to sunlight for one day.
3. Remove the black paper from the leaf.
4. Take some water in a small beaker and heat it on a burner.
5. Dip the leaf into the boiling water with the help of forceps. Keep it for about two minutes.
6. Remove the leaf from the boiling water and dip it completely in alcohol.
7. Heat the set-up using a burner till the leaf turns white.
8. Take out the leaf carefully using forceps and wash it with cold water.
9. Place it on the Petri-plate and pour a few drops of iodine solution over it with the help of a dropper.

Leaf boiled in water

Leaf dipped in alcohol

Adding iodine

Colour change in leaf

Observation: The portion of the leaf that was exposed to sunlight shows a blue-black colour, while the portion covered with the black paper does not show blue-black colour.

Conclusion: The blue-black colour indicates the presence of starch and is a positive result for starch test. The portion of the leaf that was exposed to sunlight was able to prepare its food and store starch. The portion covered with the black paper could not prepare its food because it did not receive any sunlight. Thus, no starch formation takes place in this part of the leaf.

Revise and recall

1. **Look at the picture of a leaf shown below and fill in the names of its parts.**

2. **Select the words from the help box and fill in the blanks.**

Oxygen, Light, Chlorophyll, Sugar, Carbon dioxide, Water

Photosynthesis is:

________ + ________ ————→ ________ + ________

INTERDEPENDENCE OF PLANTS AND ANIMALS

Plants and animals depend on each other for their survival.

Plants produce their own food by the process of photosynthesis and give out oxygen in this process. The oxygen given out by plants is necessary for human beings and animals to survive. Animals also depend on plants for food.

> **Science in Context**
>
> Plants not only provide us with food to eat and oxygen to breathe, but also provide us with medicines. Many medicines that we use are made from plants.

Herbivorous animals eat plants as their food. Carnivores depend on the herbivores for their food. Plants are eaten by herbivores, which in turn are eaten by carnivores, thus forming a chain. A chain that shows how one organism is dependent on another organism for food is called **food chain**.

A food chain

Animals help plants by carrying their seeds to far-off places for germination. Animals breathe out carbon dioxide, which is used by plants for photosynthesis.

The interdependence[1] of plants and animals creates a balance in nature. If the number of either plants or animals increases or decreases suddenly, this balance will be disturbed.

If there is a sudden decrease in the number of plants in nature, the oxygen level in the atmosphere will decrease, leading to an increase in the level of carbon dioxide. Similarly, if there is a sudden increase in the number of animals in nature, it will lead to an outbreak of diseases and insufficient food to meet the needs of the growing population.

Word Web

[1]**Interdependence**: dependence on each other

Let's Say Together

Chlorophyll Photosynthesis Carbon dioxide Oxygen Food chain

Keywords

Chlorophyll: The pigment that gives green colour to the leaves
Stomata: Tiny openings on the underside of leaves that help the plant to breathe
Petiole: The part of a leaf that holds it to the stem or the branch of the plant
Photosynthesis: The process by which plants make their own food, using water and carbon dioxide in the presence of light and chlorophyll
Food chain: The chain that shows how one organism is dependent on another organism for its food

Summary

1. The parts of a leaf are leaf blade, petiole, midrib and veins.
2. The green colour of leaves is due to the presence of a pigment called chlorophyll.
3. Plants make their own food by a process called photosynthesis, using water and carbon dioxide in the presence of light and chlorophyll.
4. The underside of leaves have small openings called stomata. Stomata are like the nostrils of a plant that help them to breathe.
5. Plants and animals depend on each other for their survival.

EXERCISE

A Choose the correct option for each of the following.

1. Leaves are green in colour due to the presence of
   (a) Stomata (b) Chlorophyll (c) Carbon dioxide (d) Oxygen
2. The part of a leaf that attaches it to the stem or branch is called
   (a) Midrib (b) Blade (c) Petiole (d) Vein
3. Plants make their own food using
   (a) Carbon dioxide (b) Sunlight (c) Water (d) All of these
4. During photosynthesis, plants produce
   (a) Sunlight (b) Sugar (c) Carbon dioxide (d) All of these
5. Which of these substances do veins transport to and from leaves?
   (a) Water (b) Minerals (c) Nutrients (d) All of these

B Fill in the blanks with the correct words.

1. The flat part of a leaf is called ____________________ . (vein/leaf blade)
2. Tiny openings on the underside of leaves of plants are called ____________________ . (stomata/vein)
3. Chlorophyll gives ____________________ colour to the plant. (white/green)
4. Plants give us ____________________ to breathe. (oxygen/carbon dioxide)
5. Animals breathe out ____________________ . (carbon dioxide/oxygen)

C Match the following.

Column A	Column B
(a) Photosynthesis	(1) Attaches the leaf to the stem or branch
(b) Chlorophyll	(2) Transport substances
(c) Veins	(3) Main vein of a leaf
(d) Midrib	(4) Preparation of food by the plants
(e) Petiole	(5) Green pigment

D State whether the following statements are true (T) or false (F).

1. The midrib branches into smaller structures called veins. ☐
2. Leaves need light to make food. ☐
3. Leaves give out oxygen through the veins. ☐
4. Iodine changes the colour of a leaf containing starch to red. ☐
5. Animals do not depend on plants for food. ☐
6. In a food chain, one organism is the food for another organism. ☐

E Name the following.

1. Bean-shaped structure that surrounds the stomata ____________
2. The pigment that helps plants in absorbing sunlight ____________
3. The form in which extra food is stored in plant parts ____________
4. A gas which is the product of photosynthesis ____________

F Answer the following questions briefly.

1. What is the function of veins in a leaf?
2. How do stomata help a leaf?
3. What is photosynthesis?
4. How does chlorophyll help in photosynthesis?
5. What is a food chain? Give your own example of a food chain.

G Answer the following questions.

1. Explain the parts of a leaf with the help of a labelled diagram.
2. Name the four things that the plants use to make food and the sources from which they get them.
3. Why is the interdependence of plants and animals important?

H HOTS (Higher Order Thinking Skills)

1. Why is the upper part of all green leaves darker in colour than the underside of the leaves? (Hint: Chlorophyll gives green colour to the leaves.)
2. What would happen if you take a potted plant and lock it up inside a dark room for one week? (Hint: Plants use light to prepare food.)

I Complete the photosynthesis chart.

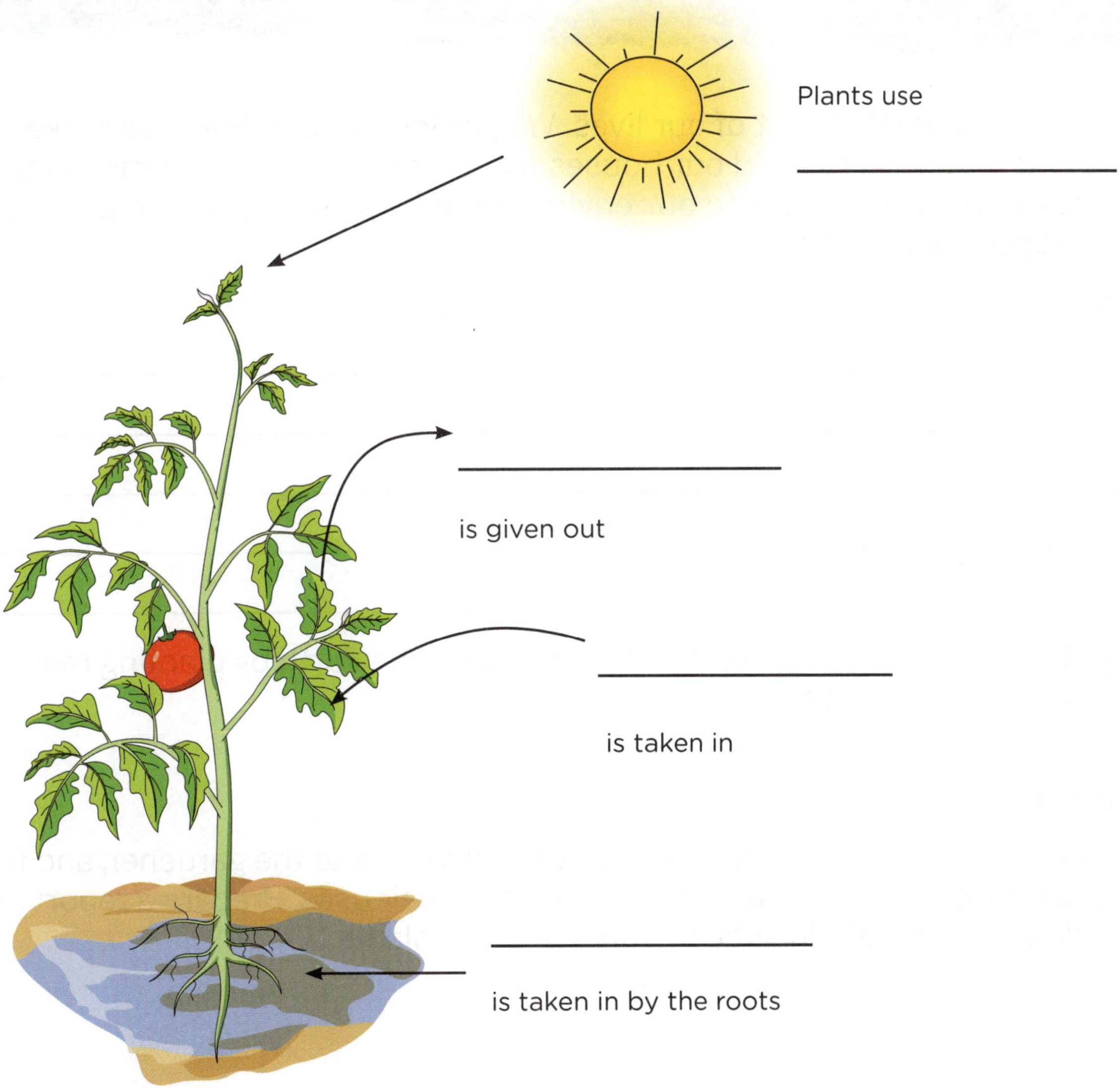

J Life Skills

Read the story of the tree and the woodcutter.

Plants are an important part of our lives. We get food to eat, fibres to make clothes and materials to build our houses from plants. We also get medicines from plants. Trees contribute to our environment by providing oxygen, preserving soil and supporting wildlife.

Now based on the story, write any five uses of trees.

1. ______________________________
2. ______________________________
3. ______________________________
4. ______________________________
5. ______________________________

Grow potted plants in and around your home. Save the Earth by planting more trees rather than cutting them down.

K Project

Visit a greenhouse or a nursery in your city or town. Talk to the gardener, and find out the names of any five plants grown there and their uses. Prepare a report on your findings; if possible, include pictures of those plants.

Find out the names of the following plants or trees.

1. I am the national tree of India. I have aerial roots and I am always green. Who am I?

____

2. I am a popular tree and my fruit is considered as the 'king of fruits'. Who am I?

____

3. My fruit is sour to taste and is used in cooking to add flavour. Who am I?

____

4. I am known as the 'blessed tree' and my leaves are of medicinal value. Who am I?

____

5. I am a very useful tree, my leaves are woven to make baskets and I am used for cooking. My fruit has water inside it. Who am I?

____

2 Adaptations in Plants

Learning Checklist

- Plant adaptations—aquatic, terrestrial, insectivorous, non-green, parasitic

Let's Get Started

Plants are seen growing at all places. Look at the following pictures and use the words given in the box to fill in the blanks.

gardens	**ponds**	**deserts**	**forests**

Wild plants are found in ________	Cacti are found in ________	Lotus plants are found in ________	Ornamental plants are found in ________

The place where an organism naturally lives is called its **habitat**. The special features acquired by an organism to adjust itself in a habitat are called **adaptations**.

In this chapter, we will learn about different adaptations shown by plants.

PLANT ADAPTATIONS

Different kinds of plants grow in different places.

These plants adapt certain features to survive in their habitat. According to the habitat they grow in, plants can be broadly grouped into two categories: aquatic plants and terrestrial plants.

Aquatic Plants

Plants that grow and live in water are called **aquatic plants**. The following figure shows the different types of aquatic plants.

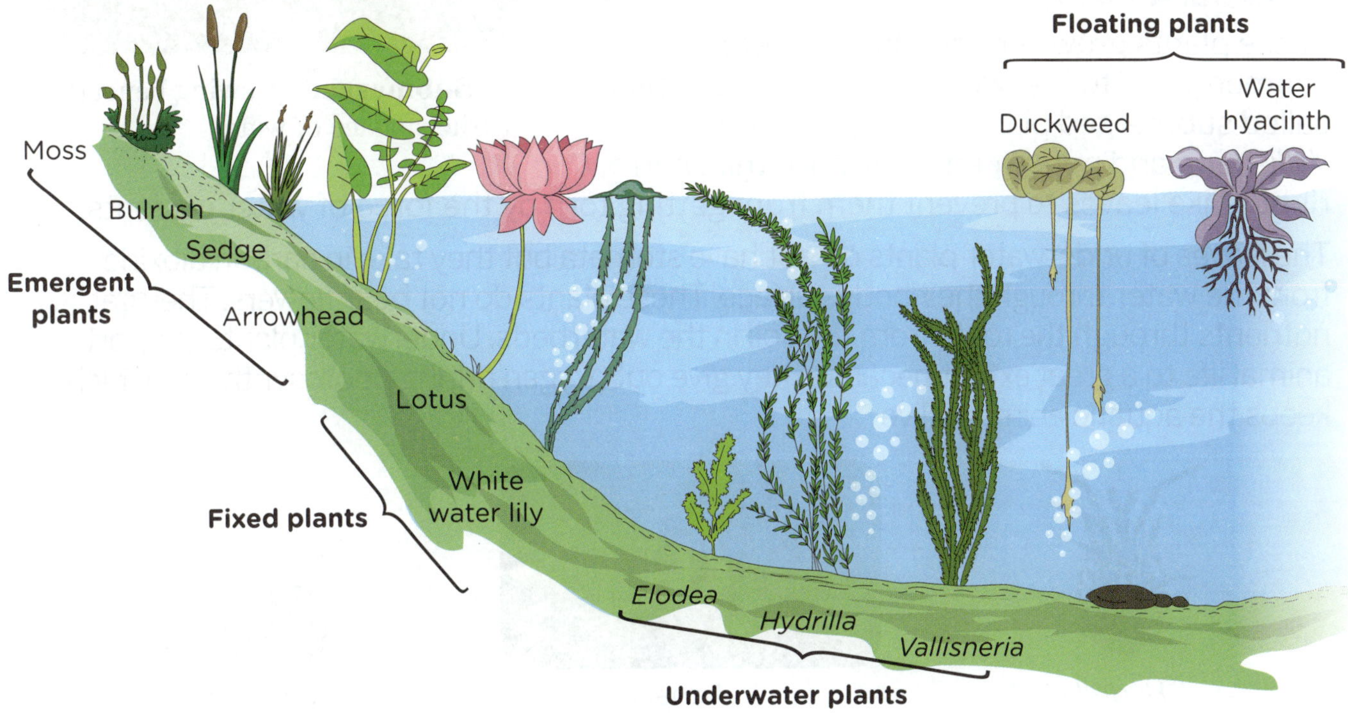

Emergent Plants

Some water plants are called emergent plants because even when their roots are fixed in the soil of the shallow waterbed, their leaves and stems extend out of the surface of the water body they are growing in. Examples of emergent plants are bulrush, cattail, arrowhead and sedge.

Bulrush

Sedge

Fixed Plants

These plants are fixed to the waterbed with the help of strong roots. Hence, they are called fixed plants. Examples are lotus and water lily. They have thin, long stalks[1] that are hollow and light in weight. These keep the flowers and leaves floating on the surface of the water. The leaves of these

Lotus

Water lily

Word Web

[1]**Stalk**: a thin stem that supports the leaves and flowers of a plant

plants have a waxy coating that prevents them from getting wet. The leaves have stomata on the upper side instead of the lower side. Fixed plants absorb nutrients from the soil in the waterbeds through their roots.

Underwater Plants

These plants grow and remain completely submerged[1] into the water. Hence, they are also called submerged plants. Examples are *Hydrilla*, *Vallisneria* and pondweed. They have thin, narrow, ribbon-like leaves to prevent them from getting torn by the force of water currents.

> **Word Web**
>
> [1]**Submerged**: growing beneath the surface of water

The leaves of underwater plants do not have stomata but they take in carbon dioxide from the water through their body surface. These plants do not bear flowers. They get nutrients through the roots from the soil in the waterbeds. Underwater plants support animal life to a great extent because they give out oxygen during photosynthesis, which keeps the aquatic animals alive.

Hydrilla

Vallisneria

Pondweed

Floating Plants

Plants that float on water are called floating plants. Examples are duckweed, water lettuce and water hyacinth. These plants float on water because either they have air filled inside their stems, for example, water hyacinth, or they are very small and light in weight, for example, duckweed. The roots of the floating plants absorb nutrients directly from the water.

Duckweed

Water lettuce

Revise and recall

State whether the following statements are true (T) or false (F).

1. Water lettuce floats on water. ☐
2. Sedges are fixed in water and hence are called fixed plants. ☐
3. Fixed plants have stomata on the upper side of their leaves. ☐
4. Duckweed is an example of emergent plant. ☐
5. The arrowhead plants have leaves and stems emerging out of the water surface. ☐

Terrestrial Plants

Plants that grow on land are called **terrestrial plants**. Terrestrial plants grow in deserts, mountains and hills, plains, marshy areas, forests, coastal areas, etc. Let us learn about the different types of terrestrial plants and their adaptations.

Plants in Deserts

Desert plants are also called **xerophytes**. They are adapted to grow in very hot and dry conditions. Examples of plants that grow in deserts are cacti, prickly pear and date palms.
Desert plants show the following adaptations:

(a) The stem of a cactus is thick and fleshy. This helps the plant to collect and store water, which is required for photosynthesis.
(b) The leaves of these plants are modified to spines[1]. Spines protect the plants and reduce water loss.
(c) These plants also have long roots that grow deep into the ground. They help in absorbing groundwater.

Word Web

[1]**Spines**: sharp, pointed structures on a plant

A cactus growing in a desert

Science in Context

Saguaro is a type of cactus found in deserts. It can live up to 200 years and can store up to 800 litres of water.

Plants on Mountains and Hills

Plants on mountains and hills are adapted to grow in very cold temperatures. Examples of such plants are pine, cedar, spruce and fir. The following adaptations are seen in these plants:

(a) The trees are straight, tall and cone-shaped so that snow can easily slide off their branches.
(b) Their leaves have a waxy coating and are needle-shaped, which helps the snow to slide off and prevents rotting of the plant.
(c) These plants have cones with seeds instead of flowers.

Pine tree

Plants in Plains

These plants are adapted to survive in varying climates of both hot and cold weather. Examples of plants that grow in plains are mango, banyan and teak. The following adaptations are seen in these plants:

(a) They have many branches with plenty of leaves and flowers.
(b) Some trees shed their leaves in autumn which grow back again during spring. Such trees are called **deciduous trees**.
(c) Some trees shed their leaves and grow new ones throughout the year. Such trees are called **evergreen trees**.

Mango tree

Plants in Marshy Areas

Marshy areas are places that have wet, clayey and sticky soil with water covering their surface. The plants growing in such areas develop roots that emerge out from the surface of the marsh. These roots help the plant to breathe. Hence, they are called breathing roots. Most of the plants that grow in marshy areas are called **mangroves**. Some examples are *Avicennia* and *Rhizophora*.

Mangroves

Plants in Forests

Forests usually have warm climates and get a lot of rain throughout the year. The plants that grow in forests grow tall with broad and abundant leaves, which can capture sunlight for photosynthesis. Examples of plants that grow in forests are redwood, mahogany, maple and oak.

Forest

Plants in Coastal Areas

Plants that grow in coastal areas usually grow tall and straight. They are adapted to survive in conditions of salty water and heavy rainfall. An example is coconut tree.

Coconut tree

Insectivorous Plants

Some plants live in a habitat where the soil is poor in nutrients or in thick forests where enough sunlight is not available to carry out photosynthesis. These plants feed on small insects for nutrition. Hence, they are called **insectivorous plants**. Some examples are pitcher plant and Venus flytrap.

Insectivorous plants show unique features that help them to catch their prey. The Venus flytrap has two lobes with hair-like spikes on their edges. These lobes snap shut when an insect sits on it.
The pitcher plant is shaped like a pitcher. Its edges secrete a slippery substance due to which the insects sitting on it slip and fall inside the pitcher, thus getting trapped.

Venus flytrap

Pitcher plant

Know the Fact!

There are about 600 types of carnivorous plants found all over the world except in Antarctica.

Non-green Plants

Some plants do not contain the green pigment chlorophyll and hence cannot carry out photosynthesis. Such plants are called **non-green plants**. These plants are adapted to absorb their food from dead plants and animals. Examples are coralroot and Indian pipe.

Indian pipe

Parasitic Plants

There are certain plants that depend on other plants partially or completely for their nutrition. They grow on other plants and absorb nutrients from them. Such plants are called **parasitic plants**. They often harm the plant on which they grow. Examples are *Cuscuta* and mistletoe.

Cuscuta

Revise and recall

Write an example for each of the following.

1. Desert plant ______________________
2. Mountain plant ______________________
3. Plant in plains ______________________
4. Plant in marshes ______________________
5. Insectivorous plant ______________________

Go Green

Walk through a park or a garden carefully. Tramping on small plants might kill them.

Let's Say Together

Adaptation Aquatic Terrestrial Mangroves Insectivorous Parasitic

Keywords

Habitat: The place where an organism naturally lives
Adaptation: The special features acquired by an organism to adjust itself in a habitat
Aquatic plants: Plants that grow and live in water
Terrestrial plants: Plants that grow on land
Xerophytes: Plants that grow in deserts
Breathing roots: The roots developed by the plants growing in marshes, which emerge out from the surface of the marsh
Insectivorous plants: Plants that trap insects for obtaining nutrients
Parasitic plants: Plants that grow on other plants and absorb nutrients from them

Summary

1. Plants adapt themselves to survive in their habitat.
2. Aquatic plants have special features to either float or stay completely under the water.
3. Aquatic plants are of these types: emergent, fixed, underwater and floating.
4. Insectivorous plants trap and eat insects, and non-green plants absorb food from dead plants and animals.
5. Plants that grow on other plants and absorb nutrients from them are called parasitic plants.

EXERCISE

A Choose the correct option for each of the following.

1. Which of these plants floats on water?
   (a) Duckweed (b) Moss (c) Water lily (d) *Hydrilla*
2. Which of the following is a xerophyte?
   (a) Cactus (b) Teak (c) Pine (d) Maple
3. Plants that are adapted to grow in deserts have
   (a) Spines (b) Thin stem (c) Short roots (d) Many leaves
4. Terrestrial plants are found in
   (a) Deserts (b) Plains (c) Mountains (d) All these places
5. An example of a non-green plant is
   (a) Cedar (b) Coralroot (c) Venus flytrap (d) Oak

B Fill in the blanks with the correct words.

1. Arrowhead is an example of ________________ plant. (floating/emergent)
2. Mountain plants have ________________ leaves. (broad/needle-like)
3. Mangroves grow in ________________. (deserts/marshy areas)
4. ________________ traps and eats insects. (Cactus/Pitcher plant)
5. Non-green plants do not have ________________. (chlorophyll/stems)
6. *Cuscuta* is a ________________ plant. (parasitic/non-green)

C Match the following.

Column A	Column B
(a) Prickly pear	(1) Mountain plant
(b) Pines	(2) Plains
(c) Banyan	(3) Insectivorous plant
(d) *Rhizophora*	(4) Desert plant
(e) Venus flytrap	(5) Mangroves

D State whether the following statements are true (T) or false (F).

1. Water lily is a floating plant. ☐
2. Terrestrial plants can grow both on land and in water. ☐
3. Desert plants have thin stems. ☐
4. The leaves of deciduous trees are shed in autumn. ☐
5. Plants growing in coastal areas cannot survive in water. ☐

E Name the following.

1. Plants having cones with seeds instead of flowers ____________________
2. Plants that trap and eat insects ____________________
3. Plants that remain completely submerged in water ____________________
4. Plants that absorb food from dead plants and animals ____________________
5. Plants that grow on other plants and often harm them ____________________

F Answer the following questions briefly.

1. What is adaptation?
2. Give two adaptations of underwater plants.
3. Give two examples each of emergent plants and parasitic plants.
4. Why do desert plants have thick stems?
5. Non-green plants cannot carry out photosynthesis. Why?

G Answer the following questions.

1. What are the different types of aquatic plants? Give one example for each.
2. List any two types of terrestrial plants and give one adaptation of each type.
3. Explain the adaptations shown by mountain plants.
4. Discuss the adaptations of plants that grow in plains.
5. What are insectivorous plants? Explain with examples.

H HOTS (Higher Order Thinking Skills)

1. A plant with broad leaves will not survive in a desert. Do you think this statement is correct? Explain. (Hint: Role of spines)
2. What would happen to a mountain plant if the climate changes from very cold to hot and humid?

I Match the adaptation to the plant type. One has been done for you.

These plants are adapted to live in very cold places.

These plants trap and eat insects to get nutrients.

These plants have roots that grow above the ground.

These plants have roots fixed to the soil of the waterbed but their leaves float on the surface of water.

These plants can live in very dry places as they have long roots to absorb the groundwater.

These plants grow in shallow waters but their leaves and stems are found growing out into the air.

J Life Skills

We can take care of plants by following small steps mentioned below:

1. We know that paper is made from plants. So, we should not waste paper and reuse it whenever possible. We should always use both sides of the paper.
2. Whenever you go out to play in a park, do not pluck leaves and flowers. Stop others also if they are doing so. The leaves of many plants are home to insects, birds and small animals.
3. Plant small herbs and shrubs around your home. These plants will give us fresh air to breathe.
4. Do not litter plastic in your surroundings. They are harmful to the plants.

K Project

Find out the different types of forests and the places where they are found. Refer to the books in your school library or use the Internet to get the information. Write the special features of plants that are adapted to grow in forests.

L Fun Activity (Cross-curricular)

Write a letter to the forest authority telling them the benefits of plants and trees so that they do not allow cutting down of trees in the future.

Letter

To,

The Forest Authority
Forest Department
India

From,
(Your name): ____________________
(Your school): ____________________
(Address): ____________________

Dear Sir/Madam,

____
____
____
____
____

Thanking you,

______________ Date: ______________

______________ Place: ______________

1 Look at the given pictures for hint and choose the correct option for the following.

1. This plant is adapted to grow in the mountains.
   (a) Pineapple (b) Pine (c) *Cuscuta*

2. This plant is adapted to grow under the water.
   (a) *Rhizophora* (b) *Vallisneria* (c) Water lily

3. This plant is adapted to digest insects.
   (a) Pitcher plant (b) Mistletoe (c) *Vallisneria*

2 Identify the emergent, floating, fixed and underwater plants in the picture given below.

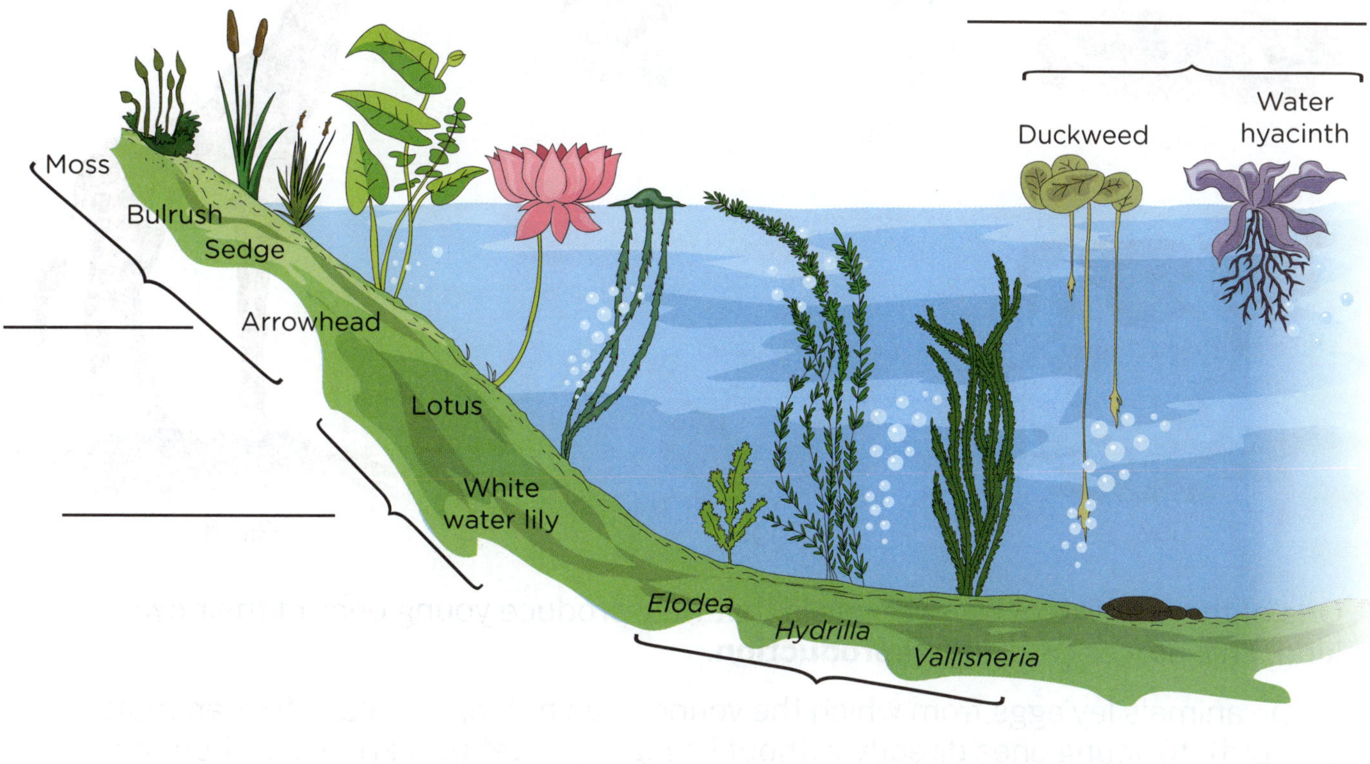

3 Animals and Their Young Ones

Learning Checklist

- Animals that lay eggs
- Animals that give birth to babies

Let's Get Started

The eggs belong to which of these animals? Take the animal to its eggs by drawing a line.

Dog

Cat

Hen

Giraffe

Cow

Eggs

One of the features of living things is that they produce young ones of their own kind. This process is called **reproduction**.

Some animals lay eggs from which the young ones hatch, whereas other animals give birth to young ones directly without laying eggs. Let us learn more about how animals reproduce.

ANIMALS THAT LAY EGGS

The animals that reproduce by laying eggs are called **egg-laying animals**. Examples are birds, frog, fish, snake, lizard and insects like cockroach and butterfly.

The eggs are kept in a warm place or the parent animals sit on their eggs to keep them warm. This process is known as **incubation**.

Science in Context

Egg-laying animals are also called oviparous animals.

Birds

Birds lay eggs in their nests and incubate the eggs by sitting on them until the eggs hatch into young ones. When the eggs hatch, chicks come out. They cannot fly as they are featherless and cannot see. The parent birds help them in feeding and take care of them until they develop feathers and learn to fly.

Hen sitting on eggs to incubate them

Chicks hatching from eggs

Structure of an egg

Eggs produced by all the birds have the same kind of internal structure. The thin, hard outer layer that protects the contents of the egg is called the **egg shell**. The jelly-like white-coloured substance that is present inside the egg shell is called the **albumen**. The yellow-coloured substance present within the albumen is called the **yolk**.

The yolk consists of the essential nutrients required for the development of a growing baby called an **embryo**. The embryo ultimately develops into a young one.

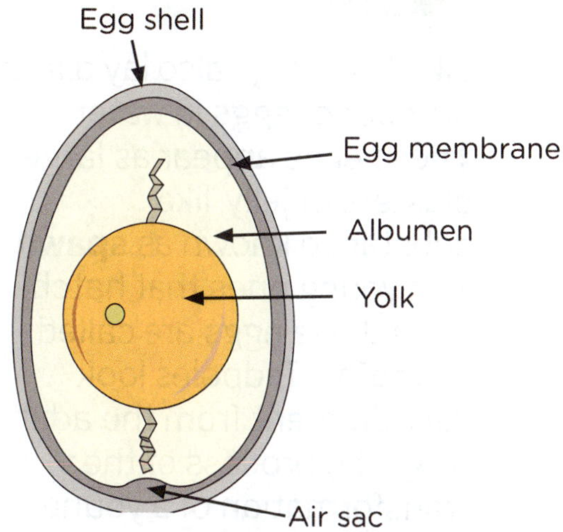

Structure of an egg

The different stages of the development of an embryo into an adult are called the **life cycle** of an animal.

Science in Context

Yolk is rich in nutrients like fats, minerals and vitamins, and albumen is rich in proteins.

Life cycle of a hen

Fish

Fish lay plenty of eggs in water at a time. Out of these, only a few develop into baby fish as some of the eggs get eaten by larger fish and other animals. Generally, these eggs obtain warmth for incubation from the sunrays.

Frogs

Like fish, frogs also lay a large number of eggs in water. These eggs appear as large clusters of jelly-like substance known as **spawn**. The young ones that hatch from these eggs are called **tadpoles**. Tadpoles look very different from the adult frog. The process of the transformation of a young one into an adult that looks completely different is called **metamorphosis**. After undergoing metamorphosis, the tadpole becomes an adult frog.

Life cycle of a frog

Butterfly

The life cycle of a butterfly has four stages. Butterflies lay their eggs on leaves. A small worm-like **caterpillar** hatches from the eggs. This stage is called **larva**. The caterpillar grows in size by eating the leaves of the plants and develops a protective covering around itself. This stage is known as **pupa**. The pupa sheds its old skin many times. The process of shedding old skin by animals is called **moulting**. Finally, the adult butterfly comes out from the pupa.

Life cycle of a butterfly

Science in Context
Maggot is the larval form of a housefly. Wriggler is the larval form of a mosquito.

Grasshoppers and Cockroaches

The life cycle of grasshoppers and cockroaches involves three main stages. The tiny larvae that hatch from the eggs are called **nymphs**. The nymphs closely resemble their parent, but do not have wings. A nymph undergoes moulting several times and eventually develops into an adult.

Life cycle of a grasshopper

Reptiles

Reptiles such as snakes and lizards lay their eggs on the ground. Out of these eggs, only a few develop into adults with the help of the sunrays that provide warmth to these eggs. Some of the eggs are eaten by other animals.

Revise and recall

State whether the following statements are true (T) or false (F).

1. Lizards reproduce by laying eggs. ☐
2. The eggs produced by all the birds have the same kind of internal structure. ☐
3. Fish lay only one egg in water at a time. ☐
4. The young ones that hatch from the eggs of frogs are called pupa. ☐

ANIMALS THAT GIVE BIRTH TO BABIES

Animals that give birth to young ones and suckle[1] them with milk are called **mammals**. Dogs, cats, cows, monkeys, rabbits, elephants, kangaroos, giraffes, lions and human beings are examples of mammals.

The complete development of the young ones takes place inside the mother's body. The mother feeds the young ones with her milk after they are born.

Mammals have a well-developed brain. Most of them have hair on their body and most of them live on land. They breathe through their lungs.

Word Web

[1]**Suckle**: feed young ones with one's own milk

Science in Context

Mammals are also called viviparous animals.

Know the Fact!

Bats are mammals even though they are able to fly like birds.

Kangaroo with its joey

Cow with its calf

Some mammals such as dolphins and whales live in water. They are called **aquatic mammals**. They do not have hair on their body. They breathe through lungs and often come up to the water surface to breathe in air.

Dolphin

Whale

Know the Fact!

Blue whale is the largest mammal.

Science in Context

Duckbilled platypus and spiny anteater reproduce by laying eggs. But they are still called mammals because they feed their young ones with their milk, have hair on their body and breathe through lungs.

Mammals Care for Their Young Ones

Mammals take care of their young ones for a long time. They keep their babies clean and warm. They feed their babies and protect them from enemies. Most fish, reptiles and insects do not take care of their young ones. They lay their eggs in a safe place and leave the young ones to live on their own.

Mammals care for their young ones

Wonder!

The *Tilapia* fish carries its eggs in its mouth until they hatch. The small fish hide in the parent's mouth when faced with danger.

Revise and recall

State whether the following statements are true (T) or false (F).

1. In mammals, the complete development of the young ones takes place inside the mother's body. ☐
2. Mammals do not have well-developed brains. ☐
3. All mammals have hair on their body. ☐
4. Human beings do not take care of their young ones. ☐

Let's Say Together

Incubation	Albumen	Yolk	Embryo	Metamorphosis
Tadpole	Moulting	Larva	Pupa	Mammals

Keywords

Incubation: The process of keeping eggs warm, often done by parent birds by sitting on them until they hatch into young ones

Metamorphosis: The process of the transformation of a young one into an adult that looks completely different

Spawn: A cluster of eggs laid by a frog which looks like jelly-like substance

Nymph: Larva of grasshoppers and cockroaches

Caterpillar: The larval stage of a butterfly

Moulting: The process of shedding old skin by animals

Mammals: Animals that give birth to young ones and suckle them with milk

Summary

1. Living organisms produce their young ones by the process of reproduction.
2. Some animals lay eggs. When the eggs hatch, young ones come out.
3. Eggs of birds contain egg shell, albumen and yolk.
4. The transformation of a young one into an adult that looks completely different is called metamorphosis.
5. The shedding of old skin by some insects to develop into an adult is called moulting.
6. The life cycle of animals involves different stages of development from an embryo to an adult.
7. Animals that give birth to young ones and feed them with their milk are called mammals.
8. In mammals, the complete development of the young ones takes place inside the mother's body.

EXERCISE

A Choose the correct option for each of the following.

1. Identify the animal that does not reproduce by laying eggs.
   (a) Housefly (b) Deer (c) Butterfly (d) Fish
2. The jelly-like white-coloured substance that is present inside the egg shell is
   (a) Albumen (b) Yolk (c) Egg shell (d) Embryo
3. The process of shedding old skin by animals is called
   (a) Incubation (b) Metamorphosis (c) Moulting (d) Life cycle
4. Identify the egg-laying animal from the following.
   (a) Hippopotamus (b) Zebra (c) Frog (d) Cat
5. In which of these animals, does the development of the young one take place inside the mother's body?
   (a) Grasshopper (b) Housefly (c) Rabbit (d) Lizard

B Fill in the blanks with the correct words.

1. Birds reproduce by ______________. (laying eggs/giving birth to young ones)
2. The large cluster of frog's eggs is called ________________. (spawn/nymph)
3. Lizards lay their eggs ________________. (in water/on the ground)
4. Animals that feed their young ones with their own milk are called ______________. (mammals/insects)
5. Mammals breathe with the help of ________________. (skin/lungs)

C Match the following.

Column A	Column B
(a) Butterfly	(1) Calf
(b) Hen	(2) Caterpillar
(c) Frog	(3) Tadpole
(d) Grasshopper	(4) Chick
(e) Cow	(5) Nymph

D **State whether the following statements are true (T) or false (F).**

1. All animals reproduce by laying eggs. ☐
2. Yolk is the yellow-coloured substance that is present inside the egg. ☐
3. Mammals like dolphins come up to the surface of water to breathe in air. ☐
4. After hatching, the tiny caterpillar that comes out from the eggs of a butterfly is known as pupa. ☐
5. A tadpole looks similar to an adult frog. ☐

E **Give two examples for each of the following.**

1. Egg-laying animals ____________ ____________
2. Animals that give birth to young ones ____________ ____________
3. Aquatic mammals ____________ ____________
4. Animals that lay eggs in water ____________ ____________
5. Animals that undergo moulting ____________ ____________

F **Answer the following questions briefly.**

1. Define reproduction.
2. What are the different ways in which animals reproduce?
3. What is incubation?
4. What is metamorphosis?
5. How do mammals take care of their young ones?

G **Answer the following questions.**

1. Describe the structure of an egg with the help of a diagram.
2. Describe the life cycle of a butterfly.
3. What are aquatic mammals? Mention their specific features.

H **HOTS (Higher Order Thinking Skills)**

1. Rahul says the young ones of all animals look like their parents. Do you agree? Why or why not? (Hint: Read the life cycle of frog and butterfly.)
2. A dolphin lives in water but does not have gills like other fish. Why? (Hint: Dolphin is an aquatic mammal.)

I **Name the stages of the life cycle of a frog shown in the pictures given below.**

______________ ______________ ______________

J **Life Skills**

Put a tick mark (✓) against the correct statements and cross out (✗) the wrong ones.

1. We should not pluck leaves or pull them unnecessarily as they are home to some insects. ☐
2. We should destroy or disturb birds' eggs. ☐
3. We should not throw waste in ponds as they are home to some aquatic animals. ☐
4. We should try to keep water and some grains or fruits in our balcony for birds. ☐

K **Project**

1. Collect pictures of various animals from old newspapers and magazines. Group them as egg-laying animals and the animals that give birth to young ones. Paste these pictures in a scrapbook. Display your scrapbook in the classroom.
2. Take a chart paper and paste or draw various stages involved in the life cycle of a butterfly/frog/grasshopper. Write the description about each stage and display the chart in your classroom.

WORKSHEET

1 **Label the stages involved in the life cycle of a butterfly.**

2 **In the table below, names of some animals are given. Write down what the young ones of these animals are called. Also, write whether these animals give birth to young ones or lay eggs to reproduce.**

Name of the Animal	Young Ones	Gives Birth to Young Ones/Lay Eggs
Cow		
Hen		
Frog		
Kangaroo		
Grassshopper		
Cat		

4 Adaptations in Animals

Learning Checklist

- Adaptations to environment
- Adaptations for food
- Adaptations for protection
- Extinct and endangered animals

Let's Get Started

Look at the pictures of animals given and identify the habitats they live in. Write in the space provided below each animal.

Land Water Tree

____________ ____________ ____________

Like plants, animals also undergo changes over a period of time to adapt to their surroundings. Let us learn about the adaptations of different animals in detail in this chapter.

ADAPTATIONS TO ENVIRONMENT

Based on the environment in which they live, animals are grouped as terrestrial, aquatic, amphibian, aerial and arboreal.

Terrestrial Animals

Animals that live on land are called **terrestrial animals**. The climatic conditions on land vary from place to place.

Polar regions are extremely cold. Animals like polar bears, Arctic foxes, penguins, seals and walruses live there. To protect themselves from cold, these animals have thick, hairy skin. Animals like polar bear and walrus also have a thick layer of fat under the skin called **blubber**.

Polar bear

Penguin

Due to the scarcity of food during cold periods, animals like bear, frog and snake prefer to sleep throughout the winter and remain inactive. This long winter sleep is called **hibernation**.

Mountains are also very cold. Animals that live on mountains such as the mountain sheep, mountain goats and yaks have thick fur on their body, which keeps them warm during cold weather. These animals have strong hooves[1] that help them to walk on the slopes of mountains.

Yak

Word Web

[1]**Hooves**: the hard covering present in the foot of some animals

Camel

Deserts are usually very hot. Animals that live in deserts such as camels have thick skin and less hair on their body. This helps to prevent water loss from their body.

Some animals like snails, lizards and earthworms sleep for a long time during summer months to escape the heat. This long summer sleep is called **aestivation**.

Science in Context

A camel drinks a large amount of water at a time. Therefore, it is able to stay without water for long periods of time. The hump of the camel contains a large amount of stored fat. This is used when there is a scarcity of food. It has long legs and flat hooves, which help it to walk easily on the loose desert sand without the feet sinking in. A camel has double eyelids, which prevent the sand from entering its eyes. A camel is also called the ship of the desert.

Aquatic Animals

Whale

Turtle

Animals that live in water are called **aquatic animals**. Fish, whale, turtle and octopus are a few examples of aquatic animals. Fish have fins, and whales and turtles have paddle-like flippers that help them in swimming. Most aquatic animals respire through gills.

Amphibians

Animals such as frog and salamander that can live both in water and on land are called **amphibians**. Most amphibians have lungs that help them to breathe on land and moist skin that helps them to breathe underwater. Frogs have well-developed, strong hindlimbs that help them to hop on land and webbed feet to help them swim in water.

Frog

Aerial Animals

Animals that can fly and spend their maximum time in the air are called **aerial animals**. Birds are examples of aerial animals. They have hollow bones, boat-shaped body, wings and feathers to help them fly. Bats are the only mammals that can fly. Insects such as butterflies and dragonflies have thin, papery wings that help them to fly.

Bird

Arboreal Animals

Animals that spend a majority of their time on trees are called **arboreal animals**. Monkeys, squirrels, tree lizards and koala bears are examples of arboreal animals. These animals have strong limbs and sharp claws that help them in climbing trees. The tail of monkeys helps them to hang on the branches of trees.

Monkey

Koala bear

ADAPTATIONS FOR FOOD

Based on the type of food that animals eat, they are grouped into the following categories:

Herbivores

Animals that eat only plants are called **herbivores**. These animals have strong and broad teeth in the front to bite off leaves and grass, and strong chewing teeth with space in between them (for grinding) at the back. They are able to travel long distances with the help of their long and strong legs in search of food. Examples include deer, giraffe and elephant.

Deer

Science in Context

Plant products are rich in a substance called cellulose. Human beings cannot digest cellulose. Most herbivores have microbes in their digestive tract that help them to digest cellulose.

Carnivores

Animals that eat the flesh of other animals are called **carnivores**. These animals have pointed, sharp, long and curved canines to tear the flesh of their prey. Carnivores chew the flesh and bones with the help of broad and flat grinding teeth present at the back of their mouth. Examples include wolf, tiger and lion.

Tiger

Omnivores

Animals such as bears, crows and human beings eat both plants and the flesh of other animals. They are called **omnivores**.

Crow

Scavengers

Animals that feed on dead and decaying animals are called **scavengers**. Examples include vultures, jackals, wild dogs and hyenas. Scavengers have sharp teeth for ripping and tearing flesh.

Hyena

Parasites

Roundworm

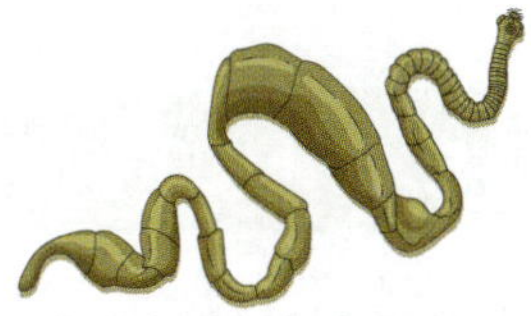

Tapeworm

Organisms that live on or inside the body of other living organisms and depend on them for food are called **parasites**. The animal on or inside which the parasite lives is called the **host**. Roundworms, hookworms and tapeworms are parasites that live inside the body of the host.

Louse

Flea

Lice (singular: louse), ticks and fleas are parasites that live on the surface of the host's body. The mouth of these organisms is adapted to suck blood from the host's body.

ADAPTATIONS FOR PROTECTION

Animals show different types of adaptations to protect themselves from danger.

(a) Rabbits, deer, fish and mice can move very fast to protect themselves from their enemies.

(b) The thick skin of elephants and hippopotamuses helps in protecting them from the hot climate.

(c) Insects like cockroaches have a hard outer body covering for protection.

(d) The hard shell of crabs and turtles protects their soft bodies.

(e) The sharp spines of porcupines protect them from their enemies.

The features of animals (colour and shape) that help them to mix or merge with their surroundings are called **camouflage**. Most animals escape from their enemies or catch their prey by camouflaging themselves.

(a) Polar bears have white fur that blends with snow. It helps them to hide in snow.

(b) Tigers have black stripes over an orange-coloured body, which helps them to blend with the forest or the grassland.

(c) Some insects have the structure of the leaves (leaf insect) or a twig (stick insect) so that they can hide from their enemies.

(d) Chameleons can change the colour of their skin to match themselves to their surroundings.

Porcupine

Leaf insect

Stick insect

Chameleon

EXTINCT AND ENDANGERED ANIMALS

Animals such as dodos, passenger pigeons, Caribbean monk seals and Tecopa pupfish are some of the species that are no longer found on the Earth. These animals are called **extinct animals**.

Dodo

Animals that are unable to adapt to their surroundings die and eventually become extinct. Millions of years ago, huge animals called dinosaurs lived on the Earth. When it became very cold, they were not able to adjust to the cold climate and became extinct.

Indian rhinoceros

Many animals are in danger due to the destruction of forests by human beings for their needs. The numbers of some animals such as tigers, cheetahs, giant pandas and Indian rhinoceros are fast declining and they may soon disappear completely from the Earth. These animals are called **endangered animals**.

Revise and recall

State whether the following statements are true (T) or false (F).

1. Walrus is a terrestrial animal that lives in polar regions. ☐
2. Rabbit undergoes aestivation. ☐
3. Koala bear is an arboreal animal. ☐
4. Wolf is an omnivore. ☐
5. Roundworms live inside the body of the host. ☐

Let's Say Together

Hibernation Aestivation Parasites Camouflage Extinct Endangered

Keywords

Hibernation: The long sleep of animals during winter months
Aestivation: The long sleep of animals during summer months
Aerial animals: Animals that can fly and spend their maximum time in the air
Arboreal animals: Animals that spend a majority of their time on trees
Parasites: Organisms that live on or inside the body of other living organisms and depend on them for food

Camouflage: The characteristics of animals (colour and shape) that help them to merge with their surroundings in order to escape from their enemies or to catch their prey
Extinct animals: Animals that are no longer found on the Earth
Endangered animals: Animals that are in danger of becoming extinct and may disappear soon

Summary

1. The features and habits that enable living organisms to live and grow in their surroundings are called adaptations.
2. Animals that live on land are called terrestrial animals.
3. Animals that live in water are called aquatic animals.
4. Animals that can live both in water and on land are called amphibians.
5. Animals that can fly and spend their maximum time in the air are called aerial animals.
6. Animals that spend a majority of their time on trees are called arboreal animals.
7. Based on the type of food they eat, animals are grouped into herbivores, carnivores, omnivores, scavengers and parasites.
8. Animals protect themselves from their enemies by adopting special features such as fast movement, having thick skin and by camouflage.
9. Many animals are in danger due to the destruction of forests by human beings for their needs.

EXERCISE

A Choose the correct option for each of the following.

1. Identify the animal that sleeps throughout the summer months.
   (a) Bear (b) Snail (c) Rabbit (d) Frog
2. Aquatic animals respire mostly through their
   (a) Skin (b) Lungs (c) Gills (d) Lungs and skin
3. Identify the parasite that lives on the host's body.
   (a) Roundworm (b) Hookworm (c) Lice (d) Tapeworm
4. Identify the animal that cannot protect itself by camouflaging.
   (a) Chameleon (b) Tiger (c) Hippopotamus (d) Polar bear
5. Identify the extinct animal from the following.
   (a) Giant panda (b) Indian rhinoceros (c) Dodo (d) Tiger

B **Fill in the blanks with the correct words.**

1. A polar bear has ________________ to keep it warm. (blubber/flesh)
2. Winter sleep is also called ________________. (hibernation/aestivation)
3. Eagle is an example of an ________________ animal. (aerial/arboreal)
4. Koala bear is ________________ animal. (an arboreal/a terrestrial)
5. Crow is ________________. (a herbivore/an omnivore)

C **Match the following.**

Column A	Column B
(a) Deer	(1) Aquatic animal
(b) Seal	(2) Terrestrial animal
(c) Salamander	(3) Arboreal
(d) Birds	(4) Amphibian
(e) Koala bear	(5) Aerial

D **State whether the following statements are true (T) or false (F).**

1. All terrestrial animals undergo aestivation. ☐
2. The thick fur of the yak helps in protecting it from the cold weather. ☐
3. Insects such as butterflies have thin, papery wings that help them to fly. ☐
4. Amphibians breathe through lungs as well as moist skin. ☐
5. Bear is an example of herbivore. ☐

E **Give two examples for each of the following.**

1. Arboreal animals ________ ________
2. Animals that undergo hibernation ________ ________
3. Carnivores ________ ________
4. Scavengers ________ ________
5. Parasites that live inside the host's body ________ ________

F **Answer the following questions briefly.**

1. Why do some animals undergo hibernation?

2. Mention the adaptations shown by arboreal animals.
3. Distinguish between parasites and scavengers.
4. Define camouflage.
5. How are extinct animals different from endangered animals?

G Answer the following questions.

1. Describe in brief about the various adaptations of terrestrial animals.
2. Describe the adaptations of aquatic animals and amphibians.
3. Describe in brief about the grouping of animals according to their eating habits.
4. Describe the various adaptations shown by animals for their protection.

H HOTS (Higher Order Thinking Skills)

1. How is a camel different from yak even though both are terrestrial animals?
(Hint: Recall about various adaptations of terrestrial animals.)
2. Can endangered animals become extinct soon? How can they be protected from becoming extinct? (Hint: Human activities like hunting and destruction of forests)

I Look at the pictures shown below and circle the odd one out. Give a reason for your selection.

1.    

____

2.    

____

J Life Skills

Which of the following images shows the correct way of treating animals? Put a tick mark (✓) against the correct actions and cross (✗) against the wrong ones.

1. Rohit is hurting the butterfly.

2. Akhil is observing the structure of a butterfly.

3. Shivam is killing the ants.

4. George is trapping the mouse.

5. Hiyang is harming the frog.

6. Medhansh is feeding the bird.

K Project

Collect pictures of various animals from old newspapers and magazines. Group them according to their habitat as terrestrial, aquatic, amphibian, aerial and arboreal animals, and paste the pictures in a scrapbook. Write a few lines about the adaptations shown by the animals in each habitat. Display your scrapbook in the classroom.

L Fun Activity (Cross-curricular)

1. Unscramble the jumbled words to form words related to the habitat of animals. One has been done for you.

LETRTSERRAI	TERRESTRIAL
TQAICAU	
LRAIAE	
BEOARLRA	
AHIMANPIB	

2. Classify the following animals based on their habitat in the table given below.

Fish, Cow, Horse, Monkey, Tiger, Flying squirrel, Bird, Polar bear, Penguin, Seal, Koala bear, Camel, Lizard, Whale, Tree lizard

Terrestrial Animals	Aquatic Animals	Aerial Animals	Arboreal Animals

Let's make a polar bear using paper

Materials required: Chart paper, crayons/markers, glue, scissors, paper bag and thread/string

Procedure:

1. Take an empty paper bag.
2. Carefully fold the edges of the paper bag along the dotted line as shown below to get the shape of a polar bear's head.
3. Take a chart paper and with the help of scissors, cut small eyes, ears, paws and claws of the polar bear.
4. Paste them in the relevant places using glue.
5. With the help of markers/crayons, draw the mouth and nose on the polar bear's head.
6. Make a small hole at the centre of the paper bag and attach a thread/string to hang it on the wall.

Your paper polar bear is ready.

WORKSHEET

Solve the crossword puzzle with the help of the clues given below.

Across	Down
3. I am also called the ship of the desert.	1. I am a scavenger.
4. I am an omnivore.	2. I can live both in water and on land.
6. I can protect myself by changing my colour.	5. I am an insect and have a hard outer body covering.
9. I am a herbivore.	7. I am an aquatic mammal.
10. I live inside the host's body.	8. I am an extinct animal.
12. I am the national animal of India and in danger of becoming extinct.	11. I love hanging from the branches of trees.

5 Human Body: Circulatory and Excretory Systems

Learning Checklist

- Circulatory system
- Excretory system

Let's Get Started

Our body has different organs. According to their functions, organs are grouped into different organ systems. In Class 3, we learned about the circulatory and excretory systems in brief. Can you recall the names of the organs that make up the circulatory and excretory systems from the images given below?

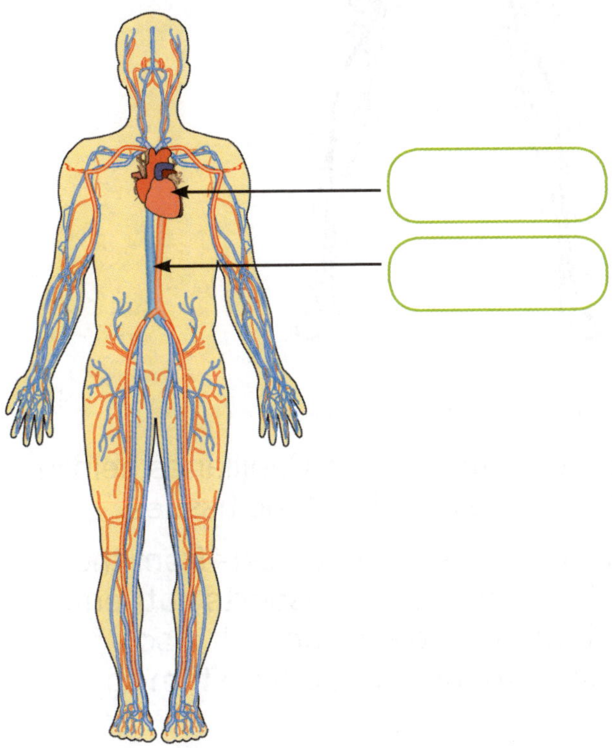

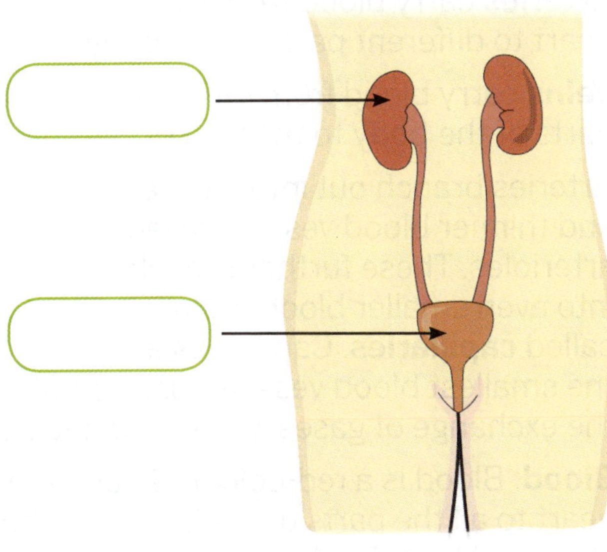

In this chapter, we will learn more about the organs and functions of the circulatory and excretory systems.

CIRCULATORY SYSTEM

The circulatory system transports substances inside our body. It consists of the heart, a network of blood vessels and blood.

Heart: The heart is a muscular organ that pumps blood into the larger blood vessels, which branch into smaller ones to reach all the organs of a human body. The heart also receives blood from all the organs of the body.

Blood vessels: These are thin tube-like structures that start from the heart and run through the entire body forming a network. They carry blood from the heart to all the parts of the body, and from different parts of the body back to the heart. The blood vessels are of three types—arteries, veins and capillaries.

Arteries carry blood from the heart to different parts of the body.

Veins carry blood from different parts of the body to the heart.

Arteries branch out into smaller and thinner blood vessels called arterioles. These further branch into even smaller blood vessels called **capillaries**. Capillaries are the smallest blood vessels. Many capillaries reunite to form veins. Capillaries help in the exchange of gases, water and nutrients between the blood and the tissues.

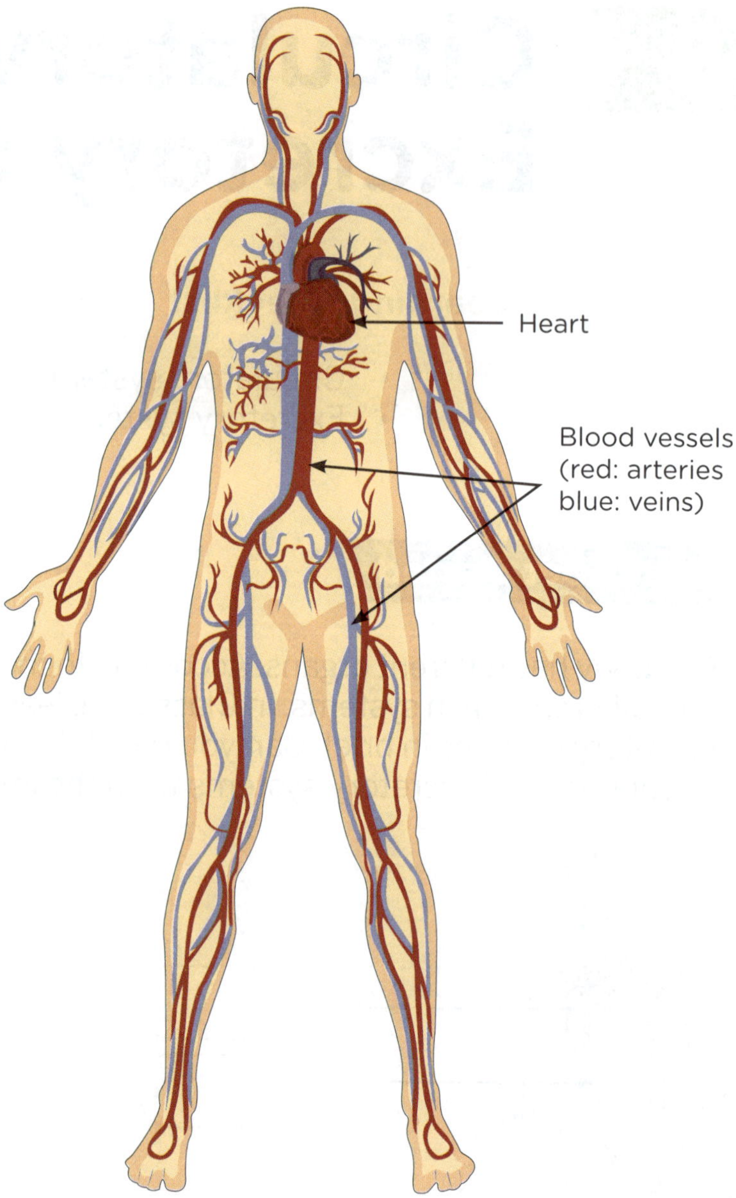

Human circulatory system

Blood: Blood is a red-coloured fluid that flows through the blood vessels from the heart to all the parts of the body and then back to the heart. It transports nutrients absorbed from food, oxygen, carbon dioxide and water inside the body. It also transports the waste products produced in the body to the excretory system so that they can be removed from the body.

Revise and recall

Who am I?

1. I am a muscular organ that pumps blood. ________________
2. I carry blood from the heart to all parts of the body and then back to the heart. ________________
3. I am the smallest blood vessel. ________________
4. I am the blood vessel that carries blood from the heart to different parts of the body. ________________
5. I am the blood vessel that carries blood from different parts of the body back to the heart. ________________
6. I flow through the blood vessels. ________________

EXCRETORY SYSTEM

The excretory system removes wastes from our body. The organs of the excretory system include a pair of kidneys, a pair of tubes called ureters, a urinary bladder and a urethra.

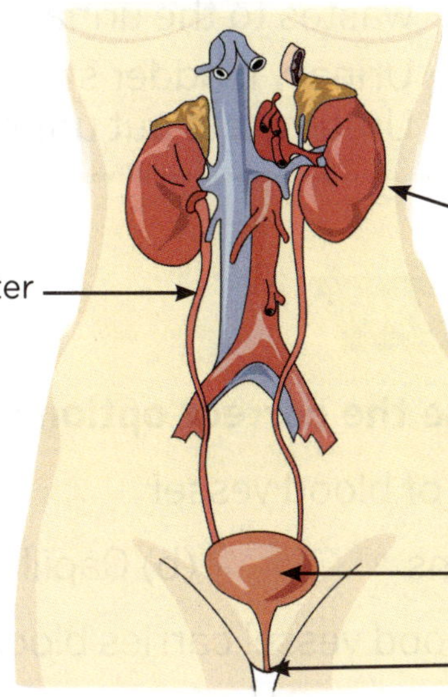

Human excretory system

Kidneys are bean-shaped structures that act like filters to collect harmful wastes such as urine and excess salts from the blood. **Ureters** are a pair of tubes that carry these wastes from the kidneys to the urinary bladder. **Urinary bladder** stores the urine until it is released from the body. **Urethra** is a tube that lets out the urine from the urinary bladder and thus out of the body.

Let's Say Together

Arteries Veins Capillaries Kidneys Ureters Urinary bladder Urethra

Keywords

Circulatory system: The organ system that helps to transport substances to different parts of our body

Excretory system: The organ system that helps to remove wastes from our body

Summary

1. The circulatory system consists of the heart, a network of blood vessels and blood.
2. The heart is a muscular organ that pumps blood to all the parts of the body and also receives back blood from different parts of the body.
3. Blood vessels are thin tubes that carry blood from the heart to all parts of body and then back to the heart.
4. Blood vessels are of three types—arteries, veins and capillaries.
5. Blood is a red-coloured fluid that flows through the blood vessels.
6. The excretory system consists of a pair of kidneys, a pair of ureters, a urinary bladder and a urethra.
7. Kidneys filter wastes from the blood, and ureters carry these wastes to the urinary bladder.
8. Urinary bladder stores urine till it is released from the body. Urethra lets out urine from the body.

EXERCISE

A Choose the correct option for each of the following.

1. A type of blood vessel

   (a) Veins (b) Capillaries (c) Arteries (d) All of these

2. This blood vessel carries blood from the different parts of the body to the heart.

   (a) Artery (b) Vein (c) Capillary (d) Ureter

3. The function of the excretory system is to remove

   (a) saliva (b) waste (c) blood (d) water

4. Which of these is an organ of the excretory system?

   (a) Blood vessel (b) Urinary bladder

   (c) Heart (d) Blood

5. Ureters carry wastes from the

   (a) Kidney to the blood vessel (b) Heart to the blood vessel

   (c) Kidney to the bladder (d) Bladder to the kidney

B Fill in the blanks with the correct words.

1. The heart pumps ______________________ to all the organs. (wastes/blood)
2. The __________ system removes wastes from the body. (excretory/circulatory)
3. ____________________________ filter waste from the body. (Heart/Kidneys)
4. _______________ are the tubes that connect the kidneys to the urinary bladder. (Urethra/Ureters)
5. Urine gets stored in the ______________________. (urinary bladder/kidneys)

C Match the following.

Column A	Column B
(a) Kidneys	(1) A pair of tubes
(b) Blood vessels	(2) Red-coloured fluid
(c) Blood	(3) Muscular organ
(d) Heart	(4) Bean-shaped
(e) Ureters	(5) Network of thin tubes

D State whether the following statements are true (T) or false (F).

1. Circulatory system removes wastes in the form of urine from the body. ☐
2. The heart pumps blood into the blood vessels. ☐
3. Blood vessels carry blood to only the hands and legs in the body. ☐
4. Our body has only one kidney. ☐
5. Kidneys act as a filter to remove wastes from the body. ☐

E Name the following in one word.

1. A muscular organ that pumps blood ______________________
2. The body part where urine is stored ______________________
3. The tubes that carry wastes from the kidneys to the urinary bladder __________
4. Blood vessels that carry blood from different organs back to the heart __________
5. Smallest blood vessels ______________________

F **Answer the following questions briefly.**

1. Name the organs of the circulatory system.
2. What is the function of the circulatory system?
3. Name the three types of blood vessels.
4. Name the organs of the excretory system.

G **Answer the following questions.**

1. Write a note on blood vessels.
2. Describe the organs and function of the human excretory system with the help of a diagram.

H **HOTS (Higher Order Thinking Skills)**

1. Why does your heart beat faster when you exercise? (Hint: The more active the body is, more oxygen it needs.)
2. What would happen if we did not have an excretory system? (Hint: Think about the function of the excretory system.)

I **Label the parts of the organ system shown below and also name the organ system.**

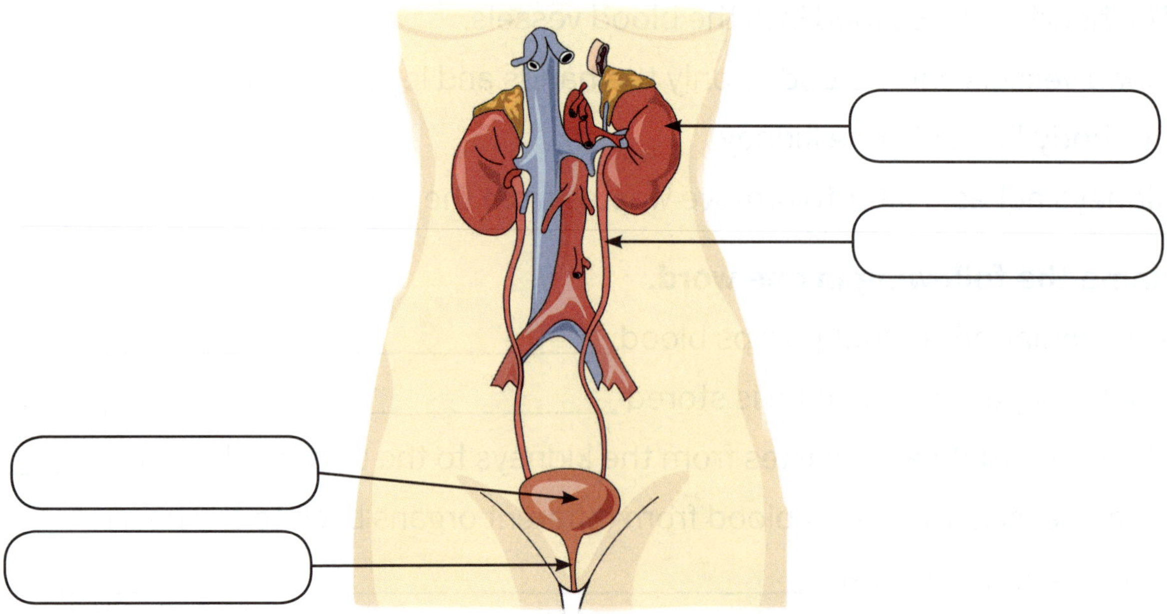

Name of the organ system: ____________________

J Life Skills

1. The number of times a heart beats in a minute is called the heart rate or pulse. We can feel the pulse in our body at those places where an artery passes close to the skin.

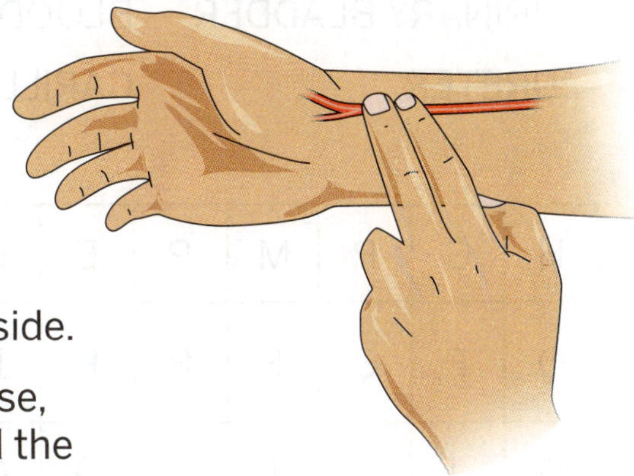

   Feel your pulse by placing two fingers on your wrist as shown in the picture given alongside.

2. When we do some physical activity like exercise, more blood has to be sent to the muscles and the heart rate increases.

   Carry out the activities given in the table and count your heart rate after each activity. Fill in the boxes and observe how your heart beats after performing every action.

Action	Heart Rate
Sitting	
After marching for a minute	
After jogging in one place for a minute	
After walking around the room for a minute	
After lying down for a minute	

K Project

1. Every person has a different blood type called blood group. Find out about the different types of blood groups that are found in human beings. Make a list of the different blood groups in your family and find out with whom your blood group matches.
2. Draw the human circulatory and excretory systems on a chart, and display it in your class.

WORKSHEET

Find the words given below in the grid and circle them. One has been done for you.

URINARY BLADDER   BLOOD VESSELS   HEART   KIDNEYS   URETHRA
URETER   CAPILLARIES   VEINS   ARTERIES

H	G	P	M	P	E	U	A	M	R	T	G	Z	M	L	I
Q	F	Q	F	R	R	F	F	N	G	N	X	X	Q	J	S
D	J	Z	T	E	G	O	M	I	K	N	X	F	B	H	E
E	N	F	O	D	L	D	H	E	H	K	Q	Y	T	Q	I
K	J	O	V	D	J	F	N	K	T	V	V	T	E	M	R
R	U	P	Z	A	A	G	I	R	H	V	J	E	M	H	A
H	Q	S	S	L	E	S	S	E	V	D	O	O	L	B	L
E	M	P	H	B	O	U	M	G	L	O	U	V	X	C	L
A	E	V	T	Y	S	E	I	R	E	T	R	A	H	L	I
R	H	V	G	R	U	C	X	U	R	E	T	E	R	B	P
T	J	N	N	A	Z	J	S	V	E	I	N	S	N	Z	A
O	B	W	Y	N	R	E	V	B	K	K	M	V	Y	P	C
R	W	H	W	I	E	G	A	R	H	T	E	R	U	S	Q
X	H	O	X	R	S	Q	K	I	D	N	E	Y	S	I	Z
V	N	N	X	U	E	A	E	C	C	M	O	D	U	M	T
H	S	L	Q	L	R	P	A	F	N	Y	O	G	I	R	M

6 Food: Importance and Preservation

Learning Checklist

- Food groups
- Balanced diet
- Preservation of food
- Rest, posture and exercise

Let's Get Started

Classify the following food items into plant and animal products, and fill in the given table.

Butter

Dried grapes

Bread

Ghee

Maize

Cashew nuts

Pepper powder

Fish fry

Plant products	Animal products

WHY DO WE NEED FOOD?

In our day-to-day life, we do many activities such as going to school, studying, playing, going for a walk, dancing, swimming, etc. To do these activities, we need energy. Where do we get energy from?

Food gives us the energy to do the everyday activities. We should eat healthy food in order to stay fit.

Walking

Dancing

FOOD GROUPS

Substances present in food that help the body to grow and stay healthy are called **nutrients**. The main nutrients found in food are carbohydrates, proteins, fats, vitamins and minerals. Food also contains roughage and water. Based on what nutrients the food contains, they are grouped into three food groups: energy-giving food, body-building food and protective food.

Carbohydrates

Carbohydrates are known as **energy-giving food**. There are two types of carbohydrates present in food—sugar and starch. Wheat, rice, potato and sweet potato contain starch. Food items such as pastries and bananas contain sugar.

Carbohydrates

People who do more physical work need more energy. Therefore, an athlete needs more carbohydrates in his diet than a person who sits and works in office all day.

Proteins

Proteins help in the growth of the body and the repair of worn-out tissues and cells. They build our muscles too. Hence, proteins are known as **body-building food**. Growing children need more proteins than adults. Food items such as milk, cheese, egg, fish, meat and pulses contain proteins.

Proteins

Science in Context
Lack of protein in the diet causes a disease called kwashiorkor.

Fats

Fats are present in food items such as oil, butter, ghee, cream, cheese, paneer and nuts. Fats also give us energy. They provide more energy than carbohydrates. Our body needs fat in very small amounts. Consumption of excess fat is not good for health as they get stored in the body and increase the body weight.

Butter

Cream

Oil

Cheese

Vitamins and Minerals

Eggs

Fruits and vegetables

Our body requires vitamins and minerals in very small quantities. Vitamins and minerals help us to stay healthy and protect us from diseases. Hence, they are known as **protective food**.

Fresh fruits, leafy vegetables, cereals and milk are some important sources of vitamins.

Milk

Nuts

Cereals

Minerals such as iron and calcium are also required to keep our body healthy and strong.

Calcium makes bones and teeth strong. Milk, curd and nuts are some of the calcium-rich foods.

Lack of iron in our body makes us feel tired and weak. Green leafy vegetables, oranges and apples are some of the iron-rich foods.

To get minerals, we should eat vegetables, fruits, egg, fish, milk, salt and cereals.

Roughage and Water

Roughage is the fibre present in some green vegetables, fruits, cereals, etc. It cannot be digested and does not provide any nutrient to our body, but it helps in the movement of food through the intestines and in removal of wastes from the body.

Water is very important for our body. It helps in digestion and maintains the body temperature. Our body loses water through sweat, breath and urine. In order to make up for this loss, we should drink plenty of water every day.

BALANCED DIET

A balanced diet is a meal that contains carbohydrates, proteins, fats, vitamins, minerals, water and fibre in the right proportion[1]. To stay healthy, we should always have a balanced diet.

Word Web

[1]**Proportion**: amount

Revise and recall

State whether the following statements are true (T) or false (F).

1. Carbohydrates are known as energy-giving food. ☐
2. Consumption of fat in excess is good for health. ☐
3. Vitamins are known as body-building food. ☐
4. Roughage is the fibre present in the food. ☐
5. To stay healthy, we should not drink water. ☐

PRESERVATION OF FOOD

Cooked or uncooked food gets spoilt when it is kept exposed to air and moisture for a long time. The process of treating food to prevent it from getting spoilt is called **preservation**.

Following are some ways of preserving food:

(a) **Refrigerating**: Keeping fruits, vegetables and cooked food in the fridge prevents them from getting spoilt.

(b) **Drying**: In this method, water is completely removed from the food item. One simple way is to keep the food item out in the open under the sun. For example, dates and raisins are preserved as dry fruits.

(c) **Canning**: The moisture in the air can spoil food. Hence, food can be kept in airtight containers to prevent them from getting affected by moisture. For example, *rasgullas* and *gulab jamuns*.

(d) **Pickling (using salt)**: Salt and oil forms a concentrated solution that is used to preserve pickles (e.g., mango or chilly pickle).

(e) **Jellying (using sugar)**: Keeping fruits or vegetables in sugar syrups is one of the ways of preserving food (e.g., mixed fruit jam).

Refrigerating

Drying

Canning

Pickling

Jellying

REST, POSTURE AND EXERCISE

In addition to a balanced diet, sufficient amount of rest, a good posture and regular exercise are essential to stay healthy.

Rest

Rest is very important for the body. We need at least 6 to 8 hours of sleep in a day. Lack of sleep makes us feel tired and it can also make us fall sick.

Posture

Posture is the position in which we keep our body while standing, sitting or walking. Having the correct posture helps us in many ways:

(a) Our bones and muscles stay healthy.
(b) We do not get tired quickly.
(c) We do not get backaches and muscle cramps.
(d) We look good.

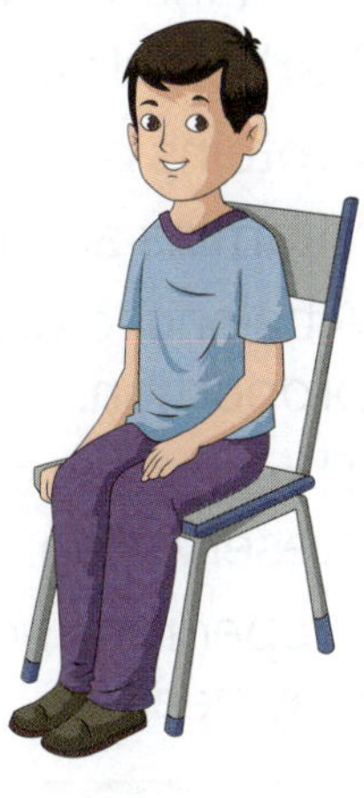

Sitting

Standing

Exercise

Regular exercise like running, walking, cycling and playing different sports helps us to stay healthy and fit. Nowadays, Yoga has also become a popular form of exercise.

If we exercise regularly, then

(a) our bones and muscles get stronger.
(b) we sleep well.
(c) we do not feel tired.
(d) we have more energy to work.

Exercise

Let's Say Together

Nutrients Carbohydrates Proteins Fats Vitamins Minerals Preservation

Keywords

Nutrients: Substances present in food that help the body to grow and stay healthy
Roughage: The fibre present in green vegetables, fruits and cereals
Balanced diet: A meal that contains carbohydrates, proteins, fats, vitamins, minerals, water and fibre in the right proportion
Preservation: The process of treating food to prevent it from getting spoilt

Summary

1. The main nutrients found in food are carbohydrates, proteins, fats, vitamins, minerals, roughage and water.
2. Carbohydrates and fats provide us energy.
3. Proteins help in the growth and repair of our body parts.
4. Vitamins and minerals protect our body from diseases.
5. A balanced diet is a meal that contains all the nutrients in the right proportion.
6. The process of treating food to prevent it from getting spoilt is called preservation.
7. Proper rest, good posture and exercise keeps us fit and helps us to stay healthy.

EXERCISE

A Choose the correct option for each of the following.

1. Which of these is essential for people who do more physical work?

   (a) Proteins (b) Carbohydrates (c) Vitamins (d) Roughage

2. Proteins are also known as

   (a) Iron-rich food (b) Body-building food (c) Fibre-rich food (d) None of these

3. Which of these, when eaten in excess, will increase the body weight?

   (a) Fats (b) Proteins (c) Carbohydrates (d) Vitamins

4. Drying is a method of preserving food by

   (a) Adding salt (b) Adding sugar (c) Freezing (d) Removing water

5. Posture refers to the body's

   (a) Position (b) Bones (c) Muscles (d) None of these

B Fill in the blanks with the correct words.

1. Food contains ________________, which help us to grow and stay healthy. (nutrients/preservatives)
2. Food items that are rich in ________________ are called energy-giving foods. (carbohydrates/vitamins)
3. Oil, butter, ghee, cream and cheese are rich in ________________. (proteins/fats)
4. Roughage is the ________________ present in some green vegetables, fruits and cereals. (fibre/nutrient)
5. The process of treating food to prevent it from getting spoilt is called

   ________________. (balanced diet/preservation)

C Match the following.

Column A	Column B
(a) Carbohydrates	(1) Prevent diseases
(b) Fat	(2) Prevents food from getting spoilt
(c) Vitamins	(3) Helps in formation of bones and teeth
(d) Preservation	(4) Butter
(e) Calcium	(5) Potato and sweet potato

D Name the following.

1. The diet that contains all the nutrients in the right proportion ________________
2. Position of the body while standing, sitting or walking ________________
3. The fibre present in some green vegetables, fruits and cereals ________________
4. Substances in food that help the body to grow and stay healthy ________________

E Answer the following questions briefly.

1. What are carbohydrates?
2. Why do athletes need more carbohydrates than a person sitting in office?
3. What is the role of roughage?
4. Why is water essential in our diet?
5. What is a balanced diet?

F Answer the following questions.

1. Name the different food groups. Explain proteins and vitamins with examples.
2. Name the different ways of preserving food and give examples for each.
3. How does the correct posture help us?

G HOTS (Higher Order Thinking Skills)

1. Food does not get spoilt quickly in winter as compared to summer. Why? (Hint: High and low temperature)
2. Renu falls sick very often. Which food items would you suggest she should eat to prevent her from falling sick? (Hint: What is the role of protective food?)

H Write B for body-building foods, E for energy-giving foods and P for protective foods.

 ☐

 ☐

 ☐

 ☐

 ☐

 ☐

 ☐

 ☐

I Life Skills

Often, the tasty food we eat contains less nutrients and more fat. (Example: Deep fried items such as potato chips). We should avoid eating such food items on a regular basis.

Make a list of five food items that you should avoid eating or eat in very small amounts.

J Project

Names of some food items are given below. Find out the nutrients present in these food items.

Name of the Food Items	Name of the Nutrients Present
Cheese pizza	
Vegetable burger	
French fries	
Pav bhaji	
Gulab jamun	

K Fun Activity (Cross-curricular)

Special food items are prepared during all festivals. Some of the famous food items are given below.

Unscramble the words to identify the names of the dishes.

Dishes	Answers	Religious Festivals
MLPU AKCE (two words)		Christmas
EESWT KLMI (two words)		Diwali
EERKH		Ramzan

Given below are pictures of different food items. Write the nutrients that they contain and also explain how the nutrient is helpful to us. The first one has been done for you.

Food Items	Name of the Nutrient	How Does It Help Us?
 Curd and milk	Calcium	Calcium helps in formation of strong bones and teeth.
 Rice  Boiled potatoes		
 Eggs  Pulses		
 Fruits and vegetables		

7 Digestion of Food

Learning Checklist

- Structure and types of teeth
- Care of teeth
- Digestive system
- Microbes

Let's Get Started

Teeth help us to bite and chew the food we eat. They also help us to speak. Clean and white teeth give us a beautiful smile. Teeth can be healthy only if they are taken good care of.

Put a tick mark (✓) against the things you do to take care of your teeth.

1. Brush twice daily ☐
2. Have milk daily ☐
3. Eat chocolates daily ☐
4. Visit a dentist regularly ☐

In this chapter, we will learn about the types of teeth, and how teeth and other organs in our body help in the breakdown of food.

TEETH

A newborn baby does not have any teeth; it starts developing teeth when it is six months old. This first set of teeth is called the **milk teeth**. Milk teeth are about 20 in number.

Between the age of 6 and 12, the milk teeth begin to fall off one by one. Hence, the milk teeth are also called the temporary teeth. New teeth start growing in their places. This second set of teeth is called the **permanent teeth**. There are 32 permanent teeth in total, 16 in the upper jaw and 16 in the lower jaw. The permanent teeth last till old age.

> **Science in Context**
>
> Some people have only 28 teeth in the permanent set of teeth. The remaining 4 teeth appear later during the age of 17–21 and are called **wisdom teeth**. Some people do not have wisdom teeth at all!

Structure of Teeth

A tooth has three parts:

Crown: The visible part of the tooth above the gums is called the crown.

Neck: The part of the tooth below the crown touching the gums is called the neck.

Root: The part of the tooth inside the gums is called the root.

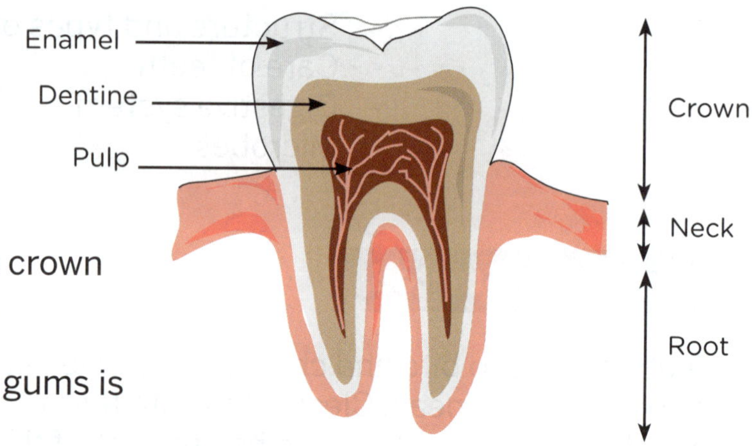

Structure of a tooth

The hard, white outer covering of a tooth is called the **enamel**. Enamel is the hardest part of our body.

There is another layer below the enamel called the **dentine**. Below the dentine lies the pulp. **Pulp** is the soft part of the tooth. It has blood vessels and nerves inside it, which are connected to the gums.

Types of Teeth

Teeth are mainly classified into four types based on their functions: incisors, canines, premolars and molars.

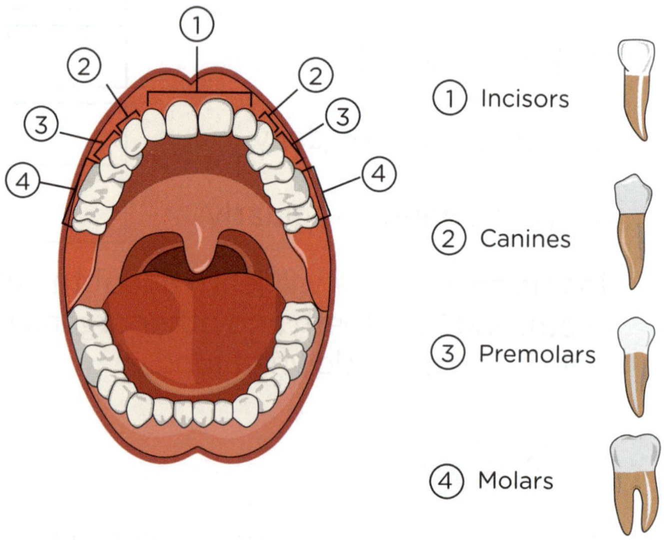

Let us learn more about each type.

Incisors

These teeth help in cutting and biting off pieces of food. There are four incisors in the upper jaw and four in the lower jaw. They are placed in the front in both the jaws.

Canines

These teeth are seen on either side of the incisors in both the upper and lower jaws. They help in holding and tearing the food. There are a total of four canines, two in the upper jaw and two in the lower jaw. Carnivores have canines that are longer and sharper as they are modified to tear flesh faster and with ease.

Premolars

These teeth help in crushing and grinding the food. There are four premolars each in the upper and lower jaws. They are found next to the canines. These teeth are usually broader than other types of teeth.

Molars

These teeth are found towards the back of the mouth. They help in chewing and grinding the food. There are 12 molars in total, six in the lower jaw and six in the upper jaw. These teeth grow at different stages. They are bigger and broader than other teeth.

> **Science in Context**
>
> Herbivores use incisors to bite off the leaves from plants and molars to grind the bitten off leaves.

CARE OF TEETH

When we eat food, tiny food particles get stuck to the surface of the teeth and also in the spaces between them. If these food particles are not removed regularly, germs start growing in these areas. These germs first attack the enamel, then the dentine and finally move into the pulp. Eventually, the germs attack the nerves, resulting in toothache.

Here are a few ways by which you can keep your teeth clean and healthy:

1. Brush your teeth properly in the morning and at night before going to bed. Moving your toothbrush upwards and downwards in a circular motion is the right way to brush your teeth. You should brush the inner and outer surfaces of teeth and also on the sides of teeth.

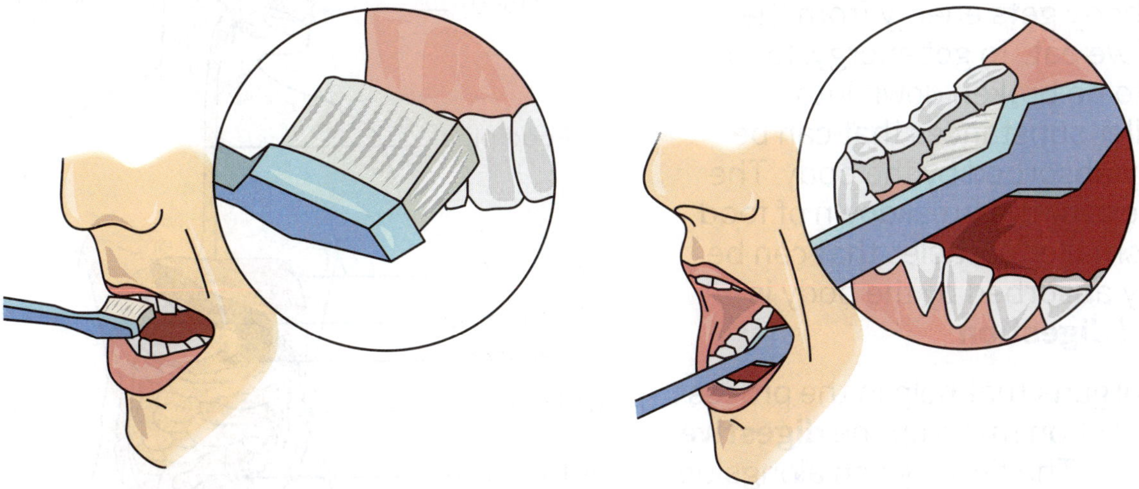

Teeth should be brushed properly to keep them healthy

2. Gargle[1] and rinse your mouth after every meal.
3. Use a mouthwash and dental floss[2], if possible.
4. Avoid eating too many candies and chocolates.
5. Eat lots of salads and fruits.
6. Drink milk and eat food items that are rich in calcium such as cheese, eggs, etc.
7. Visit a dentist[3] regularly to know how healthy your teeth are and get them treated, if required.

Word Web

[1]**Gargle**: clean the mouth with water or a mouthwash

[2]**Dental floss**: a soft thread used for cleaning the spaces between the teeth

[3]**Dentist**: a person qualified to treat people suffering with tooth problems

Revise and recall

Put a tick (✓) against the correct statements and cross (✗) against the wrong ones.

I can take care of my teeth by:

1. Brushing them only once a day. ☐
2. Eating only chocolates. ☐
3. Gargling my mouth after every meal. ☐
4. Visiting the dentist only when I have a toothache. ☐

DIGESTIVE SYSTEM

Our body gets energy from the food we eat. To get energy, food has to be broken down into smaller substances that can be easily absorbed by the body. The process of the breakdown of food into smaller particles that can be easily absorbed by the body is called **digestion**.

The organs that help in the process of digestion make up the **digestive system**. The figure given alongside shows the human digestive system.

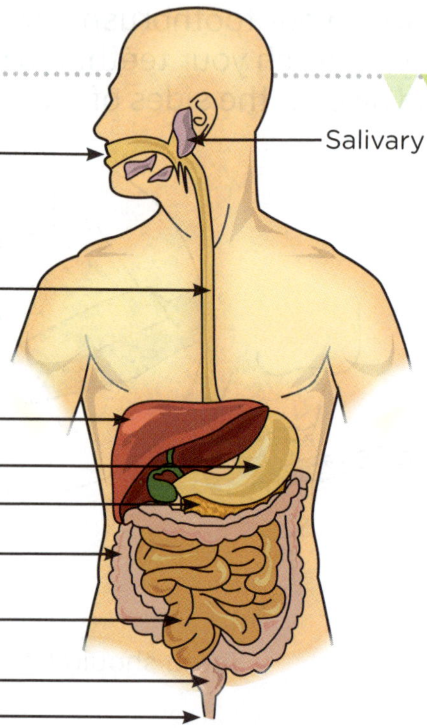

Human digestive system

Process of Digestion

Digestion of the food we eat starts in the **mouth**. The teeth bite and chew the food into smaller pieces. Saliva is a digestive juice secreted in the mouth by structures called **salivary glands**. Saliva mixes with the food and makes it soft, moist and easy to swallow. The soft and moist food is now called the **bolus**. Food that contains starch, such as rice, is broken down into sugar by the saliva and hence tastes sweet.

The bolus then enters the **food pipe**. The food pipe moves by contracting and relaxing alternatively. This movement helps in pushing the food down into the **stomach**. It is a sac-like organ where the food stays for many hours and some part of digestion takes place. Stomach produces acid and digestive juices that help to digest the food.

From the stomach, the remaining undigested food is pushed into a long coiled tube called the **small intestine**. Here, the digestive juices produced by the small intestine, the **liver** and the **pancreas** mix with the food and digest it.

> **Science in Context**
>
> The rumbling sound in your stomach occurs when there is no food in the stomach and the stomach and intestines contract.

All the useful nutrients from the digested food get absorbed by the walls of the intestine. These nutrients are then absorbed by the blood vessels, which carry them to different parts of the body.

The undigested food enters the **large intestine** where the extra water and minerals are absorbed. The remaining solid waste is stored in the **rectum** until it passes out from the body through the **anus**.

Revise and recall

Fill in the blanks using the names of the organs of the digestive system.

From the mouth, the food enters the ________________ and then passes into the ________________. From the stomach, the digested food then moves into a long coiled tube called the ________________. The food is completely digested as the juices of the ________________, ________________ and ________________ also mix with the food. The undigested food passes into the ________________ where the extra water and minerals are absorbed. The remaining solid waste is stored in the ________________ until it passes out of the body through the ________________.

MICROBES

Microbes are tiny living things that cannot be seen with the naked eye. They can only be seen under a microscope[1]. They grow everywhere: on food, in soil, in water and even inside and outside our body.

Word Web

[1]**Microscope**: an instrument that makes very small objects appear big

The main categories of microbes are bacteria, viruses, fungi and protozoa.

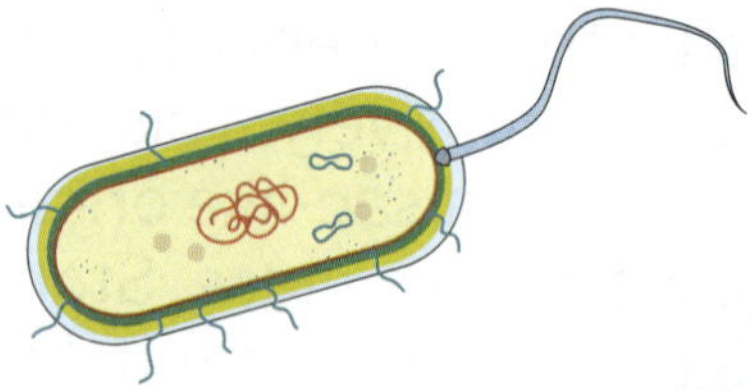

A bacterium

Bacteria

Bacteria (singular: bacterium) are made up of only one cell. They can be of different shapes such as rod shaped, round or spiral.

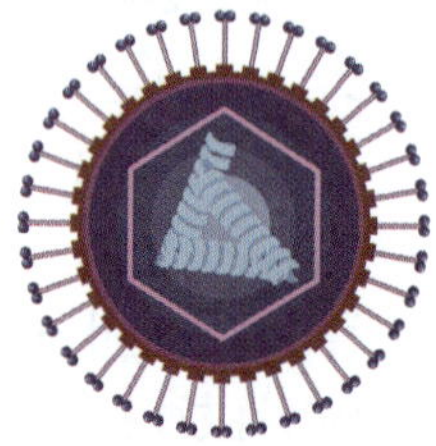

A virus

Viruses

Viruses are the smallest living things that can only be seen under a very powerful microscope.

Fungi

Fungi

Fungi (singular: fungus) are the microbes that grow mainly on dead and decaying matter.

Protozoa

Protozoa (singular: protozoan) are single-celled microbes.

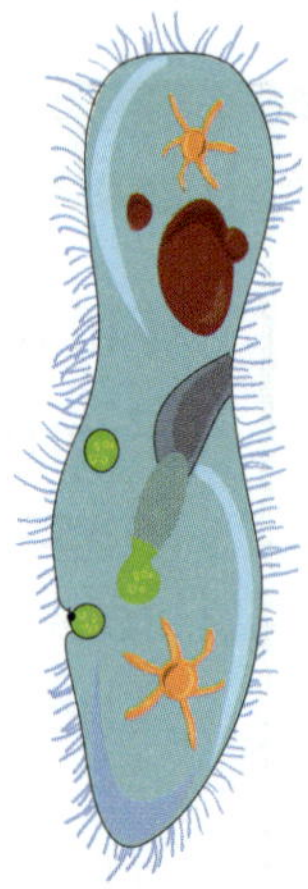

A protozoan

Some microbes are useful to us. Useful microbes help us in the following ways:

(a) Bacteria help in changing milk into curd.
(b) Bacteria and fungi help in breaking down dead matter.
(c) Protozoa are used as soil fertilizers.
(d) Fungi like yeast help in making bread.
(e) Some bacteria help in digesting the food we eat.
(f) We obtain medicines from some bacteria and viruses.

Some microbes are harmful to us and cause diseases. These microbes are called **germs** or **pathogens**.

(a) Bacteria cause diseases such as typhoid, tetanus and cholera.
(b) Viruses cause diseases such as flu, chicken pox, dengue, mumps and even common cold.
(c) Fungi mainly cause skin diseases such as ringworm, candidiasis and athlete's foot.
(d) Protozoa cause diseases such as dysentery and malaria.

Let's Say Together

Incisor	Canine	Premolar	Molar	Saliva
Food pipe	Stomach	Intestine	Pancreas	Liver
Microbes	Bacteria	Virus	Protozoa	Fungi

Keywords

Crown: The visible part of the tooth above the gums

Enamel: The hard, white outer covering of a tooth

Dentine: The part of a tooth found below the enamel

Pulp: The soft part of a tooth that has blood vessels and nerves inside it

Digestion: The process of the breakdown of food into smaller particles that can be easily absorbed by the body

Digestive system: The organ system that helps in the process of digestion

Microbes: Tiny living things that can only be seen under a microscope

Summary

1. There are two sets of teeth in humans: the milk teeth and the permanent teeth.
2. The milk teeth fall off between the age of 6 and 12, and the permanent teeth start growing in their places. There are 32 permanent teeth in total, 16 in the upper jaw and 16 in the lower jaw.
3. Brushing, gargling, avoiding too many sweets and chocolates, eating healthy food like salads, fruits and milk, and visiting a dentist regularly are some of the ways to take care of our teeth.
4. The organs of the digestive system are the mouth, food pipe, stomach, liver, pancreas, small intestine, large intestine, rectum and anus.
5. The different types of microbes are bacteria, viruses, fungi and protozoa.
6. Microbes can be harmful or useful. Harmful microbes cause diseases like cholera, typhoid, dengue and athlete's foot. Useful microbes help in preparing different kind of food items, medicines, fertilizers, etc.

EXERCISE

A Choose the correct option for each of the following.

1. The teeth that help in holding and tearing the food are
   (a) Incisors (b) Canines (c) Premolars (d) Molars
2. Toothache can be avoided by
   (a) Eating very little sweets (b) Brushing teeth regularly
   (c) Eating lots of salads and drinking lots of milk (d) All of these
3. The organ(s) of the digestive system is/are
   (a) Pancreas (b) Large intestine (c) Liver (d) All of these
4. The organ that produces acid and digestive juices to digest food is
   (a) Liver (b) Intestine (c) Stomach (d) Food pipe
5. The microbes that can be of different shapes are
   (a) Bacteria (b) Protozoa (c) Viruses (d) Fungi

B Fill in the blanks with the correct words.

1. There are ______________ teeth in the permanent set. (16/32)
2. The part of the tooth inside the gums is called the ______________. (crown/root)
3. From the stomach, the remaining undigested food is pushed into a long coiled tube called the ______________. (small intestine/large intestine)
4. ______________ grow mainly on dead and decaying matter. (Fungi/Viruses)
5. Typhoid and tetanus are caused by ______________. (protozoa/bacteria)

C Match the following.

Column A	Column B
(a) Bacteria	(1) Athlete's foot
(b) Pathogens	(2) Common cold
(c) Virus	(3) Malaria
(d) Protozoa	(4) Harmful microbes
(e) Fungi	(5) Cholera

D State whether the following statements are true (T) or false (F).

1. Milk teeth are formed after the permanent teeth fall off. ☐
2. Digestion is the breaking down of food into smaller particles. ☐
3. Saliva is a digestive juice secreted in the mouth. ☐
4. The undigested food is stored in the stomach. ☐
5. Microbes cannot be seen with the naked eye. ☐

E Answer the following in one word.

1. The first set of teeth that is formed ____________
2. The hard, white outer covering of the tooth ____________
3. The structures in the mouth that produce saliva ____________
4. Tiny living things that can only be seen under a microscope ____________
5. Microbes that help in making bread ____________

F Answer the following questions briefly.

1. Name the parts of a tooth.
2. List the organs of the digestive system.
3. What is the function of the stomach in the digestive system?
4. What are germs? Give an example.
5. What are the different shapes of bacteria?

G Answer the following questions.

1. Describe the structure of a tooth with the help of a diagram.
2. Name the different types of teeth and write their functions.
3. List four ways by which you can take care of your teeth.
4. How are microbes useful to us?

H HOTS (Higher Order Thinking Skills)

1. Richa, who is 12 years old, has 14 teeth in her upper jaw. Her father, who is 40 years old, has 16 teeth in his upper jaw. Can you explain why? (Hint: What are wisdom teeth?)
2. Kriti often swallows food without chewing it properly. Is it a good practice? Why or why not?

I **Use different crayons to colour the organs of the digestive system. Label each organ.**

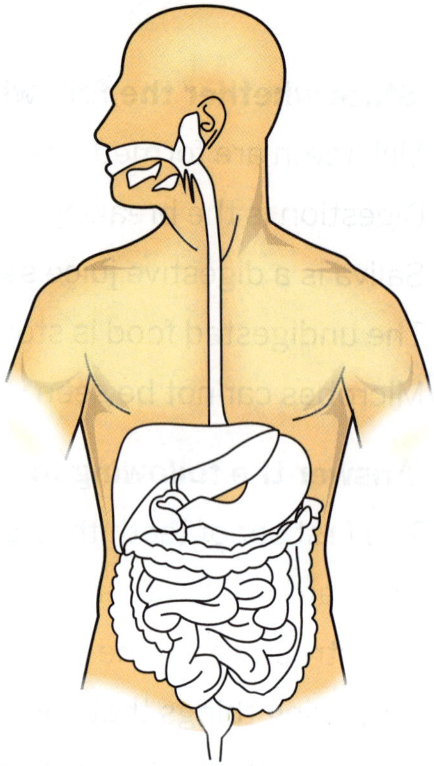

J Life Skills

Join the happy tooth with the action that makes it healthy and happy. One has been done for you.

I will drink a lot of milk.

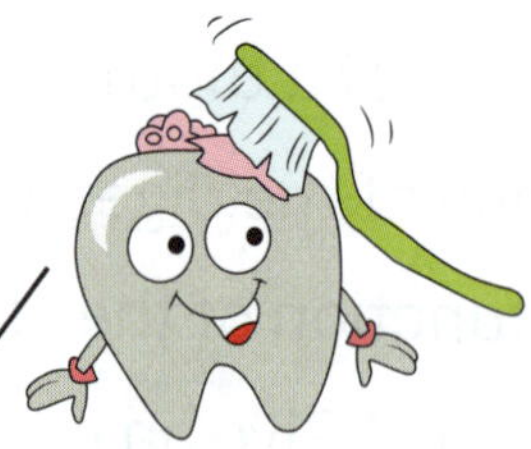

I will brush regularly.

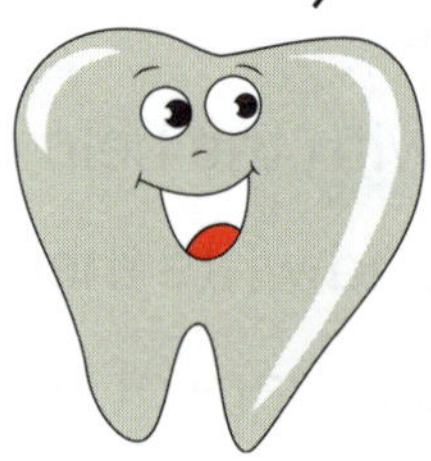

Happy tooth

I will brush my teeth only sometimes.

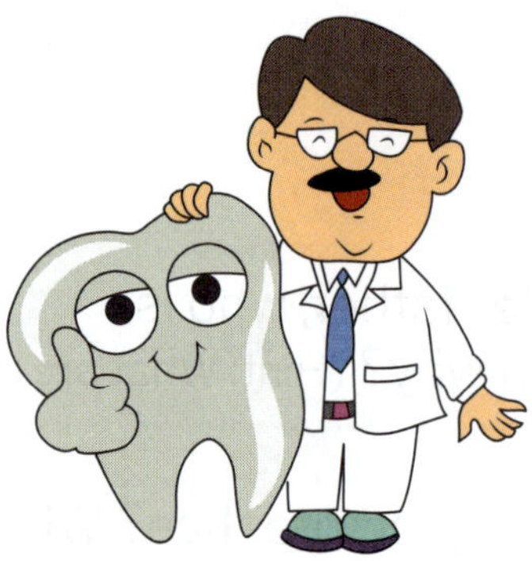

I will visit my dentist.

I will eat lots of candies and chocolates.

I will eat lots of salads and fruits.

Look at the pictures of different types of microbes and fill in the blanks.

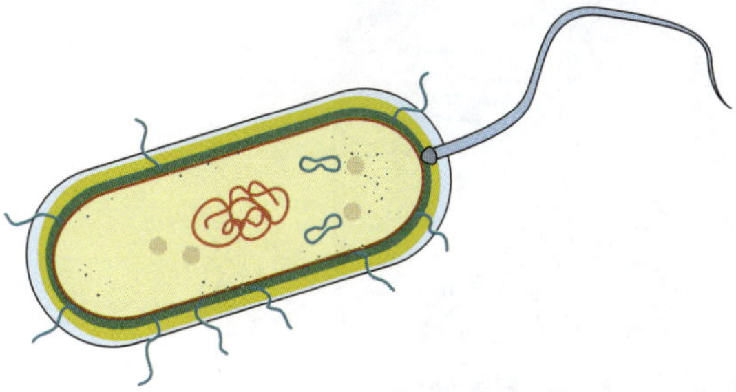

Bacterium

One use of bacteria:

____

____

A disease caused by bacteria:

____

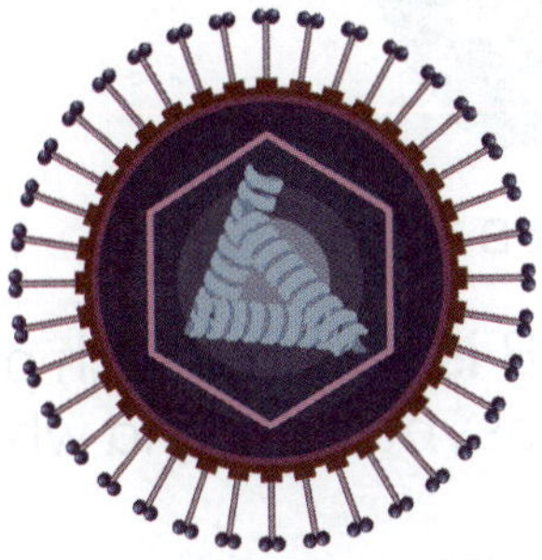

Virus

One use of virus:

____

____

A disease caused by virus:

____

Fungi

One use of fungi:

____

____

A disease caused by fungi:

____

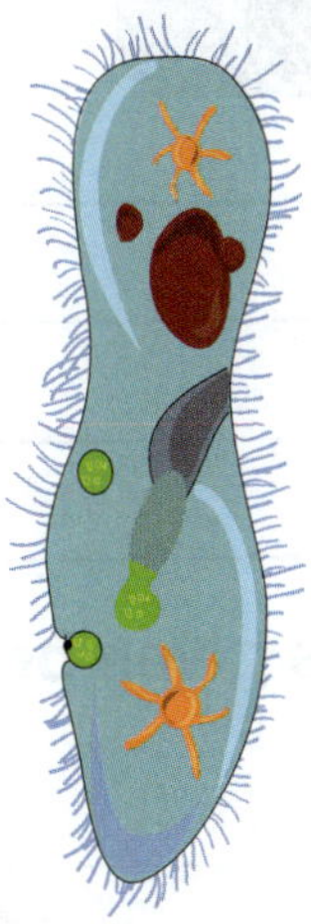

Protozoan

One use of protozoa:

____

____

A disease caused by protozoa:

____

A Answer the following question with the help of the given images.

Pot A Pot B

Pot A is kept in the open and watered regularly, but Pot B is covered with plastic bag and kept in dark room. Which pot's plant will show photosynthesis and why?

____

____

____

____

B Identify and write the name, type and adaptations of the plants given below.

1. 

Name: ______________

Type: ______________

Adaptations: ______________

____

2. 

Name: ______________

Type: ______________

Adaptations: ______________

____

C Answer the following questions based on the pictures given below.

1. The letter 'Y' can be substituted by which of the following options?

   (a) Legs (b) Antenna (c) Wings

2. Label the stages involved.

D Who am I? Find the name of the animals using the clues given below.

1. I live inside the body of host and I have a shape in my name. ____________
2. I can live on land and water. I hop when I am on land. ____________
3. I am a bird but I don't fly. I have thick fat under my skin. ____________
4. I am a bird and I feed on dead and decaying animals. ____________

E Fill in the blanks with the words given in help box to complete the following sentences.

Ureters	Kidneys	Urinary bladder	Urethra

1. ____________ are bean-shaped structures that act like filters to collect wastes and excess salts from the blood.
2. These wastes are carried from the kidneys to the urinary bladder by a pair of tubes called ____________.
3. The urine is stored in ____________ until it is released from the body.
4. ____________ lets out the urine from the urinary bladder and thus out of the body.

F Write the name of the food group to which these food items belong. Also write two sources of it.

1. ____________ ____________
2. ____________ ____________
3. ____________ ____________

G Sequence the following organs to represent the order in which food passes through the digestive system.

Large intestine	Stomach	Mouth	Food pipe	Anus
Small intestine	Rectum			

____

____

LOOKING BACK

SOCIAL STUDIES

1 Our Country India

Observe and Reflect

- Which continent does this map represent?
- How many water bodies surround India?
- Which water body is named after India?

India is the seventh largest country in the world and the third largest country in Asia. Located in the southern tip of Asia, it is surrounded by the Bay of Bengal on the east, the Arabian Sea on the west and the Indian Ocean on the south.

The countries that are located next to a particular country are known as its **neighbouring countries**. The neighbouring countries of India are Nepal, Bhutan, Pakistan, Bangladesh, Afghanistan, Sri Lanka, Maldives, China and Myanmar.

Afghanistan and Pakistan lie to the west of India. Sri Lanka and the Maldives lie to the south of India. Bangladesh, Nepal, Bhutan, Myanmar and China border its east.

Find Out

Look at the world map. Find out the largest and the smallest country in Asia.

Fact Zone

Maldives is an **archipelago** in the Indian Ocean. It has 1190 coral islands.

Find Out

What is a subcontinent? Which countries make up the Indian subcontinent?

Political Divisions of India

Look at the political map of India. It represents the states and territories of India.

You already know that for the **convenience** of administration of the central government, India is divided into 28 states and eight union territories. The central government, called the Government of India, looks after the entire country, while the state governments look after their **respective** states. In India, the union territories are directly under the rule of the central government.

The city that is the base of all important government activities of a state is known as the **capital** of the state. The capital of a state is the seat of power of the state.

Look at the list of the 28 states and eight union territories with their respective capitals.

Political divisions of India

State	Capital
Andhra Pradesh	Hyderabad/Amaravati
Arunachal Pradesh	Itanagar
Assam	Dispur
Bihar	Patna
Chhattisgarh	Raipur
Goa	Panaji
Gujarat	Gandhinagar
Haryana	Chandigarh
Himachal Pradesh	Shimla
Jharkhand	Ranchi

State	Capital
Manipur	Imphal
Meghalaya	Shillong
Mizoram	Aizawl
Nagaland	Kohima
Odisha	Bhubaneshwar
Punjab	Chandigarh
Rajasthan	Jaipur
Sikkim	Gangtok
Tamil Nadu	Chennai
Telangana	Hyderabad

State	Capital
Karnataka	Bengaluru
Kerala	Thiruvananthapuram
Madhya Pradesh	Bhopal
Maharashtra	Mumbai

State	Capital
Tripura	Agartala
Uttar Pradesh	Lucknow
Uttarakhand	Dehradun
West Bengal	Kolkata

Union Territory	Capital
Jammu and Kashmir	Srinagar (summer), Jammu (winter)
Ladakh	Leh
Andaman and Nicobar Islands	Port Blair
Chandigarh	Chandigarh

Union Territory	Capital
Dadra and Nagar Haveli and Daman and Diu	Daman/Silvassa
Lakshadweep	Kavaratti
Delhi – National Capital Territory	New Delhi
Puducherry	Puducherry

Do It Yourself

Look at the map and answer the questions.

1. When was this new state carved out?
2. The capital of this state is also the capital of the new state. Name the capital city.
3. Name the proposed new capital city of Andhra Pradesh.

Physical Features of India

When we look at the physical map of India, we see great diversity in the landforms in India.

Broadly, the six physical features of India are:

- The Northern Mountains
- The Northern Plains
- The Great Indian Desert
- The Southern Plateau
- The Coastal Plains
- The Islands

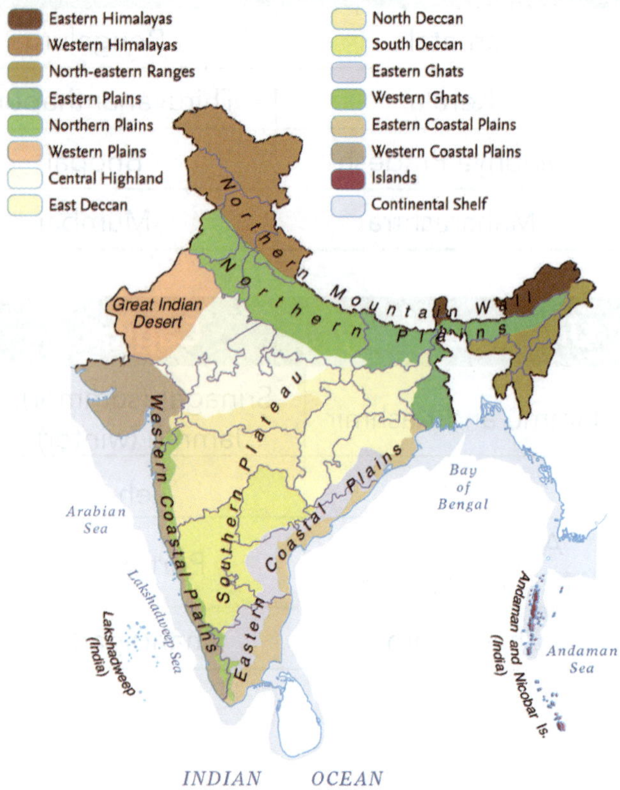

Physical features of India

Eco Zone

New Delhi, India's capital city, is one of the most polluted cities in the world. What steps can we take to prevent pollution?

Remember

» Pakistan, Afghanistan, Maldives, Myanmar, Bhutan, Nepal, Bangladesh and Sri Lanka are the neighbouring countries of India.

» India is divided into 28 states and eight union territories.

» India has six physical divisions.

Review Zone

A Fill in the blanks with the correct answers.

1. Pakistan lies to the .... of India.

   a. west b. east c. north

2. The south-east and south-west of India are bordered by the ....

   a. Coastal Plains b. Northern Mountains c. Southern Plateau

3. .... is the capital of Himachal Pradesh.

   a. Kolkata b. Shimla c. Gangtok

4. Chandigarh is the capital of ....
   a. Haryana   b. Bihar   c. Assam

5. The Great Indian Desert region consists of the state of ....
   a. Maharashtra   b. Rajasthan   c. Punjab

B Write T for True and F for False.

1. Sri Lanka is one of India's neighbours. ☐
2. West Bengal has two capitals. ☐
3. The Andaman and Nicobar Islands are administered by their own state government. ☐
4. Hyderabad is the capital of Telangana. ☐
5. The Great Indian Desert is located in the north-east of India. ☐

C Answer these questions in brief.

1. Name all the neighbouring countries of India.
2. India is divided into how many states and union territories.
3. Name the capitals of any three southern states of India.
4. State the capitals of three north-eastern states of India.
5. Who looks after the administration of the union territories?

D Read the capital cities in different regions of India. Circle the odd one out.

1.	Srinagar	Shimla	Mohali	Chandigarh
2.	Agartala	Imphal	Itanagar	Jorhat
3.	Kochi	Bengaluru	Chennai	Hyderabad
4.	Mumbai	Agra	Bhopal	Gandhinagar
5.	Patna	Ranchi	Siliguri	Kolkata

E Answer these questions in detail.

1. Describe India's location in Asia.
2. Name the neighbouring countries of India.
3. Name all the physical features of India and name one state which falls in each region.

Think Zone

A What do you think would happen if the political divisions of India were dissolved? Discuss in class.

B **Look at the picture and answer the questions.**

1. What do you see in the picture?
2. What are these called?
3. Where can these be found in India?

Life Skills Zone

How can the people of a region contribute to the wealth of that region?

Value Zone

A state is known by its people and their work. We must appreciate and respect people from all regions.

Activity Zone

Take a quick quiz on India and answer these questions.

1. The third largest country of Asia: ....
2. The government that looks after all the states and union territories of India: ....
3. A city that serves as the capital of two states of India: ....
4. A landlocked neighbouring country of India: ....

2 The Northern Mountains

Observe and Reflect

- Which physical feature of India can you see in this picture?
- Where in India can we find such a landform?
- Name two states that have this type of landscape.

Look at the map of northern India. India is the land of the highest mountain **ranges** in the world, the Himalayas. They form the **crest** of the country. The **Northern Mountains** region stretches from the state of Arunachal Pradesh in the east to Jammu and Kashmir in the west. The total length of the Northern Mountains is around 2500 km. The width varies from 250 to 400 km. The Himalayan, Karakoram and Kailash ranges are all the part of the Northern Mountains.

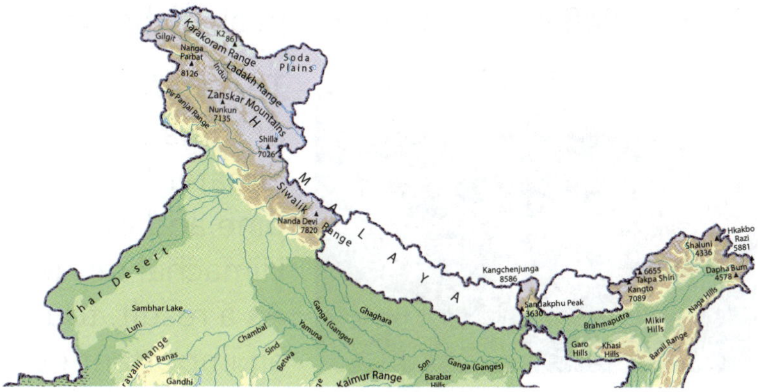

Northern Mountains

Importance of the Northern Mountains

The Northern Mountains play an important role in determining the climate of India. They block the cold winds that blow from the north. The Himalayas are the natural barrier for rain-bearing clouds. As a result, the Northern Plains receive rains and have a moderate climate. The Himalayas are also the source of many important rivers. These rivers are the **lifeline** of the plains of India. The thick forests of the Northern Mountains are sources of timber and rich wildlife.

Parts of the Northern Mountains

The Northern Mountains consist of three ranges that run parallel to each other.

1. The Greater Himalayas or Himadri
2. The Middle Himalayas or Himachal
3. The Lesser Himalayas or Shiwalik

Find Out

Who were the first people to successfully climb Mt Everest and when?

Fact Zone

Khardung La, is the highest motorable road in the India.

Nanda Devi peak

Just as the name suggests, the **Greater Himalayan range** is the highest of all the three ranges. Also known as Himadri, the mountains of this region remain covered with snow and **glaciers** throughout the year and have an extremely cold climate. These glaciers are the source of many important rivers like Ganga, Yamuna, Indus and Brahmaputra. The vegetation is sparse as only a few plants like lichens, moss and wildflowers can survive the cold climate. Yak, snow leopard, goat and sheep are the only wildlife found in this region. Kangchenjunga, at an **elevation** of 8,586 m, is the highest peak in India. Mt Everest, which stands at a height 8,848 m, is the highest peak in the world.

Hill station in Himachal

The **Middle Himalayas** or Himachal, lies to the south of Himadri. Since it is lower in altitude than the Greater Himalayas, it is not so cold here. With thick pine and deodar forests, the scenic beauty of the Himachal range has given rise to many hill stations. As a result, tourism is an important economic activity in this region.

Eco Zone

Deforestation in the hills for timber leads to landslides during heavy rains.

The **Lesser Himalayan ranges** are also known as the Shiwalik range. This range has the Shiwalik range in the north and the Purvanchal range in the north-east. The Shiwalik range merges with the foothills of the Himalayas and is about 16 km wide in some places. It runs parallel to the main Himalayan range and is separated from it only by hills and valleys. This region is the most populated region of the Himalayas. Due to favourable climatic conditions, many food crops are grown here.

Mountain ranges and hills like the Patkai, Mishmi, Naga, Manipur, Tripura and Mizo run through the Lesser Himalayas in the north-east and are collectively called the Purvanchal range.

Life in the Northern Mountains

Some of the major states and union territories that lie in this region are Jammu and Kashmir, Ladakh, Uttarakhand, Himachal Pradesh and Sikkim. Most states of the north-east, such as Arunachal Pradesh, Nagaland, Manipur, Meghalaya and Mizoram, also fall in the Northern Mountain region.

Jammu and Kashmir has two capitals—Srinagar in summer and Jammu in winter. In August 2019, the state was bifurcated into two union territories—Jammu and Kashmir and Ladakh. The capital of Ladakh is Leh. Ladakh is an important union territory of the region. Lying at the northernmost point of India, Jammu and Kashmir experience an extremely cold climate for several months at a stretch. Kashmir has a pleasant and cool summer and snowfall occurs during winters. Vegetation here varies from thick pine and cedar forests in the valleys to sparse vegetation in the Ladakh.

Find Out

Kahwa and *kangri* are two important terms in Kashmir. What are they and what do they mean?

Farming is the main occupation during the summer season. Farmers grow kidney beans (*rajma*), maize, rice and vegetables. Saffron is an exclusive product of this region. Kashmir is famous for apple, walnut and almond orchards.

Jammu and Kashmir is famous for handicrafts like woven woollen and silk clothes. The place is also famous for embroidered shawls and carpets, walnut wood handicrafts and papier-mâché products.

People speak in Urdu and Kashmiri in Srinagar and Kashmir, Dogri in Jammu and Ladakhi in Ladakh.

Wular lake

Do It Yourself

Look at the picture and answer the questions.

1. What is the boat known as?
2. Where in India can we find these boats?
3. What is the climate of this place?

Kashmir is known for it's scenic Wular and Dal lakes. Tourists enjoy staying in houseboats, taking boat rides in the *shikaras*, trekking in Pahalgam and skiing in Gulmarg. The Vaishno Devi temple, the Amarnath caves, the city of Srinagar, the Sonmarg hill station and the town of Pahalgam are all places to visit here. Ladakh with its monasteries is another important tourist destination of the northern mountain region.

Himachal Pradesh is another important state in the Northern Mountains. Farming is a major occupation and the people here grow maize, barley, rice and vegetables. The state is known for its fruit orchards.

Shimla

Himachal Pradesh is particularly famous for all its hill stations like Shimla, Kullu, Manali and Dalhousie. Many tourists visit them during the summer months. People here speak in Hindi, Punjabi, Kinnauri and Pahari. The state is famous for its warm *kullu* shawls with colourful woven borders.

Valley of Flowers

The beautiful state of **Uttarakhand** in the northern mountains is known for its Rhododendron forests. UNESCO World heritage site, the Valley of Flowers is located here. People here speak in Hindi or the Pahari language.

Sikkim

Farming and tourism are the two major occupations in the state. Tourists visit pilgrimage sites, such as Hemkund Sahib, Haridwar, Badrinath, Kedarnath, Gangotri and Yamunotri. Many hill stations like Ranikhet, Nainital and Mussoorie are located here too.

Bordered by Bhutan, Tibet and Nepal, **Sikkim** has cool summers and cold winters. It experiences heavy rainfall during the rainy season. People here speak Nepali, Sikkimese and Lepcha.

Tea plantations

Sikkim is a popular tourist destination. Farming and weaving are the two major occupations of the people of Sikkim. The red panda is found in this state.

Fact Zone

In 2013, flash floods damaged the Kedarnath shrine and left many pilgrims stranded.

Darjeeling, a hill station in the state of West Bengal, also comes under the Northern Mountains region. Vast plantations in Darjeeling produce tea, which is exported throughout the world.

In the north-east, five states, namely Arunachal Pradesh, Meghalaya, Manipur, Nagaland and Mizoram, are part of the Northern Mountains.

The largest state in the northeast is **Arunachal Pradesh**. It shares international borders with China, Myanmar and Bhutan. Farming and weaving are the two most important occupations. The state produces paddy, maize and wheat. Tourist places in Arunachal Pradesh are the Tawang Monastery and the Namdapha National Park which is famous for its snow leopard.

Tawang Monastery

Find Out

Why do people in some parts of Arunachal Pradesh live in **stilt** houses?

The northeastern state of **Meghalaya**, land of the Khasi, Garo and Jaintia hills, shares its international borders with Bangladesh. Mawsynram, a village in Meghalaya, is the wettest place in the world with high annual rainfall. Shillong, its capital, is a beautiful hill station. Farmers grow paddy, potato and maize. Meghalaya is known for its pineapple and banana plantations.

Meghalaya

Manipur shares its border with Myanmar. The beautiful Loktak Lake in Manipur is the largest freshwater lake in north-east India. The climate is generally pleasant throughout the year and cold only during the winter months. Farmers produce cash crops, such as rubber, cardamom, tea and coffee in the hills. The Manipuri classical dance originated here.

The state of **Nagaland** also shares an international border with Myanmar. The Naga hill range makes the terrain mountainous and the climate wet and cool. Farmers grow rice, millets, pulses, sugarcane, oilseeds and potatoes. Weaving and woodwork are the other major occupations.

Mizoram, a landlocked state in the northeast, shares its international border with Bangladesh and Myanmar. Agriculture is the main occupation of the Mizo people. They also make a variety of bamboo products. Mizoram has one of the highest literacy rates in India.

Mizoram

Remember

- The Northern Mountains consists of three parallel ranges—the Greater Himalayas, the Middle Himalayas and the Lesser Himalayas.
- The states and union territories that fall under the Northern Mountains are Jammu and Kashmir, Ladakh, Himachal Pradesh, Uttarakhand, Sikkim, parts of West Bengal, Arunachal Pradesh, Meghalaya, Manipur, Nagaland and Mizoram.

Review Zone

A Fill in the blanks with the correct answers.

1. Jammu and Kashmir is located in the .... part of India.
   a. western b. eastern c. northern
2. The Lesser Himalayas are also known as the .... range.
   a. Shiwalik b. Himachal c. Terai
3. Pahalgam is located in ....
   a. Jammu and Kashmir b. Himachal Pradesh c. Uttarakhand
4. Patkai is a hill which is part of the .... range.
   a. Himachal b. Himadri c. Purvanchal
5. Rhododendron forests are found in the state of ....
   a. Sikkim b. Uttarakhand c. Himachal Pradesh

B Name the following.

1. The highest of the three parallel ranges of the Himalayas: ....
2. A place in Kashmir that tourists visit to ski: ....
3. Shawls with colourful borders made in Himachal Pradesh: ....
4. A state in north-east India shares its international borders with Myanmar: ....
5. The north-eastern state with a high literacy rate: ....

C Write T for True and F for False.

1. No vegetation is found in the Middle Himalayas. ☐
2. The river Ganga has its source in the Himadri. ☐
3. Mizoram has thick bamboo forests. ☐
4. People grow crops in Jammu and Kashmir during the summer months. ☐

5. The Loktak Lake is located in Manipur. ☐

D Answer these questions in brief.

1. Name the three parallel ranges of the Northern Mountains.
2. Which is the second highest peak in the Himalayas?
3. Name two famous lakes of Kashmir.
4. Which state has many pilgrimage sites?
5. In which states of north-east India do the Northern Mountains lie?

E Answer these questions in detail.

1. Describe briefly the Northern Mountain region of India.
2. What do you know about the Purvanchal range?
3. Briefly state the life and activities of the people of Jammu and Kashmir.
4. Discuss the lifestyle of the people living in any one north-eastern state.
5. Write about the vegetation found in the states in the Northern Mountains.

Think Zone

A There are houseboats in Kashmir as well as in Kerala. Find out the similarities and differences between the houseboats of both the states.

B Look at the picture and answer the questions.

1. Which state has apple orchards?
2. Name two famous hill stations of this state.
3. What do the people of this state generally wear?

Life Skills Zone

How do you think the climate of a region affects the life of the local people?

Value Zone

The Northern Mountains have a rich wildlife and vegetation. We must respect the land and take steps to preserve its natural flora and fauna.

Activity Zone

Divide the class into five groups. Let each group choose a state of north-east India. The group should collect information about the climate, vegetation, major crops, people and major places of interest. Make a PowerPoint presentation and present it in the class.

3 The Northern Plains of India

Observe and Reflect

- What do you see in the picture?
- In which regions of India can you see such lands?
- What is the climate like in such places?

We know that plains are low-lying flat lands. A large part of India is occupied by the Northern Plains. These plains are fertile since they are watered by the **perennial rivers** which flow down from the Himalayas.

Importance of the Northern Plains

The Northern Plains are an important physical feature of India as it has a suitable climate for agriculture and other economic activities. The **alluvium** deposited by the rivers makes the plains fertile. Rivers help in the **irrigation** of fields. Since, the plains provide a means of livelihood to the people, many people settle here. Towns and cities easily develop along the banks of the rivers and **river basins**. A river basin is an area watered by a river and its **tributaries**. The river basins are ideal for agriculture and irrigation. The three major basins of the Northern Plains in India are the Indus basin, the Ganga basin and the Brahmaputra basin.

The Northern Plains

Eco Zone

Important river basins formed by the rivers Narmada, Tapti, Cauvery, Godavari, Krishna and Mahanadi are a source of irrigation and hydroelectric power.

The Indus Basin

The Indus river originates in the Tibetan Plateau. It flows through four countries, namely, India, Pakistan, China and Afghanistan. In the Northern Plains, the main tributaries of the Indus are the rivers Chenab, Jhelum, Satluj, Beas and Ravi. These rivers drain Jammu and Kashmir, Punjab, Haryana and Himachal Pradesh.

The Indus river

The Ganga Basin

The Ganga, originating from the Gangotri glacier in the Himalayas, is the most important river of India. Flowing through the states of Uttar Pradesh, Uttarakhand and Bihar, it is in West Bengal that the Ganga branches out into small streams called distributaries.

Ganga at Devprayag

A few tributaries of the Ganga are Gomti, Ghaghara, Kosi and Gandak. Some of the rivers that meet Ganga from the south are Son, Chambal and Betwa. The Ganga river basin is the most fertile region of the Northern Plains.

Find Out

Where does the Ganga meet its largest tributary, the Yamuna?

River Brahmaputra

The Brahmaputra Basin

Another important basin of India is the Brahmaputra basin. The river Brahmaputra originates in Tibet. It enters India through the state of Arunachal Pradesh where it is called river Dihang and flows into Assam as Brahmaputra. The Brahmaputra, like the Ganga, breaks off into distributaries before it finally drains into the Bay of Bengal. The Ganga and Brahmaputra rivers form the world's largest delta known as the Sunderbans Delta.

Fact Zone

The word 'delta' is derived from the Greek letter delta '□', which is also triangular in shape.

Do It Yourself

List the rivers of the three major river basins of the Northern Plains.

Indus basin	Ganga basin	Brahmaputra basin

Life in the Northern Plains

Some of the most important states that lie in the Northern Plains are Punjab, Haryana, Uttar Pradesh, Bihar, West Bengal, Assam and Tripura. The union territory of Delhi is also located in the Northern Plains. Let us find out about the life of the people in the states that lie in this region.

Punjab is located in the Indus and Satluj river basins. It has very hot summers and cold winters with rainfall mainly during the monsoons. Punjab receives water from the rivers Satluj, Ravi and Beas which make the land fertile and ideal for agriculture. Being the largest producer of wheat, this state is known as the 'wheat bowl' of India. Other crops, such as rice, millet, sugarcane, mustard, oilseeds and gram are grown here.

The capital of Punjab is Chandigarh. A few other important cities of this state are Patiala, Amritsar, Jalandhar and Ludhiana. The Golden Temple in Amritsar is a famous pilgrimage site. People mainly speak Punjabi and Hindi. Though agriculture is the main occupation of the people in Punjab, many industries like food, paper and textile are found in the state.

Golden Temple

Fact Zone

The popular Punjabi folk dances are *Gidda* and *Bhangra*.

Haryana lies in the Satluj basin. Chandigarh is the capital city. Haryana too has hot and dry summers, cold winters and receives rainfall during the monsoon months. The main crops of the state are wheat and rice. Farmers use pumps and tube wells for irrigation.

Rice fields in Haryana

The people in the state speak mainly in Hindi and Haryanvi. Many cities of Haryana are part of the National Capital Region of Delhi.

One of the important states of the Ganga basin is **Uttar Pradesh**. Yamuna and Ganga are the two main rivers that run through the state. The summer months are very hot and the winter months are very cold. Heavy or light rainfall might occur in the monsoons. The major crops of the state are rice, wheat, sugarcane, corn and pulses. People speak in Urdu, Bhojpuri and Hindi. The state is known for its sugar mills, leather and textile industries. Many service industries like tourism and hospitality flourish here. The cities of Agra, Mathura, Varanasi and Lucknow are major tourist destinations.

Varanasi

Nalanda university

Bihar lies on the Ganga basin. Its capital is Patna. Rice, wheat, jute and sugarcane are the major crops that are grown here. Bihar experiences hot summer months and cold winter months. Patna is an ancient city and the relics of the ancient university of Nalanda are found here. People here mainly speak Hindi, Urdu, Bhojpuri and Maithili.

West Bengal receives water from the Ganga and Brahmaputra rivers, making it very fertile. Jute and rice are the main crops of this region. The summer months are hot and humid, while the winter months are cool with heavy rainfall during the monsoons. Kolkata is the capital of West Bengal. People here mainly speak in Bangla and Hindi. The major occupation of the people is farming and manufacturing, which is an important industry in West Bengal.

Howrah bridge

The Northern Plains extend eastwards to the north-eastern states of **Assam** and **Tripura**. Both the states experience hot and humid summers, pleasant winters and heavy rainfall during the monsoon.

The Brahmaputra river flows through Assam, making the land fertile. Jute and rice are the major crops. Tea cultivation and silkworm rearing is also practised here.

The capital of Assam is Dispur. Guwahati is one of the most important cities of Assam. People here speak Assamese and Hindi.

Tripura, surrounded by Bangladesh on three sides, is a small state in the northeast. People here grow jute, rice and bamboo. The main river of Tripura is Gumti.

Assam

Remember

- The Northern Plains of India consist of mainly three river basins—the Ganga basin, the Brahmaputra basin and the Indus basin.
- States that lie in the Northern Plains are Punjab, Haryana, Delhi, Uttar Pradesh, Bihar, West Bengal, Assam and Tripura.

Review Zone

A Fill in the blanks with the correct answers.

1. The ancient university of Nalanda is located in the state of ....
   a. Haryana b. Uttar Pradesh c. Bihar
2. .... receives water from the Ganga and Brahmaputra rivers.
   a. West Bengal b. Bihar c. Uttar Pradesh
3. The capital of West Bengal is ....
   a. Lucknow b. Kolkata c. Chandigarh
4. Ganga rises from the .... glacier.
   a. Gangotri b. Yamunotri c. Tibetan Plateau
5. The Golden Temple is located in ....
   a. Tripura b. Amritsar c. Chandigarh

B Write T for True and F for False.

1. Assam is surrounded by Bangladesh on three sides. ☐
2. The Indus river passes through four countries. ☐
3. Yamuna is one of the major distributaries of the Ganga river. ☐

4. The Brahmaputra river drains into the Arabian Sea. ☐
5. Tea is grown in Assam. ☐

C Answer these questions in brief.

1. Define a river basin.
2. From where do the Ganga and Brahmaputra rivers originate?
3. Name the countries through which the Indus river flows.
4. Name the languages spoken by the people of Bihar.
5. In which basin does the state of Haryana lie?

D Answer these questions in detail.

1. Why are the Northern Plains so fertile?
2. Describe the life of the people living in Punjab.
3. Which state receives water from two major rivers? How is the life of the people in this state?
4. What kind of life do people have in the states of Assam and Tripura?

Think Zone

A Imagine that you have to plan a trip to Assam. What should you keep in mind while planning the trip? What are the places that you plan to visit?

B Look at the picture and answer the questions.

1. Which monument is depicted in the picture?
2. In which state is it located?
3. In which river basin does this state lie?

Life Skills Zone

Both Haryana and Bihar lie in the same physical region of India, namely, the Northern Plains. However, the life of the people in both states is different. Why do you think there is a difference? Find out two reasons for it.

Value Zone

All states in India have a rich cultural heritage. One must respect and protect one's cultural heritage.

Activity Zone

Circle the names of rivers found in the Northern Plains in the word search.

- Beas
- Bhagirathi
- Brahmaputra
- Chenab
- Dihang
- Gandak
- Ganga
- Ghaggar
- Gomti
- Gumti
- Hooghly
- Kosi
- Ravi
- Satluj
- Son
- Yamuna

E	T	O	O	M	J	L	W	A	V	M	B	I	E	Y
B	E	A	S	U	R	S	G	K	G	R	B	T	L	L
G	A	O	L	D	X	A	G	V	A	N	W	M	G	H
V	G	T	D	B	S	C	G	H	R	Q	A	U	Z	G
Y	A	Q	E	X	U	J	M	G	U	A	Z	G	N	O
S	A	C	H	E	N	A	B	I	A	S	G	V	C	O
K	K	M	M	Q	P	U	G	E	Y	H	U	G	P	H
N	O	F	U	U	I	H	T	A	R	I	G	A	H	B
M	M	S	T	N	G	W	A	S	K	J	W	N	Q	V
H	S	R	I	F	A	D	W	C	Y	C	Y	D	A	W
E	A	D	L	V	I	S	K	Z	I	F	F	A	X	V
K	E	X	I	H	N	O	D	Z	Q	F	K	K	U	R
W	H	V	A	X	E	B	W	R	L	V	B	B	S	X
C	A	N	S	X	G	R	H	J	I	G	Q	R	O	V
R	G	I	T	M	O	G	R	U	A	N	R	O	N	R

4 The Western Desert

Observe and Reflect

- Which landform is shown in the picture?
- Who is called the ship of the desert and why?
- Name two such famous landforms from around the world.

Take a look at the map. It shows the extent of the Great Indian Desert. You already know, a desert is covered with sand and gets very little rain.

The Western Desert

The **Great Indian Desert** is also known as the **Thar Desert**. It stretches from the Rann of Kutch in Gujarat to the borders of Haryana. A large part of Rajasthan lies in the Thar Desert. The Aravalli range is located to the east of the Thar Desert.

The Thar Desert is a dry and hot desert. It has many **sand dunes**. Sandstorms are a regular feature of the desert. Small streams and underground water are the only natural sources of water in this region. Sometimes, underground water comes to the surface and forms water bodies known as **oases**. The lands around these water bodies are fertile and hence, villages develop around them. Date palms are a characteristic feature of oases.

Fact Zone

Deserts like the Gobi Desert get snow during the winter months and are known as cold deserts.

Camels are important to the people of the desert. They provide milk and are used for travelling and transporting goods from one place to another. Camels are also used to draw water from wells and to plough fields.

Find Out

Which river flows through the Thar Desert and why is it not of much use?

Cactii in desert

The climate in the Thar Desert remains very hot and dry throughout the year. While temperatures are high during the day, the nights are always cold. This region receives little or **scanty** rainfall.

Due to the **scarcity** of water, only plants that can draw underground water or store water can survive here. Cactus, keekar and babool are a few examples of such plants. People build houses with thick walls and small windows to keep away the heat.

Eco Zone

The clearing of forests and overgrazing increases the spread of desert land.

Do It Yourself

Look at the picture and answer the questions.

1. Which physical feature is surrounding the water source?
2. Which tree can be seen growing around the water body?
3. What is this water body called?

Life in the Region

Rajasthan, known as the 'desert state', is located in the Western Desert region. Bikaner and Jodhpur are two cities in this region. Agriculture, sheep rearing, textile printing, tourism and making handicrafts are the main occupations of the people of Rajasthan. They grow bajra and oilseeds. Due to the scarcity of water, people sometimes move in groups from one place to another looking for water. These people are called *banjaras*.

The people of Rajasthan speak in Hindi and Rajasthani. Men wear white *dhoti* with colourful *kurta* and tie *pagri* on their head to keep the heat away. Women wear colourful *ghaghra*, *odhni* and *choli*. They wear large silver jewellery and several white bangles that completely cover their

Find Out

Why is making handicrafts an important occupation of people living in the deserts?

forearms. Jaisalmer, Jaipur and Chittorgarh have famous forts. Rajasthan is also known for its national parks and sanctuaries.Rann of Kutch is known for its uniquely embroidered clothes. The area is also known for animals like the wild ass and the desert fox.

Remember

- The Great Indian Desert is also known as the Thar Desert.
- It stretches from the Rann of Kutch in Gujarat to the borders of Haryana.
- A large part of Rajasthan lies in the Thar Desert.
- Desert areas receive very little rainfall.

Review Zone

A Fill in the blanks with the correct answers.

1. The Aravalli range lies to the .... of the desert region.
   a. southwest b. east c. south
2. Hot and .... winds blow in the deserts.
   a. cold b. moist c. dry
3. .... is one of the commonly found plants in the desert region.
   a. Eucalyptus b. Cactus c. Pine
4. .... is an important city of the desert region in Rajasthan.
   a. Udaipur b. Bikaner c. Ajmer
5. The desert region is .... populated.
   a. thickly b. sparsely c. highly

B Name the following.

1. A place in the desert that has a water source and date palms: ....
2. Rajasthani men wear this on their heads to stay cool in the heat: ....
3. Hills lying to the east of the Thar Desert: ....
4. A cold desert: ....

C **Write T for True and F for False.**

1. The winter months are very cold in the deserts. ☐
2. The Thar is a wet and white desert. ☐
3. The Rann of Kutch lies in the desert region. ☐
4. All types of vegetation are found in deserts. ☐

D **Answer these questions in brief.**

1. Where is the Thar Desert located?
2. What languages do the people of Rajasthan speak?
3. What are camels used for in deserts?
4. Why do villages develop around oases?
5. Name four important cities of Rajasthan.

E **Answer these questions in detail.**

1. How do desert plants adapt to the conditions of water scarcity?
2. Describe the clothes worn by the men and women of Rajasthan.
3. Why do deserts have cold nights?
4. What are the kind of houses that can be found in a desert and why?

Think Zone

A The Thar Desert is located in the western part of India. What are the factors that influence the climate of this regions?

B **Look at the picture and answer the questions.**

1. What bird is this—the stork or the Great Indian Bustard?
2. In which region is this bird found?
3. Name two animals found in the region where this bird is found.

Life Skills Zone

Rajasthan in a well-known tourist destination. Why do you think tourists like to visit Rajasthan?

Value Zone

People in the desert regions are generally hardworking. Life is much more difficult for them than it is in other areas.

Activity Zone

Puppetry is a popular art performance in Rajasthan. Let us make sock puppets.

You will need an old pair of socks, buttons, some wool, paper, glue, scissors and different-coloured sketch pens.

1. Take an old pair of socks.
2. Mark the place for the eyes. Now, either glue buttons for the eyes or sew them on to the socks.
3. Take some wool for the hair of the puppet and stick it on the socks where the puppet's head should be. You can style the hair however you like.
4. Now that the puppet is ready, give it a name.
5. Wear the socks on your hand. You are now ready to stage a puppet show.

5 The Southern Plateau

Observe and Reflect

- Which part of India does this picture show?
- Name the seas on the western side and the eastern side of this part of India.
- What is the name of the neighbouring country visible in the picture?

Do you know what a plateau is? A plateau is a large stretch of high or elevated land that has a flat upper part.

The Southern Plateaus, also known as the 'peninsular plateaus', form a distinct physical feature of India. The rocky plateau is wide in the north and **tapers** as we travel towards the south. They are outlined by the Western Ghats in the west, the Aravalli hills and the Rajmahal hills in the north, the Eastern Ghats in the east and the Nilgiri hills in the south. The rivers in the Southern Plateaus are mainly rain-fed and flow with a great speed. Some flow into the Bay of Bengal and the others, like river Narmada and Tapi, flow into the Arabian Sea.

The Southern Plateau is divided into two parts by river Narmada. The northern part is called the **Central Highlands** and the southern part is called the **Deccan Plateau**.

The Central Highlands consist of the **Malwa Plateau** and the **Chhota Nagpur Plateau**. The Malwa Plateau is of volcanic origin. It is drained by the Chambal and Betwa rivers and bordered by the Aravalli and the Vindhya ranges. The southernmost part of Rajasthan and most of Madhya Pradesh fall in this plateau region.

Southern Plateau

^ Chhota Nagpur Plateau

The Chhota Nagpur Plateau also known as the 'mineral belt' of India is bordered by the Satpura range in the north-west and drained by river Damodar. It includes Jharkhand, northern Odisha and north-eastern Chhattisgarh.

The Central Highlands is rich in black soil, which is excellent for cultivating cotton and sugarcane. The region has vast resources of minerals like coal, iron, bauxite, manganese and mica.

The Deccan Plateau is surrounded by the Eastern Ghats and the Western Ghats, extending upto the southern tip of peninsular India. It is drained by the Godavari, Indravati, Krishna, Kaveri and Mahanadi rivers which flow eastwards into the Bay of Bengal. Some areas in the region have red soil, which is good for crops, such as groundnut, tobacco, millets, potato and sugarcane.

^ Western Ghats

Find Out

The area with black soil is also known as Deccan Trap. Find out why is it called so?

Life in the Plateau Region

Many states of India including Madhya Pradesh, parts of Maharashtra, Karnataka, Jharkhand, Odisha, Chhattisgarh, Andhra Pradesh, Telangana and Tamil Nadu lie in the plateau region. Let us look at the life of the people in these states.

Eco Zone

The Southern Plateau is rich in minerals yet, due to exploitation of these minerals, frequent landslides occur.

Madhya Pradesh lies in the centre of India in the Central Highlands region. It has a dry and wet climate.

^ Kanha National Park

Agriculture is the main occupation of the people here. Wheat, sugarcane, pulses, oilseeds and cotton are the main crops. Panna is a well-known diamond mine of the state. The state has rich forest reserves and has more than ten national parks. The Kanha National Park and Bandhavgarh National Park serve to protect tigers. The people of Madhya Pradesh speak Hindi and Marathi.

In the year 2000, the state of **Chhattisgarh** was formed out of Madhya Pradesh. The climate in the state is hot and humid. Chhattisgarh has both hills as well as plains. The main occupation of the people is farming and mining. The Bhilai steel plant, situated in Chhattisgarh, is a major producer of steel in the country. Chhattisgarh has scenic waterfalls, such as Chitrakote Falls, which attract tourists. The people here speak Hindi.

Fact Zone

Anamudi is the highest peak, Jog Falls, the highest waterfall, and Godavari is the longest river of the Deccan Plateau.

Some parts of **Odisha** towards southeast Chhattisgarh are located in the Central Highlands. Rice and jute are the main crops of this region.

Maharashtra lies in the north-western part of the Deccan Plateau. The state has an irregular monsoon climate. Farming is the main occupation of the people in the state. Mumbai is the capital. The black soil that is found abundantly in parts of Mumbai is suitable for growing cotton and sugarcane. Other crops include groundnut, wheat, *jowar*, pulses and *bajra*. Maharashtra has many textile industries. The people of Maharashtra speak Marathi, Hindi and Konkani.

Do It Yourself

Name this famous festival that is celebrated in Maharashtra during the monsoon season. Find out why this festival is celebrated.

Eco Zone

The tribal people living around the Southern Plateau worship nature and protect parts of the forests as sacred groves.

Jharkhand was carved out from the state of Bihar in the year 2000. The climate of the state is hot and humid. Jharkhand is rich in minerals and forest reserves. Farming, animal rearing and mining are the important occupations of Jharkhand. The major crops grown here are paddy, oilseeds, millets and sugarcane. A large section of the population in the state is tribal. The people of Jharkhand mainly speak Hindi, Bihari, Odia, Santhali and Munda.

A part of the state of **Andhra Pradesh** is located in the Deccan Plateau region. Farming, mining, animal rearing and handicrafts are the important occupations of the people. The region has rich deposits of mica and limestone. Farmers here grow rice, *jowar*, tobacco, sugarcane and groundnut. The state is the largest producer of tobacco in India. People speak in Telugu and Urdu.

Charminar

In 2014, a new state named **Telangana** was created from some parts of Andhra Pradesh. Farmers here grow rice, tobacco, maize and cotton. It shares its capital with Andhra Pradesh. People here speak Telugu. Nagarjuna Sagar Dam, one of the largest dams in the world, is located here.

Nilgiri Hills

Tamil Nadu lies to the south of Andhra Pradesh. Agriculture, weaving and fishing are the main occupations of the people in Tamil Nadu. Farmers grow rice, sugarcane, groundnut, bananas and oilseeds. Tea, coffee and rubber are also grown along the slopes of the Nilgiri hills. Tamil Nadu is also known for its textile and leather industry. Tamil is the main language of the people of Tamil Nadu.

The state of **Karnataka** lies to the south of Maharashtra. The farmers of Karnataka grow coffee, sugarcane, cotton, spices and jowar. The state has extensive teak and sandalwood forests and **hydroelectric** power. Karnataka has five national parks including Bandipur and Nagarhole and Nilgiri Biosphere Reserve. Kannada is the state language. It is a major centre of the information technology (IT) industry.

Jog Falls

Remember

- The Southern Plateaus, also known as the 'peninsular plateaus', form a distinct physical feature of India.
- The Narmada river divides the plateau into two parts—the Central Highlands and the Deccan Plateau.
- Madhya Pradesh, Maharashtra, Odisha, Karnataka, Tamil Nadu, Chhattisgarh and Jharkhand are the major states of the Southern Plateau region.

Review Zone

A Fill in the blanks with the correct answers.

1. The Southern Plateaus, also known as the .... plateaus, form a distinct physical feature of India.
   a. table b. peninsular c. coastal
2. The river .... divides the entire plateau region into two parts.
   a. Tapi b. Godavari c. Narmada
3. .... is the highest peak in the Deccan plateau.
   a. Mt Abu b. Anamudi c. Mt Annapurna
4. .... Plateau is of volcanic origin.
   a. Malwa b. Vindhya c. Betwa
5. .... soil is found in the Central Highlands.
   a. Alluvial b. Sandy c. Black

B Name the following.

1. A state of India that is known for its tobacco production: ....
2. A famous diamond mine located in Maharashtra: ....
3. Two rivers of the Deccan Plateau that drain into the Arabian Sea: ....
4. A type of soil suitable for growing cotton: ....
5. A state with rich tribal culture: ....

C Write T for True and F for False.

1. The Deccan Plateau is only surrounded by the Western Ghats. ☐
2. The Chhota Nagpur Plateau covers Jharkhand. ☐
3. The Godavari is the longest river in the Western Plateau. ☐
4. The people of Tamil Nadu speak Odia. ☐
5. Red soil is good for growing groundnut and tobacco. ☐

D Answer these questions in brief.

1. What is a plateau?
2. Name four rivers of the Southern Plateau that drain into the Bay of Bengal.

3. Which regions are included in the Chhota Nagpur Plateau?
4. Name three hills of the Western Ghats.
5. What are the main crops of the state of Maharashtra?
6. What is the state of Andhra Pradesh famous for?
7. Which rivers flow through the state of Karnataka?

E Answer these questions in detail.

1. Describe the Central Highlands.
2. Describe the rivers of the Deccan Plateau.
3. Write a short note on the states of Telangana and Jharkhand.
4. Describe the state of Karnataka.

Think Zone

A Why does the state of Karnataka have extensive hydroelectric power?

B Look at the picture and answer the questions.

1. In which state are these trees found?
2. What is the wood of this tree used for?

Life Skills Zone

The plateau region has rain-fed rivers flowing through it. These rivers dry up during the summer months. Find out how the people of the region cope with this situation.

Value Zone

Every time a tree is being cut, we should see to it that a new one is planted in its place.

Activity Zone

Make a chart on the rivers and dams of the Southern Plateau. Paste colourful pictures of the rivers and dams and write briefly about their location.

6 The Coastal Plains and the Islands

Observe and Reflect

- Name any two states that lie in the coastal plains.
- What is the name of the small group of islands located below the southern part of India?
- What does the green colour signify on the map?

When we visit the seaside, we see long sandy beaches where the land meets the sea. This is called a **coast**. The low-lying land along a coast is called a **coastal plain**.

Coastal plains

The Coastal Plains

We have already learned about the Deccan plateau. The coastal plains surround it from Gujarat in the west to West Bengal in the east. The coastal plains in the west are called the **Western Coastal Plains** and the coastal plains in the east are called the **Eastern Coastal Plains**. The two plains meet at Kanyakumari.

The Eastern Coastal Plains is a wide stretch of land that stretches from West Bengal in the north to Tamil Nadu in the south. It lies between the Eastern Ghats and the Bay of Bengal. Tamil Nadu, Puducherry, Andhra Pradesh, Odisha and West Bengal lie along the Eastern Coastal Plains.

The Eastern Coastal Plains has two parts. The northern part is called the **Northern Circars** and the southern part is called the **Coromandel Coast**. Many rivers, such as the Godavari, Krishna, Kaveri and Mahanadi form large deltas along this coast. The Chilka Lake, the largest saltwater lake in India, is located along the eastern coast in the state of Odisha.

The Western Coastal Plains is a thin strip of land that stretches from the state of Gujarat in the north to Kerala in the south. It falls between the Western Ghats and the Arabian Sea. The Western Coastal Plains is divided into three parts. These are the **Gujarat Coast** in the north, the **Konkan Coast** in the middle and the **Malabar Coast** in the south. The Gulf of Khambat and the Gulf of Kutch lie in the Western Coastal Plain. The western coast is narrower than the eastern coast. The states of Gujarat, Maharashtra, Goa, Karnataka and Kerala are located in the Western Coastal Plain.

Find Out

Why are the coastal areas fertile?

Fact Zone

Indira Point is the southernmost point of India.

Life in the Coastal Plains

Let us look at the life of the people that live in the different states of the coastal plains.

We have already learned about **West Bengal** in the Northern Plains. If you look at the location of West Bengal on the map, you will find that some parts of it fall under the Northern Mountains, some under the Northern Plains and some in the Eastern Coastal Plain. Which parts of West Bengal fall in the Eastern Coastal Plain?

Located on the eastern coast, **Odisha** is a fertile state. Agriculture and fishing are the two most important occupations in the state. Rice is a major crop. Lentils, oilseeds and jute are also grown here. The coastal region is hit by major cyclones almost every year. The Chilka Lake is a major tourist attraction where **migratory** birds roost.

Chilka Lake

Andhra Pradesh is the eighth largest state of India. Some parts of this state are part of the Deccan Plateau while some parts make up the coastal plains. It is home to the Visakhapatnam Port, which is an important seaport of India. The state has a shipbuilding yard, an oil refinery and an iron and steel plant.

Towards the southernmost part of India, **Tamil Nadu** has a long coastline called the Coromandel Coast. The river Kaveri, which flows through the state, provides it with water and makes the land fertile. Its capital, Chennai, is well known for cotton and silk *sarees*. The Marina Beach in Chennai is the longest beach in India.

Marina Beach

Matri Mandir

Once a French colony, **Puducherry** is now a union territory of India. It lies to the south of Chennai. The famous Aurobindo Ashram and the Matri Mandir are located here. Farming and fishing are the main occupations of the people here.

The state of **Gujarat** lies on the west coast of India. Gandhinagar is the capital of Gujarat. Ahmedabad is the largest city in this state. Farming is the main occupation of the people. The crops grown here are *jowar*, *bajra*, cotton, oilseeds, sugarcane and wheat. The famous Sabarmati Ashram is located here. Gujarat is home to the Asiatic lion, which is found in the Gir National Park.

Sabarmati Ashram

Located on the western side of the Indian peninsula, **Maharashtra** is the third largest state in the country. Mumbai, the capital of Maharashtra, is the largest seaport of India. It is also an important centre for business and industry. Bombay High is an offshore oilfield, which has large deposits of petroleum.

Eco Zone

Make no open fires. A small open fire can destroy an entire forest!

The smallest state of India, **Goa** is a land of beautiful sandy beaches, old churches, marvellous monuments, beautiful temples and well-maintained museums. Panaji is the capital of Goa. Agriculture is the main occupation of the people of Goa. The people here are also engaged in farming and fishing. Cashew nuts, rice, spices, coconuts and mangoes are the main crops grown here.

Goa

A part of the state of **Karnataka** lies on the Konkan Coast with the other parts are located in the Deccan Plateau. Bengaluru is the capital of Karnataka and is known as the information technology or IT capital of India. Karnataka has thick teak forests along its coastal areas, making the state a major producer of sandalwood products. Mangalore is an important seaport of the state.

The state of **Kerala** lies on the Malabar Coast. Thiruvananthapuram is the capital city of Kerala. The state is known for its beautiful backwaters. Agriculture is the main occupation of the people. Coconut, rubber, cocoa, coffee and spices are the main crops grown here. Kerala has the highest literacy rate in India.

Kerala backwaters

The Islands

You already know that an island is a piece of land surrounded by water. A number of islands surround the coastal plains. Of these, the two biggest group of islands are the **Andaman and Nicobar Islands** and the **Lakshadweep Islands**. Look at the map of India and you will find exactly where the two island groups are situated.

Fact Zone

The Andaman Islands are a group of 300 islands out of which only 26 are inhabited.

Andaman and Nicobar Islands

These islands are situated in the Bay of Bengal. The Andaman and the Nicobar Islands are the two island groups forming one union territory. The Andaman lies to the north and Nicobar lies to the south. The capital of this union territory is Port Blair. The main occupations are agriculture, fishing, animal rearing and construction. Rice is the main food crop along with maize, coconut and rubber.

The smallest union territory of India, the Lakshadweep Islands, lies in the Arabian Sea. The Lakshwadeep Islands are a group of 36 islands out of which only 10 are **inhabited** by people. Kavaratti is the capital of the Lakshadweep Islands. This island is formed by the **deposition** of corals. Fishing is the main occupation of the people. The main crop grown here is coconut.

Do It Yourself

This is a famous dance form of Kerala. Find out its name. Find out how and where this style of dancing originated. You can browse the Internet to find out.

Remember

- A coastal plain is the lowland that runs along a coast.
- The Eastern Coastal Plains is divided into two parts—the Northern Circars and the Coromandel Coast.

» The Western Coastal Plains is divided into three parts—the Gujarat Coast, the Konkan Coast and the Malabar Coast.

Review Zone

A Fill in the blanks with the correct answers.

1. The southern part of the Eastern Coastal Plains is called the .... Coast.
   a. Malabar b. Coromandel c. Konkan
2. Kerala is famous for its ....
   a. museums b. backwaters c. islands
3. The Chilka Lake is in the state of ....
   a. Maharashtra b. Kerala c. Odisha
4. .... is a union territory.
   a. Puducherry b. Port Blair c. Kavaratti
5. Mangalore is an important seaport in ....
   a. Goa b. Karnataka c. West Bengal

B Name the following.

1. A river of the Eastern Coastal Plains that forms a delta in the eastern coast: ....
2. The capital of the Andaman and Nicobar Islands: ....
3. A group of islands formed by coral deposition: ....
4. The longest beach of India: ....
5. A famous ashram in Gujarat founded by Mahatma Gandhi: ....

C Write T for True and F for False.

1. An island is a piece of land surrounded by water on three sides. ☐
2. The Hirakud dam is built on the river Godavari. ☐
3. The coast of Tamil Nadu is called the Coromandel Coast. ☐
4. Bombay High is located in Maharashtra. ☐
5. The Marina Beach is located in Bangalore. ☐

D Answer these questions in brief.

1. Name the four rivers that form large deltas along the Eastern Coastal Plains.
2. What are the main occupations of the people in Goa?
3. What is an island? Name the group of islands in the Arabian Sea.
4. Which is the longest beach of India? Where is it located?
5. Which are the main crops of Gujarat?

E Answer these questions in detail.

1. Describe the extent and location of the Coastal Plains of India.
2. What do you know about the Western Coastal Plains of India?
3. Briefly describe the union territory of Puducherry.
4. Describe the state of Kerala.
5. Describe the Lakshadweep islands.

Think Zone

A Kerala is suitable for growing spices. Which spices are grown in Kerala? What do we use them for?

B Look at the picture and answer the questions.

1. Who is this person?
2. What is he carrying?
3. What does he do to earn a living?

Life Skills Zone

How does the location of a place affect the occupation of the people living there? Do people living in coastal areas have different livelihoods than people living in the mountains or deserts? Explain.

Value Zone

People of India follow different traditions and beliefs. We should respect these beliefs and traditions.

Activity Zone

Find out the names of the bird sanctuaries that are located along the coastal plains. Make a chart, paste pictures and write the names of the birds that are found there.

7 Natural Resources of India

Observe and Reflect

- What do you see in the picture?
- How does it help to grow crops?
- Can it be used for drinking?

Look around you. Where do you get all these things from? Our Earth provides us with everything that we need to live. Air, water and sunlight are some of the things that we get from the Earth. They are called **natural resources**. Natural resources are the **resources** that we get from nature and that help us in our day-to-day lives.

Natural resources are mainly of two types:

- **Renewable** or **inexhaustible** resources
- **Non-renewable** or **exhaustible** resources

Renewable Resources

Renewable or inexhaustible resources are the resources that never get used up as they are abundantly available in nature. Sunlight, air, water and soil are some natural resources that will never get used up. This makes them inexhaustible. Let us learn about the uses of some renewable resources.

Eco Zone

Although air, water and soil are inexhaustible, they can get polluted. These have an adverse effect on our health.

Air is essential for all humans, animals and plants to survive. While plants use air to make their food, humans need air to breathe and live. The blanket of air on the Earth's surface also helps maintain the right temperature so that it is suitable for life. Without this blanket of air, life on the Earth would not have been possible.

Water makes up three-fourths of the Earth's surface. Just like air, water is essential for humans, animals and plants to survive.

Sunlight is one of the most important renewable resources. Sunlight warms us and provides light in the daytime. Plants use sunlight to make their food through a process called **photosynthesis**. Sunlight also serves as a source of **solar energy**. Many cars today run on solar energy. Cooking can also be done using solar energy.

Wind is another important natural resource. Windmills are used to create energy from the movement of the wind. Several states in India, like Tamil Nadu and West Bengal, produce wind energy.

Fact Zone

Electricity produced by using water is called hydroelectricity. The Tehri dam in India is the highest dam of India.

Solar panels

Forests are a rich source of plants, trees, animals and soil. Plants and trees provide us with wood, medicines, gum, perfumes and raw materials to make many things. Most importantly, plants release oxygen in the air, which is essential for humans.

Animals provide us with food like milk, eggs and meat and other things like wool and leather. They are also sometimes used as a means of transport in hilly areas and deserts.

Soil, which forms the top layer of the Earth's surface, is essential for plants to grow and live.

Forests

Non-renewable Resources

Non-renewable resources are those resources that exist in limited quantities and it takes a long time for them to be created. Their supply is slowly getting over. They are also known as exhaustible resources. Some examples of non-renewable resources are coal, petroleum, metals, minerals, oil and gas. Coal, natural gas and petroleum are called **fossil fuels**. When plants and animals die, with time, their remains get buried under the earth. They are pressed further into the ground and after many years become fossil fuels.

Find Out

In which states of India are coal reserves found?

Coal is one of the most useful non-renewable natural resources. It is used for many purposes like cooking, producing electricity and for heating. It is used both in homes as well as industries. Machines and vehicles also run with the help of coal.

Petroleum is used to form diesel and petrol, which are used to run cars, ships and aeroplanes. It is a very rare natural resource as not many countries in the world have petroleum reserves. Petroleum is also known as liquid gold. Bombay High in India is a petroleum **reserve**.

Bombay High

Metals like iron, bauxite and copper are useful natural resources used to make many important objects of daily use.

Do It Yourself

Write the names of the natural resources that are used to make the following things.

....

Conservation of Natural Resources

It is very important for us to use both renewable as well as non-renewable natural resources carefully. Since non-renewable resources take a long time to form, it is very important for us to preserve them. Therefore, people have developed ways where sunlight, water and wind are used in place of non-renewable sources to produce energy. These are called **alternative** sources of energy.

Remember

- Minerals, metals, fossil fuels, air, water and other such resources, which are useful in our daily lives are known as natural resources.
- There are two types of natural resources—renewable and non-renewable.

» Air, water and sunlight are renewable resources.

» Petroleum, coal and metals are non-renewable resources.

Review Zone

A Fill in the blanks with the correct answers.

1. Non-renewable resources are also known as .... resources.
   a. exhaustible b. exhausting c. inexhaustible

2. Water is used to produce ....
   a. hydroelectricity b. solar energy c. wind energy

3. Bauxite is an .... resource.
   a. exhaustible b. inexhaustible c. renewable

4. Fossil fuels are made up of the remains of ....
   a. solar energy b. dead plants and animals c. water sources

5. We use .... to get solar energy.
   a. hydroelectricity b. wind c. sunlight

B Each tile has a set of letters. Two or more tiles form a word in a phrase. Unscramble the tiles to reveal the phrase and read the message. The first tile has been unscrambled for you.

O U R	D W	S E R	C E S	E	A N
I L D	L I F	V E	R E S		

CON										

C Write T for True and F for False.

1. Renewable natural resources do not need to be preserved. ☐
2. Windmills require wind and sunlight to work. ☐
3. Coal and petroleum are examples of fossil fuels. ☐
4. Plants make food through the process of photosynthesis. ☐
5. Sunlight is a non-renewable resource. ☐

D **Answer these questions in brief.**

1. Name some non-renewable natural resources.
2. Define natural resources.
3. What is solar energy?
4. How does soil help us?
5. Write one difference between renewable and non-renewable natural resources.

E **Answer these questions in detail.**

1. Describe two renewable natural resources.
2. Why is it important for us to conserve both renewable as well as non-renewable natural resources?
3. How are coal and petroleum useful as natural resources?

Think Zone

A How would your life be affected if there were no more coal and petroleum in the world? List the things that you would not be able to do.

B **Look at the picture and answer the questions.**

1. What do you see in the picture?
2. Which natural resource do they require in order to work?
3. What are they used to generate?

Life Skills Zone

Find out about one type of alternative energy and write a report on it.

Value Zone

Plants and forests may be inexhaustible but if we keep cutting down forests and don't plant new ones, they will run out.

Activity Zone

Make a chart showing the renewable resources that are used to produce energy. Draw pictures along with each natural resource and explain their benefits in two or three sentences.

8 Soils of India

Observe and Reflect

- What is the man in the picture doing?
- Why does this need to be done?
- What are the natural resources plants require to live?

The uppermost layer of the surface of Earth is known as **soil**. Also known as the **topsoil**, it forms on the surface of the land. Soil is a mixture of minerals, water, air and the decaying remains of plants and animals.

Formation of Soil

Soil takes a very long time to form. Large rocks, due to wind, water and sunlight, are broken down into smaller pieces. With time, these pieces are further broken down into smaller pieces, which form sand, **silt** and the different types of soil. But this is a process that takes millions of years!

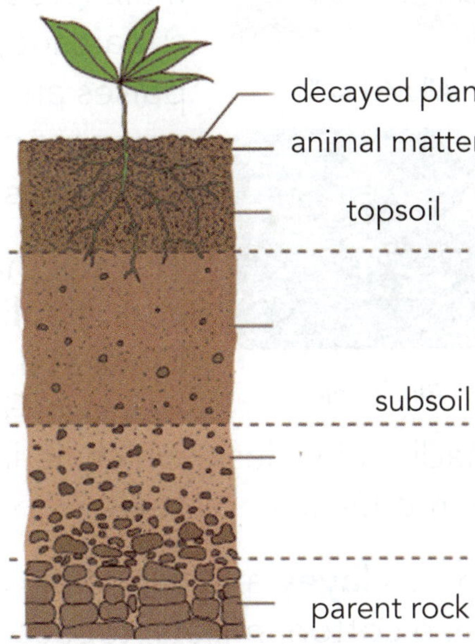

Soils profile

Why is soil such an important natural resource? This is because plants, trees and crops require soil to grow. We have learned in the previous chapter that soil is a renewable resource.

Soil differs from place to place but all types of soil are composed of **particles** of clay, sand and silt in varying quantities. The nature of soil depends upon the rocks and other materials from which it is formed. Some types of soils are very fertile, while others are not depending upon the location of a region. The soils in areas that have plenty of water supply are very fertile. When soil is fertile, crops grow well. In places where the soil is not fertile, farmers use **manure** or fertilizers to make the soil more fertile.

Different Types of Soils

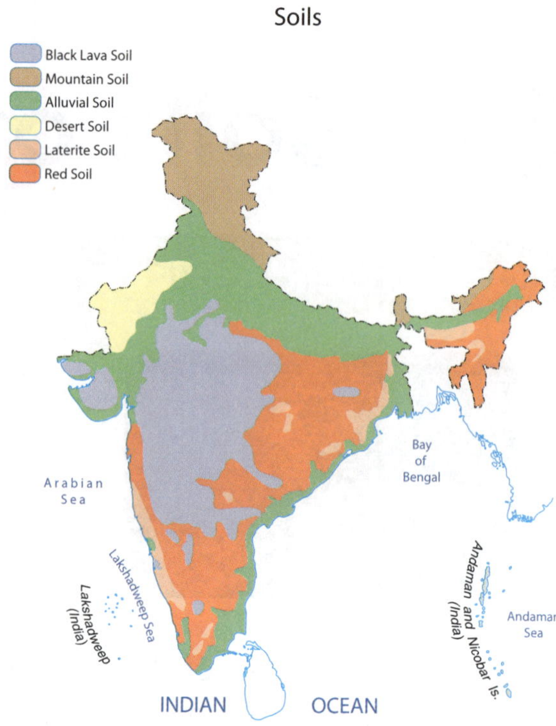

Soils in India

Different parts of India are rich in different types of soils. Look at the map and find out which part of India is rich in which type of soil.

The soil that is formed due to the deposition of silt and sand brought down by rivers is known as **alluvial soil**. This type of soil is found in plenty in the Northern and Coastal Plains of India. These deposits are very fertile and soft in nature. Alluvial soil is rich in minerals.

Alluvial soil

Alluvial soil is good for growing crops, like rice, wheat, maize, tobacco, sugarcane, oilseeds, pulses and jute amongst many others. Fruits and vegetables also grow very well in this type of soil.

Black soil

The soil that is formed from **lava** after it **solidifies** is known as **black soil**. Black soil is mainly found in Gujarat, Maharashtra and Madhya Pradesh, which lie in the north-western part of the Deccan plateau.

Find Out

Which type of soil is found in the place where you live?

This soil is **clayey** and can retain a lot of moisture. It is most suitable for growing crops like cotton, millets, tobacco, oilseeds, wheat, sugarcane and even citrus fruits.

Take a look at the picture. The soil is red in colour and hence, it is known as **red soil**. The presence of iron makes this soil appear red in colour. This soil is not very fertile, still people grow crops such as pulses, rice, millets and certain vegetables. Red soil is found mainly in the states of Jharkhand, Madhya Pradesh, Maharashtra, Odisha, Andhra Pradesh, Tamil Nadu and Telangana.

Red soil

The soil that is produced by the process of **weathering** is known as **laterite soil**. This soil is found in regions that experience a lot of rainfall. As a result of the rain, the minerals in the soil get washed away. This process of washing away of minerals is known as leaching.

Laterite soil

It is found in some parts of Bihar, Odisha, Maharashtra, Karnataka, West Bengal, Meghalaya, Andhra Pradesh, Kerala and Telangana. Farmers of these regions apply fertilizers to the soil and mainly grow coffee, tea, coconut and rubber.

Fact Zone

Soil looses fertility when one variety of crop is grown for a long period. Farmers grow different crops in the same land to keep the soil fertile. This is known as crop rotation.

The soil that is found in the deserts is known as **desert soil**. Deserts receive little to no rainfall and hence, the soil is not at all fertile. It is only with the help of irrigation and fertilizers that a few crops like wheat, barley, millets, pulses and cotton can be grown here. This soil is mainly found in the desert regions of India, namely, Rajasthan and its surrounding areas.

Desert soil

Mountain soil

The soil that is found in the slopes of the hills is known as **mountain soil**. Rich in **humus**, this soil is very good for growing fruits and practising terrace farming. When the hilly slopes are divided into steps and various kinds of crops like maize, barley, coffee, fruits and spices are grown then it is known as terrace farming.

Eco Zone

For one week every year, trees are planted in different parts of the country. This is known as *van mahotsav*.

This type of soil is mostly found in the hilly areas of Uttarakhand, Jammu and Kashmir and Himachal Pradesh.

Do It Yourself

This is a picture of terrace farming. Find out more about how and where it is practised in India.

Soil Erosion and Conservation

Often due to natural as well as human activities, the top layer of the soil gets worn away. This is known as **soil erosion**.

Natural occurrences like heavy rainfall, excessive floods and strong winds **corrode** the top layer of the soil resulting in soil erosion. Some human activities like deforestation and land pollution cause soil erosion. The roots of the plants hold the soil together. When trees are cut down, the soil becomes loose. This results in the soil getting easily worn away. As a result, the land becomes less fertile and unsuitable for growing crops.

There are a few ways through which we can control soil erosion and increase fertility of the soil:

Planting a sapling

- Plant more trees instead of cutting them down as this leads to deforestation.
- Reduce land pollution by not throwing waste anywhere.
- Chemical fertilizers should be avoided because they decrease soil fertility.
- Natural and organic fertilizers like manure and **compost** should be used.

Remember

- Soil forms the top layer of the Earth's surface.
- There are various types of soils found in India, namely, alluvial, laterite, black, red, desert and mountain soil.
- Alluvial soil is very fertile and good for growing crops.
- Black soil is formed from solidified lava.
- Red soil contains iron and hence, is red in colour.
- Laterite soil is not fertile because of leaching.
- Desert soil is not fertile and is found in the desert regions of India.
- Mountain soil is found on hill slopes and is ideal for practising terrace farming.
- The wearing away of the upper layer of soil is known as soil erosion.

Review Zone

A Fill in the blanks with the correct answers.

1. .... can prevent soil erosion.

   a. Rocks b. Trees c. Earthworms

2. The Northern Plains are rich in .... soil.
   a. laterite   b. alluvial   c. mountain
3. Spices grow well in .... soil.
   a. alluvial   b. mountain   c. desert
4. .... prevents the soil from becoming infertile.
   a. Crop rotation   b. Crop farming   c. Deforestation
5. Mountain soil is rich in ....
   a. clay   b. lava   c. humus

B Name the following.

1. The process of minerals being washed away from the soil due to rains: ....
2. The process of growing different crops in each season in the same area of land: ....
3. An organic fertilizer that makes the soil fertile without harming it: ....
4. The process by which the top layer of the soil is washed away by rains or winds: ....
5. A state in India where desert soil is found: ....

C Write T for True and F for False.

1. Land pollution results in soil erosion. ☐
2. Mountain soil is formed by the process of weathering. ☐
3. Black soil cannot retain moisture and hence, is ideal for growing cotton. ☐
4. Manure should be used instead of chemical fertilizers. ☐
5. Red soil is not very fertile. ☐

D Answer these questions in brief.

1. Define soil.
2. Name the various types of soil found in India.
3. Which crops are ideal for alluvial soil?
4. Where is black soil found in India?
5. What is leaching?

E **Answer these questions in detail.**

1. How is soil formed?
2. How and why is crop rotation practised?
3. How is laterite soil formed?
4. State a few ways in which soil erosion can be prevented.

Think Zone

A Do you think that different types of soil in different parts of India affect the lives of the people in those parts? Select a type of soil and write about how it affects the life of the people living there.

B **Look at the picture and answer the questions.**

1. What type of soil is this?
2. Where is it found in India?
3. How can crops be grown here?

Life Skills Zone

Deforestation should not be practised but still it is done in many areas. Why do you think people still cut down trees? Make a list of things that are made from trees and suggest other resources that we can use to replace wood.

Value Zone

Planting trees reduces soil erosion. Make groups and spread awareness about the importance of trees inyour neighbourhood.

Activity Zone

You know soil is made up of clay, silt and sand. It also has humus and the remains of dead plants and animals. Take some topsoil, clay, sand and silt. Feel the texture of each separately. Compare the sizes of the particles of soil and fill in the table.

Particle	Clay	Silt	Sand	Humus
Size				
Texture				

9 Forests and Wildlife of India

Observe and Reflect

- Identify the animal in the picture.
- Why are laws being made to prevent people from killing this animal?

Do you know what a forest is? A forest is a large area covered by trees, which is home to many wild animals. We have learned before that forests are an important source of renewable resources.

Importance of Forests

We know that plants take in carbon dioxide and give out oxygen which is essential for all animals and humans to survive. Trees prevent soil erosion. Soil erosion takes place when the topmost layer of soil wears away. This happens when there is too much water in a region, causing the soil to become loose. The roots of trees firmly hold the soil, thereby preventing soil erosion.

> **Eco Zone**
>
> Forests are considered as the 'lungs of the Earth' because they provide clean and fresh air, which is vital for our survival.

Forests provide food and shelter to wild animals. Trees give us products like gum, wood, medicines, fuel, furniture, paper, clothing and many more.

At least 33 per cent of a country should be covered by forests. However, only 20 per cent of India is covered by forests. Efforts have been made in various states to increase the forest cover and it has increased a little in recent times. Look at the map of India depicting India's forest cover.

Different Types of Forests

We know that like soils, there are different types of forests too. Depending upon the nature of the trees found, the forests of India can be divided into five types—evergreen, deciduous, mountainous, thorn and mangrove or tidal forests. Let us learn more about these types of forests.

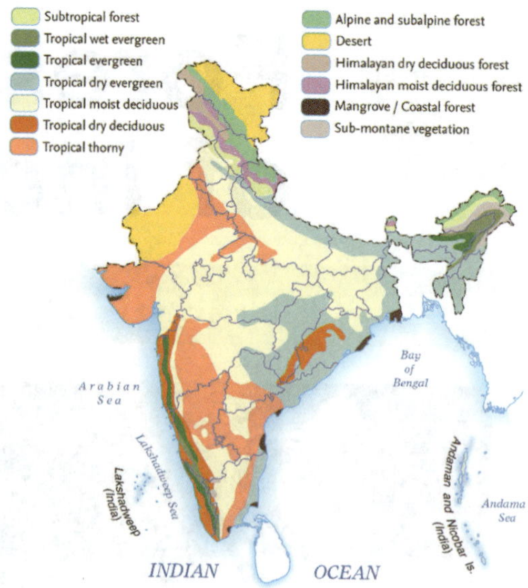

Natural Vegetation of India

Evergreen forests have trees which never shed their leaves. These evergreen trees grow very tall and have a thick and woody bark. Since the trees grow very close to each other, the leaves at the top form a roof-like cover called canopy. These canopies do not allow much light to pass through them. Sometimes it rains heavily in these areas.

Evergreen forest

Evergreen forests grow well in moist and wet places and are found mainly in the northeastern hills, the Andaman and Nicobar Islands and the hill slopes of the Western Ghats. The evergreen forests have mahogany, ebony and rosewood trees.

Find Out

Find out the names of the animals that are commonly found in evergreen forests.

The trees that shed their leaves in the summer season form **deciduous forests**. These forests grow in areas that experience moderate rainfall.

They are mainly found in the foothills of the Himalayas, in the states of Uttarakhand and in Uttar Pradesh. Such forests are also found in the states of Maharashtra, Madhya Pradesh, Karnataka, Kerala, Tamil Nadu and Odisha.

Deciduous forest

Sal, teak, sandalwood, mahua, sheesham, bamboo and semul are the major trees found in deciduous forests. They are home to animals like deer, monkeys and birds like parrots. Deciduous forests form the largest forest cover in India.

Mostly coniferous trees such as pine, fir, spruce and deodar make up **mountainous forests**. These trees are conical in shape, very tall and bear fruits, which are also known as cones because of their shape. The leaves are pointed and hence, snow does not gather on the leaves. These forests are also known as coniferous forests.

Mountainous forest

Coniferous forests are mainly found in the higher parts of the Himalayan Mountains and also in the Nilgiris. Paper is made from the **pulp** of coniferous trees.

Thorn forest

Thorn forests are mainly found in the desert regions of Rajasthan, parts of Haryana and the southern part of Punjab. The trees that have sharp thorns and small leaves to prevent loss of water, like *keekar* and *babool*, form thorn forests. The sharp thorns also keep animals away. These plants grow in desert areas and hence, they need long roots for survival. The roots of these plants spread out over a large area in order to absorb water and minerals. Various types of wild palms and cacti are also found in these forests.

Mangrove forest

The forests that are found in deltas and in areas submerged in seawater are known as **mangrove** or **tidal forests**. These trees can grow well in both freshwater and seawater.

In India, tidal forests are found in the Ganga-Brahmaputra delta. The famous *Sundari* tree, a few **ferns**, shrubs and palms grow in these forests. Boats are made out of the wood of these trees. This forest is the home of the Royal Bengal tiger, spotted deer, crocodiles and many more animals.

Conservation of Forests

A number of movements have been launched in order to protect the forest cover of India. Of these, the Chipko movement which took place in the 1970s was the most famous. A group of villagers from the Reni village of Uttarakhand clung to the trees preventing woodcutters from cutting them down. The movement was successful and spread to many parts of the country.

Wildlife in India

The wildlife of India includes a large number of birds, animals and insects. The Royal Bengal tiger, our national animal,

Royal Bengal tiger

One-horned rhino

is found in the Sundarbans. The one-horned rhinoceros found in the Kaziranga National Park is a protected animal. Rhinos, elephants, hippos and deer are also found in many forests in the north-eastern states. Deciduous forests give shelter to animals like the leopard, boar, bear and the wild buffalo. Camels and desert cats are found in thorn forests. Asiatic lions are found in the Gir forests of Gujarat. However, due to a large amount of deforestation and **poaching**, these animals are losing their natural homes. Hence, it is important for us to conserve both the forests as well as its wildlife.

In order to control poaching, the government has declared many areas as wildlife sanctuaries, bird sanctuaries and national parks. While a national park is meant to protect forest cover and wildlife, a wildlife sanctuary protects **endangered** species. Some of the important national parks and wildlife sanctuaries of India are given in the table below.

National Park	State/UT
Jim Corbett National Park	Uttarakhand
Ranthambore	Rajasthan
Gir	Gujarat
Kaziranga	Assam
Sariska	Rajasthan

National Park	State/UT
Sundarbans	West Bengal
Bandipur	Karnataka
Kanha	Madhya Pradesh
Panna	Madhya Pradesh
Periyar	Kerala
Bandhavgarh	Madhya Pradesh

Wildlife Sanctuary	States/UT
Chilka Lake	Odisha
Sultanpur	Haryana
Periyar	Kerala
Hazaribagh	Jharkhand

Wildlife Sanctuary	States/UT
Bharatpur	Rajasthan
Idukki	Kerala
Dachigam	Jammu & Kashmir

Do It Yourself

Based on the data given above, mark the locations of national parks and wildlife sanctuaries on an outline map of India. Put a ▭ for national parks and a O to show wildlife sanctuaries.

Remember

- Forests are an important renewable natural resource.
- The major types of forests in India are evergreen, deciduous, mountainous, thorn and mangrove or tidal.
- It is important to conserve both forests and wildlife.

Review Zone

A Fill in the blanks with the correct answers.

1. The pulp of .... trees is used to make paper.
   a. evergreen b. deciduous c. coniferous
2. .... trees can grow both in freshwater and seawater.
   a. Sal b. Sundari c. Teak
3. Coniferous trees are found in the ....
   a. Sundarbans b. Niligiri hills c. slopes of the Western Ghats
4. .... forests form the largest forest cover of India.
   a. Evergreen b. Deciduous c. Mangrove
5. Boats are made out of wood that can be obtained from .... forests.
   a. evergreen b. deciduous c. mangrove

B Name the following.

1. Trees that do not shed their leaves irrespective of the season: ....
2. Trees that shed their leaves in the dry season: ....
3. Trees whose pulp is used to make paper: ....
4. An animal found in the mangrove forests of Sundarbans: ....
5. An area enclosed for the protection of forest cover and wildlife: ....

C Write T for True and F for False.

1. Camels are found in the thorn forests of Rajasthan. ☐
2. The estimated forest cover of India is 33 per cent. ☐
3. Deciduous forests are found in the Andaman and Nicobar Islands. ☐

4. Mountainous forests are also known as coniferous forests. ☐
5. The Chipko Movement was launched to protest against deforestation. ☐

D Answer these questions in brief.

1. Name the types of forests found in India.
2. Which trees are mainly found in evergreen forests?
3. Write one difference between wildlife sanctuaries and national parks.
4. In which state was the Chipko Movement first launched?
5. Where are mountainous forests found in India?

E Answer these questions in detail.

1. Discuss the importance of forests.
2. Describe the mangrove forests of India.
3. What do you know about the Chipko Movement?
4. Describe the forests found in the desert regions of India.

Think Zone

A Do you think putting animals in zoos is a good way to prevent poaching? Give reasons for your answer.

B Look at the picture and answer the questions.

1. Name this animal.
2. Where is this animal mostly found?
3. In which national park can this animal be found?

Life Skills Zone

In what way, can you contribute to preserve trees and wildlife of your state?

Value Zone

Do you think animals like living in zoos?

Activity Zone

Make a group project on the topic 'Forests in India'. Divide the class into five groups. Each group can take up one type of forest found in India. Collect more information about the plants and animals in different types of forests. Make a PowerPoint presentation on it. You can also make colourful charts. Present the project report in the class.

ASSESSMENT

Assessment (Chapters 1–9) **Maximum Marks: 50**

A Put a tick (✓) near the correct option. **(1 x 10 = 10)**

1. What is the capital of Himachal Pradesh?
   a. Jaisalmer b. Shimla
2. Which is the highest of the three parallel ranges of the Himalayas?
   a. Greater Himalayas b. Middle Himalayas
3. Which is of the following a desert plant?
   a. Cactus b. Tulsi
4. Which soil is suitable for sugarcane growth?
   a. Black b. Laterite
5. Which river divides the Southern Plateau into two?
   a. Ganga b. Narmada
6. Where is the Coromandel Coast situated?
   a. Tamil Nadu b. Assam
7. Which season is characterized by long and hot days?
   a. Summer b. Winter
8. What is the process through which plants make their food called?
   a. Photosynthesis b. Transpiration
9. What is the process of washing away of minerals called?
   a. Bleaching b. Leaching
10. What prevents soil erosion?
    a. Trees b. Land

B Match the columns. **(1 x 5 = 5)**

Column A	Column B
1. Mt Everest	a. Tibetan Plateau
2. Middle Himalayas	b. Chhota Nagpur Plateau
3. Indus river	c. Small water bodies
4. Oases	d. Himachal
5. River Damodar	e. Himalayan mountains

C **Find an odd one in each line and write the reason why it is odd.** **(2 x 10 = 20)**

1.	Northern Plains	Northern Mountains	Southern Plateaus	Canal
	Reason:			
2.	Khasi	Garo	Jaintia	Alps
	Reason:			
3.	Black	Laterite	Alluvium	Wells
	Reason:			
4.	Camel	Cow	Goat	Lion
	Reason:			
5.	Kanha	Gir	Sunderban	Madhya Pradesh
	Reason:			
6.	Chennai	Karnataka	Kerala	Bihar
	Reason:			
7.	Summer	Autumn	Winter	Wind
	Reason:			
8.	Water	Sunlight	Wind	Industries
	Reason:			
9.	Satpura	Himalaya	Aravalli	Thar
	Reason:			
10.	Evergreen	Deciduous	Mountainous	Plains
	Reason:			

D **Answer the following questions.** **(3 x 5 = 15)**

1. Describe in detail why are evergreen forests called so.
2. What are the components of soil?
3. Write a note on the wildlife of India.
4. Briefly describe the islands of India.
5. How are the Himalayas important to us?

GENERAL KNOWLEDGE

VALUE EDUCATION

1 Same Sound

Some words have the same sound but have different spellings. Read the words given in the box. Complete the sentences with the correct words.

1. a. The gardener dug a ___hole___ in the ground to make a compost pit.

   b. Dev was so hungry, he ate a ___whole___ pizza by himself.

2. a. She enjoyed the storybook so much that she __________ it over and over again.

   b. My mother bought me a new __________ scarf for my birthday.

3. a. Sam was sad because the new shirt that he got was too __________ for him.

   b. Mother told Farid that if he did not keep his new badge properly, he would __________ it.

4. a. Baby __________ enjoyed eating his bowl of honey.

   b. Tina got out of bed and walked to her door in her __________ feet.

5. a. The little mouse __________ up all the cheese.

   b. He had __________ marbles in his pocket.

hole	eight	bare	loose	ate	lose	whole	bear

Fact Zone

A homophone is a word that is pronounced like another word but has a different spelling or meaning, for example *some, sum.*

2 Sports Terms

Look at the sports icons given below. Choose two correct terms used in the sport from the box and fill in the blanks.

1.  Swimming ____________ ____________
2.  Golf ____________ ____________
3.  Hockey ____________ ____________
4.  Football ____________ ____________
5.  Tennis ____________ ____________
6.  Shooting ____________ ____________
7.  Basketball ____________ ____________
8.  Boxing ____________ ____________

Hook Free Hit Ace
Free Throw Bogey Keepie-Uppie
Knockout Heat Bulls Eye
Lap Bunker Scoop Deuce
Target Tackle Layup

Fact Zone

The terms 'penhold grip' and 'loop' are associated with table tennis and 'raider' and 'lobby' are used in the sport of *kabbadi*.

3 Find the Fruits

Read the clues and name the fruits in the crossword.

Across

2. Grows in bunches of a climbing plant
5. Known as peru or amrood, this fruit has a white pulp
7. Soft, red and yellow, this fruit is juicy and pulpy inside with a hard seed in the middle
9. A small green fruit with sour juice
10. Called the king of fruits, eaten especially in summer

Down

1. A soft red fruit whose tiny seeds are on the outside
3. A round fruit whose inside is full of juicy pink-red seeds
4. A big fruit with a green and hard skin. The inside is pink or red and is full of water
6. Red or green fruits that grow in Himachal Pradesh and Kashmir
8. Small soft round fruits usually used on top of the icing on a cake

Fact Zone

Jackfruit, originally from the Western Ghats region in India, is eaten both as a fruit and a vegetable.

4 Dances of India

India is known the world over for its classical dances. Identify the classical dances with the names of their state of origin. Choose the correct options from the two help boxes given below.

1.

2.

3.

4.

5.

6.

7.

8.

Kathak Mohiniyattam Kuchipudi Odissi Sattriya Manipuri Kathakali Bharatanatyam

Kerala Tamil Nadu Assam Manipur Uttar Pradesh Odisha Andhra Pradesh Kerala

Fact Zone

The origin of the Bharatanatyam dance can be traced to Sage Bharat Muni's ancient text *Natyashastra*.

5 Signs on a Hill Station

Have you ever noticed that traffic signs are different when you travel to a hill station? Look at the picture clues of traffic signs. Choose the correct words from the box and label the signs.

compulsory ahead or right	men at work	petrol pump ahead
narrow road ahead	hairpin bend	falling rocks

Fact Zone

Street signs have been there since the time of the Romans. They built pillars or milestones to let travellers know how far they've travelled and how far they are from a place.

6 Animal Groups

Read the description and name the animal groups. Choose the correct word from the help box.

1. Animals that live in water ______________
2. Animals that live on trees ______________
3. Animals that live both on land and in water ______________
4. Animals that live on land ______________
5. Animals that give birth to young ones ______________
6. Animals that lay eggs ______________
7. Animals that live in the sea ______________
8. Flesh eating animals ______________
9. Plant eating animals ______________
10. Animals that eat both animals and plants ______________

Herbivorous	Aquatic	Arboreal
Amphibians	Marine	Omnivorous
Terrestrial	Carnivorous	
Mammals	Oviparous	

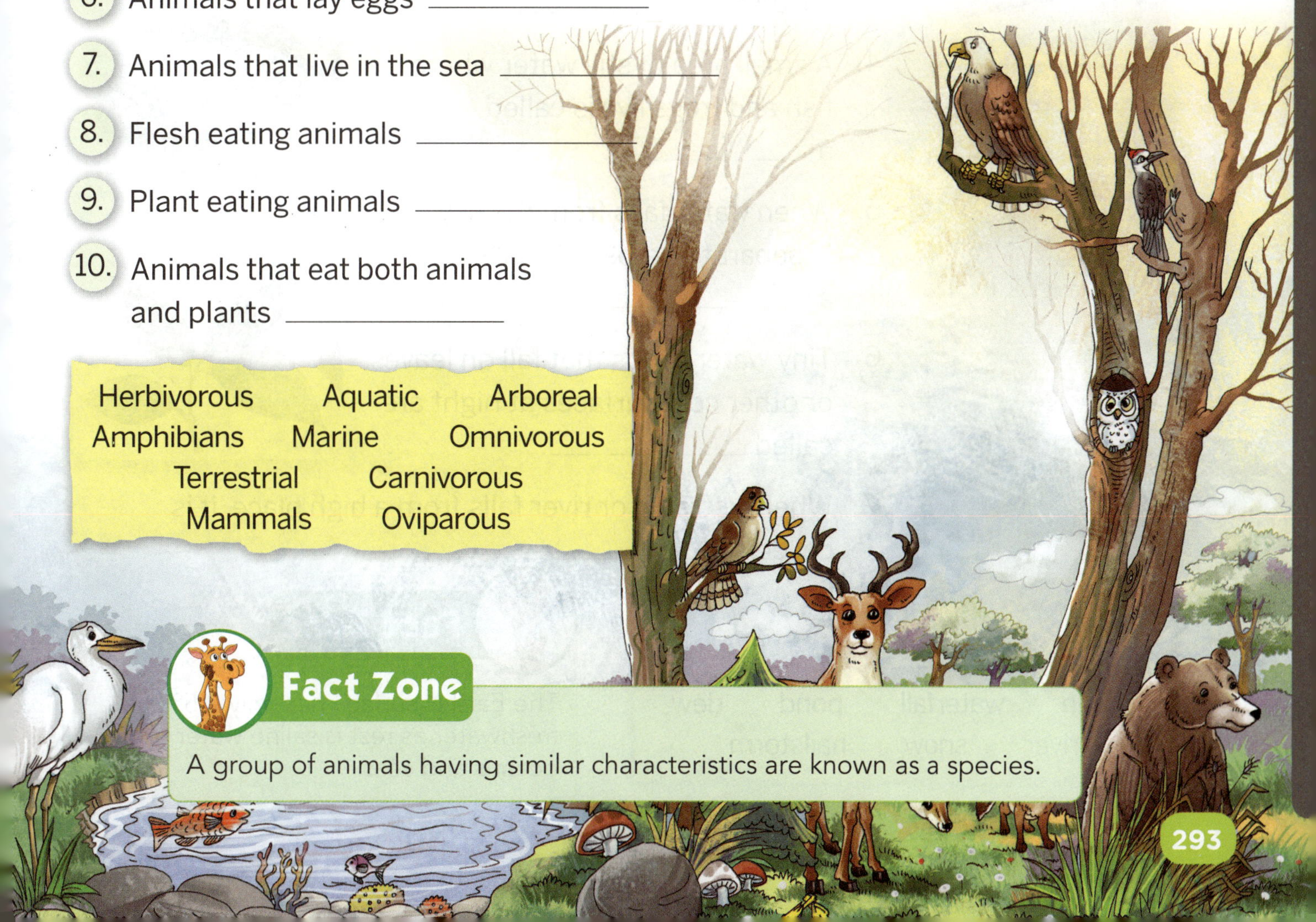

Fact Zone

A group of animals having similar characteristics are known as a species.

7 Water on Earth

Read the clues and identify the water bodies found on earth. Choose the correct word from the help box.

1. The salt water that covers the earth is called an ___ocean___.

2. Small white pieces of frozen water that falls from the sky in cold places is called ____________.

3. A natural flow of water that continues in a long line to the sea or ocean is called a ____________.

4. A small area of still water where fish and frogs live is called a ____________.

5. When water falls from the sky in separate drops, it is called a ____________.

6. Tiny water drops that fall on leaves or other cool surfaces at night are called ____________.

7. When a stream or river falls from a high place, it is called a ____________.

ocean	waterfall	pond	dew
river	snow	hailstorm	

Fact Zone

The Earth's surface has only 2.5% of freshwater as rest is saline water from oceans and seas.

8 Telling Time

Read the statements and draw hands on the clock to show the correct time these activities are completed. Write the time in the blanks too.

1. She left home at three-fifteen in the afternoon and it took forty-five minutes for her to reach the market.

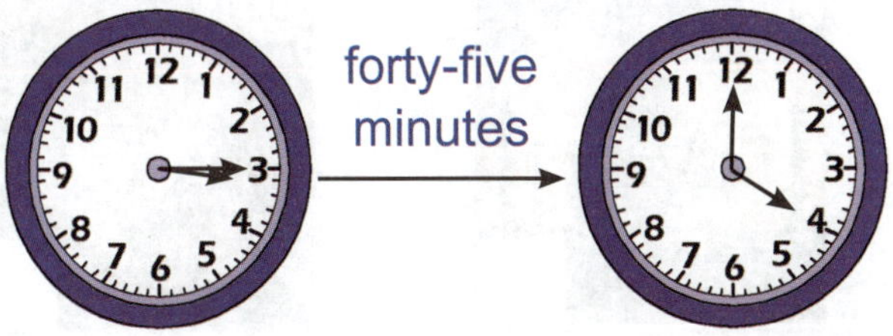

4:00 p.m.

2. Neha started cooking at ten past ten in the morning and finished in twenty minutes.

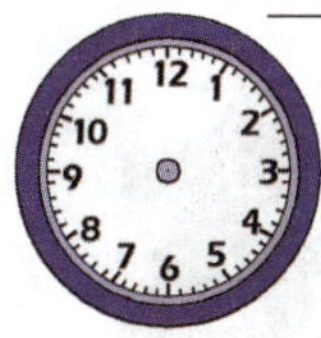

______

______

3. The show started at twelve-twenty-five and ended in two hours.

4. Sushil started studying for his test at three-forty in the afternoon and finished after two hours and thirty minutes.

______

______

5. The race started at 2 o' clock in the afternoon and lasted for eleven minutes.

6. Gurmeet wakes up at six-thirty and takes forty-five minutes to get ready for school.

______

Fact Zone

There are 24 Time Zones across the world.

9 North India

Look at the pictures of the famous places and things from the different states and union territories of north India. Match two things for each state or union territory.

1.

Taj Mahal

5.

phulkari

6.

Kullu cap

7.

shikara

2.

Jim Corbett National Park

3.

Golden Temple

4.

phiran

a. Uttar Pradesh

b. Jammu and Kashmir

c. Punjab

d. Himachal Pradesh

e. Uttarakhand

8.

Laxman Jhula

9.

Chikankari

10.

Christ Church, Shimla

Fact Zone

The Northern Plains are called the 'food bowl of India.'

10 Flags of the World

Identify the flags of different countries in the world. Choose the correct answer from the help box.

1.

____

2.
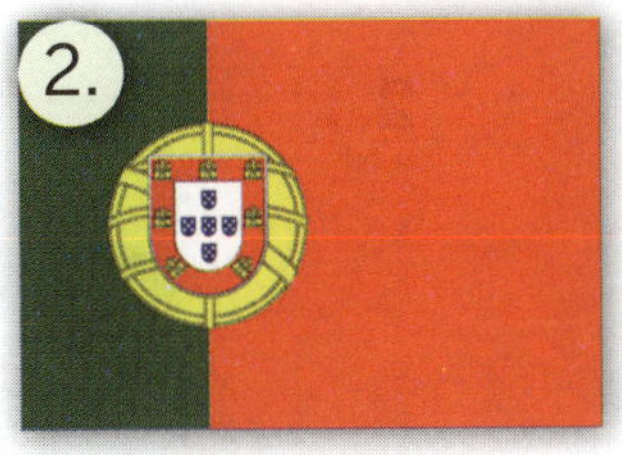
____

3.

____

4.

____

5.

____

6.

____

7.
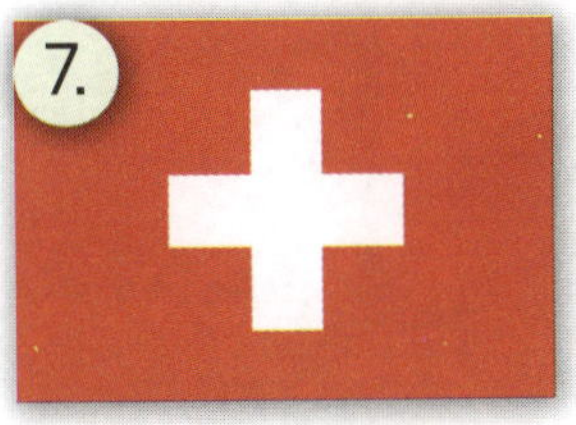
____

8.
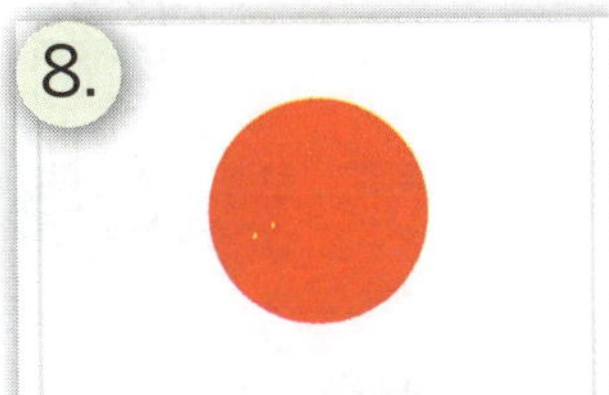
____

9.

____

10.

____

11.

____

12.

____

France Thailand Japan India China Turkey Germany
Switzerland Saudi Arabia Portugal Russian Federation Iran

Fact Zone

The flag of the Netherlands was the oldest tricolour flag in the world.

• 11 Compost Pit

Look at these pictures. They show how a compost pit is made. Number the pictures in correct sequence.

1.

2.

3.

4.

5.

6.

7.

Fact Zone

Compost pit originated with the farmers in England.

12 Word Search

Find the words related to weather in the zigzag word search. One has been done for you.

C	S	N	O	W	C	L	O	U	M
A	K	A	L	F	D	E	W	D	I
L	E	G	B	H	A	I	L	W	S
M	L	N	L	R	S	Q	R	O	T
C	I	I	I	A	I	U	A	B	S
L	G	N	Z	Z	N	A	I	N	N
E	H	T	F	A	L	L	E	R	O
A	R	F	R	R	D	D	D	S	W
M	O	O	O	W	I	N	N	T	M
S	G	G	S	T	T	H	U	O	R

BLIZZARD	CALM	CLEAR	CLOUD	DEW
FOG	FROST	HAIL	LIGHTNING	MIST
RAIN	RAINBOW	SMOG	SNOW	SNOWFLAKE
SQUALL	THUNDERSTORM		WIND	

13 Our Arms and Legs

Label the different parts of our arms and legs using the words in the help box. One has been done for you in each.

Fact Zone

Your forearm and your foot are the same length.

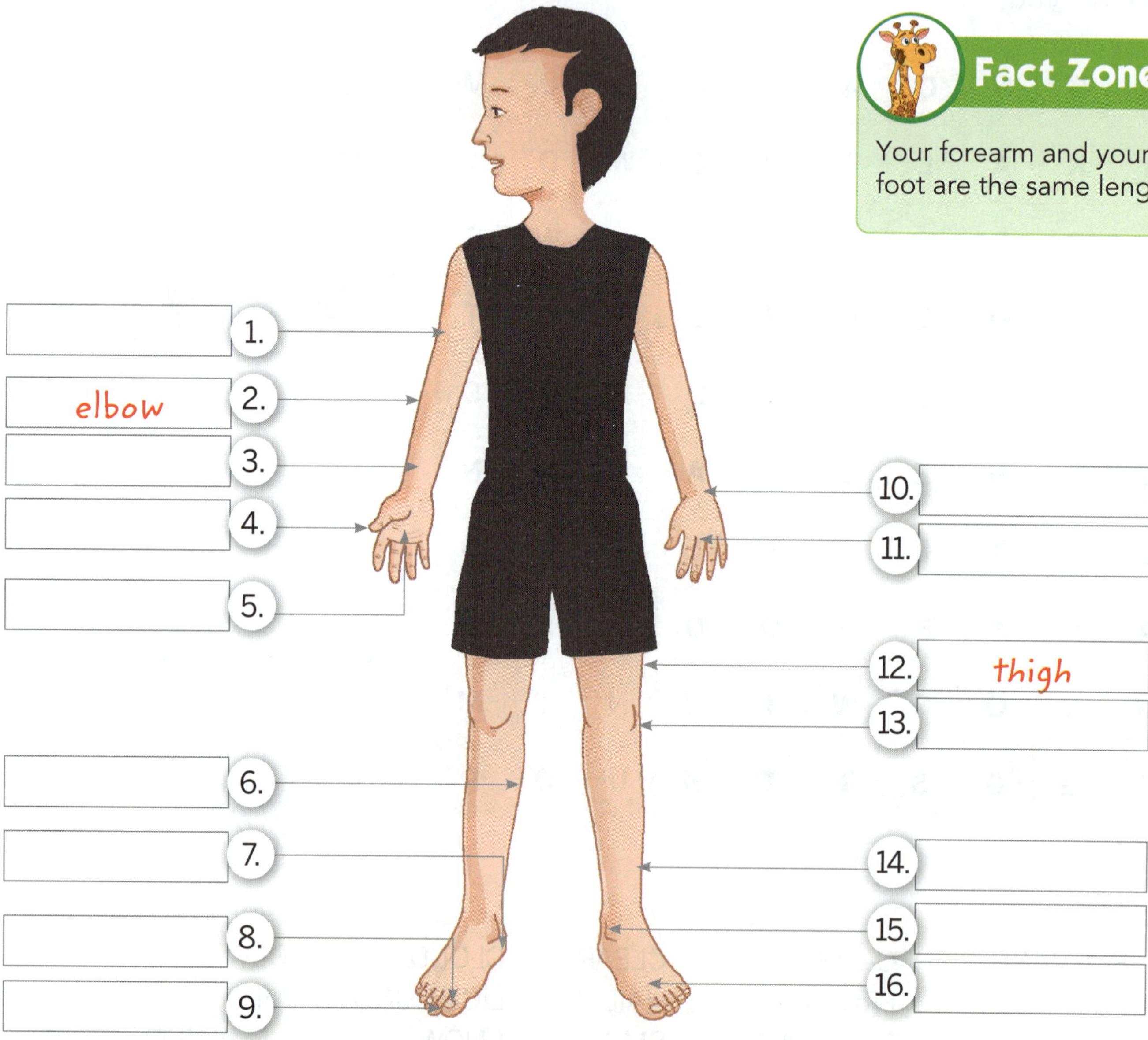

thigh	ankle	palm	thumb	knee	foot	nail	forearm
calf	knuckles	elbow	toes	wrist	shin	heel	upper arm

14 Flowers

Flowers help us in many ways. They give us oil, spices, dyes and perfumes. Look at the flowers below and write their names.

1. 

We get edible oil and yellow dye from this flower.

____

2. 

We get perfume and hair ornaments from this flower.

____

3. 

This flower is edible and is eaten as a vegetable.

____

4. 

This is an edible flower. We also get perfumes and hair ornaments from this flower.

____

5. 

This flower is used for medicinal purposes. We also get a type of spice from it.

____

6. 

This flower gives us yellow dye and is used for flavouring.

____

7. 

This flower is used to make garlands.

____

8. 

This is an edible flower.

____

9. 

We get red food colouring from this flower.

____

Fact Zone

There are some flowers that eat bugs and small animals! The Venus fly trap is an example. When an insect lands on its hairy leaves, its trap snaps and then starts digesting the insect.

A **Match the following.**

1. 

2. 

3. 

a. Uttarakhand

b. Germany

c. Bharatanatyam

d. Ocean

e. Golden Temple

f. Narrow road ahead

4. 

5. 

6. 

B **Choose the correct answer to fill in the blanks.**

1. A term associated with swimming is ____________________. (lap/ace)
2. The tiny seeds of this small, red-pink fruit are on the outside are called ____________________. (strawberry/cherry)
3. Animals that live both on land and in water are called ____________________. (amphibians/arboreal)
4. Kuchipudi is the traditional dance of ____________________. (Andhra Pradesh/Uttar Pradesh)
5. Raj went out to play at five twenty-five and returned at twenty minutes past six. Raj played for ____________________. (fifty minutes/fifty-five minutes)

1 The Mule's Lesson

Discuss

Do you also fight like Ritu and Akanksha? Do you think fighting on the court is a good habit? Discuss in class.

Read along

A trader set forth on a journey with an ass and a mule. Both of the animals were well-laden with heavy loads.

Think and Say

You need to leave to meet your cousin, but your mother has not finished the household work yet. What would you do?

Cooperation

The ass carried his load easily, as long as he walked on the plains. However, when he began to climb the steep mountain path, his load seemed heavier. He found it difficult to carry such a load. So he requested his companion, the mule, to take a small portion of his load. The mule, however, paid no attention to the ass's request.

Shortly afterwards, the ass fell down dead under his burden. The trader could not find another animal in such a wild region. He placed the ass's load on the mule, over and above the mule's own load.

The mule groaned beneath this heavy burden. He said to himself, 'If only I had helped the ass a little in his need, I would not be bearing all the load now!'

Figure out

A. Tick (✓) the correct option.

1. The mule could have helped the ass
   a. by sharing his load. ☐ b. by showing smartness. ☐
2. Did the mule cooperate with the ass?
   a. Yes. ☐ b. No. ☐
3. The ass would have remained alive
   a. had the mule helped him a little. ☐
   b. had he sat down on the road and not moved. ☐
4. How did the mule become the loser?
   a. The mule became the loser as he had to bear the load of the ass too. ☐
   b. The mule became the loser as he lost his companion, the ass. ☐
5. What lesson did the mule learn?
   a. The mule learnt that he should never travel with the ass. ☐
   b. The mule learnt that if you cooperate with others, you help not only them but yourself, too. ☐

B. Answer these questions orally.

1. Was the mule a good team player?
2. Why did the ass want to share his load?
3. At the end, did the mule have to suffer too?

Relate

Choose the best option. Draw a smiley ☺ against it.

1. You and your friend have a badminton match coming up. You know the whole school will be watching. What would you do?
   a. I would try to take all the shots by myself, so that it looks as if my efforts have won the match. ◯
   b. I would play my best and try to win as a team. After all, I win if my team wins. ◯
2. Your mother is in a hurry for her appointment at the dentist's. You have asked her to make sandwiches for you. What would you do?
   a. I would help my mother make the sandwiches so that she can reach the dentist in time for her appointment. ◯
   b. I would stay away from the kitchen so that she does not see me and ask me to help. ◯
3. Your little sister has taken a parrot as a pet. She has gone for her class and its time to feed the parrot. What would you do?
   a. I would complain that I have to feed the parrot. ◯
   b. I would feed the parrot happily. ◯

Workout

In the word search given below, find these five words related to cooperation.

team   help   friends   group   tolerance

T	E	A	M	G	J	D	V	F
T	G	E	I	R	F	F	V	R
G	R	J	K	L	G	T	B	I
T	O	L	E	R	A	N	C	E
V	U	H	H	H	O	R	C	N
G	P	T	F	F	U	G	D	D
T	H	H	E	L	P	G	V	S

Create

Draw or cut out pictures of team work and cooperation from old magazines. Make a collage of these and write a few lines about working together. Display the chart in class.

Remember

- Always cooperate with people around you.
- Cooperating makes things easier for everyone.
- If you cooperate with others, they would cooperate with you.
- Work together and you will be successful.

Enjoy

Read the book *Kid Cooperation* from your library. Discuss it in class.

Be smart

If you are the leader of a team, what qualities should you have? Unscramble the following words to find out.

meta psitir: _ _ _ _   _ _ _ _ _ _

selnessesslf: _ _ _ _ _ _ _ _ _ _ _ _

tolercane: _ _ _ _ _ _ _ _ _

tysetisinvi: _ _ _ _ _ _ _ _ _ _ _

disciliенp: _ _ _ _ _ _ _ _ _ _

Teaching tips

- Tell students how an activity can be done faster if everyone cooperates.
- Make the students play cooperation games that would enable them to understand the true meaning of cooperation.
- Include an activity in class where if everyone cooperates and quickly completes the work assigned, they can get extra time for sports, library or any other activity which they all enjoy.

2 Tina's Camping Trip

Discuss

Have you ever planted a sapling or a seed? Why or why not? Discuss in class.

Let's work together,
And build a garden of our own.
It won't take much, it won't take long,
Seeds will bloom once they are sown.

Read along

Tina's class was going on a camping trip. She was very excited. She looked forward to spending a night under the beautiful stars.

Finally after waiting for a whole week, the day for Tina's camping trip arrived. Her teacher, Roma Ma'am, took the entire class to a sanctuary nearby. Tina saw many fragrant flowers, tall trees, beautiful birds, swift squirrels and even a few deer, as they dashed through bushes and over green grass.

By the time evening fell, Tina had collected many fallen flowers, seeds and fruits. As she and her best friend, Anita, chatted about the day's events, they set up their sleeping bags. At night, Tina and Anita curled up inside their sleeping bags, warm and snug. They smelled the fragrant flowers, watched the glowing fireflies and heard the rustling of the leaves and the chirping of the grasshoppers. Happy and content, Tina, Anita, Roma Ma'am and the class soon fell asleep one by one.

When the class returned to school, the teacher asked them to make a project on the camping trip. They were to show this project after a few weeks.

For the project on the camping trip, Tina potted a plant from the seeds that she had collected on the trip. She also collected pictures of the things, seen during the trip, and made a collage.

By the time, it was time for her to show the project, her potted plant had grown pretty with greeen leaves and big red flowers. She showed the potted plant and the collage proudly to her class.

Tina was proud of her new green friend and vowed to respect nature.

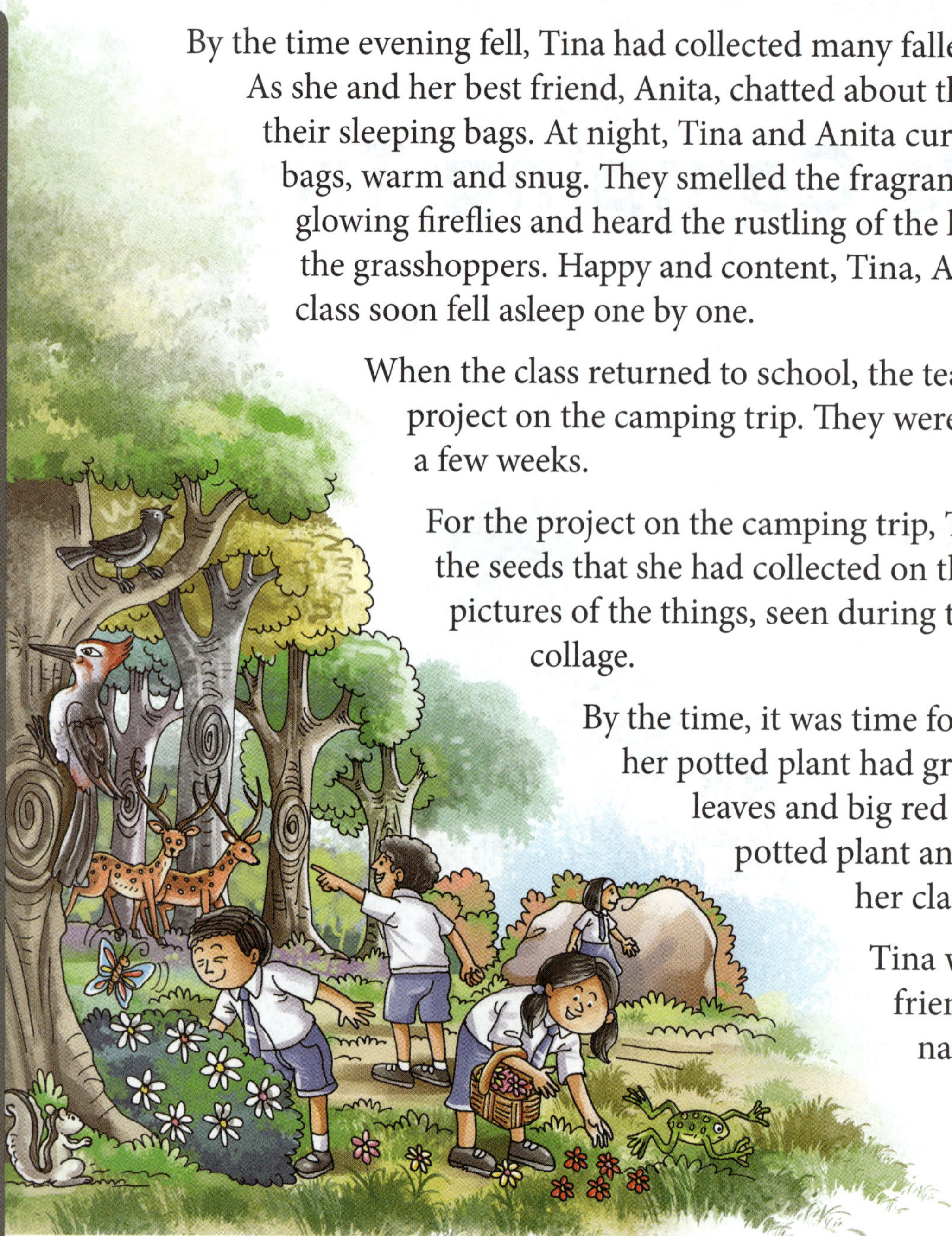

Think and Say

You notice that a tap in your bathroom is dripping. What would you do?

Figure out

A. Tick the correct option to answer the questions.

1. Which two animals did Tina see?
   a. Tina saw deer and squirrels. ☐
   b. Tina saw deer and lions. ☐

2. Who was Tina's new friend?
   a. Tina's new friend was Anita. ☐
   b. Tina's new friend was a plant that she had potted. ☐
3. What preparations did Tina make for the project on the camping trip?
   a. Tina made no preparations.
   b. Tina potted a plant and made a collage for the project on the camping trip.
4. What was Tina's collage made of?
   a. Tina's collage was made of pictures collected of the things, she had seen during the trip. ☐
   b. Tina's collage was made of random photographs. ☐
5. Was Tina excited about sleeping under the stars?
   a. Yes, she was very excited about sleeping under the stars. ☐
   b. No, as it was just another day for her. ☐

B. Answer these questions orally.

1. Who was Anita?
2. What was Tina looking forward to?
3. Enlist the things that Tina saw during the camping trip.

Relate

Choose the best option. Draw a smiley ☺ against it.

1. There is a lot of leaf litter in your garden. What would you do?
   a. I would burn the leaf litter. ◯
   b. I would collect the leaf litter in a pile and ask the gardener to use them for compost. ◯
2. You notice that your friend wastes a lot of paper by making paper planes and paper boats out of them. What would you do?
   a. I would tell him that he can use old newspapers to make paper planes and paper boats to save paper. ◯
   b. I would also start making paper planes and boats out of my own notebook sheets. ◯

3. Your younger sister wants you to pluck some flowers for her. What would you do?
   a. I would tell her that flowers look best on plants.
   b. I would pluck some flowers for her.

Workout

Your family and you went for a camping trip to a nearby hill. Write a paragraph talking about all the animals you saw, the different plants you passed by and anything else that really attracted you. Try to include everything you can think of.

Create

Save trees by making your own recycled paper.

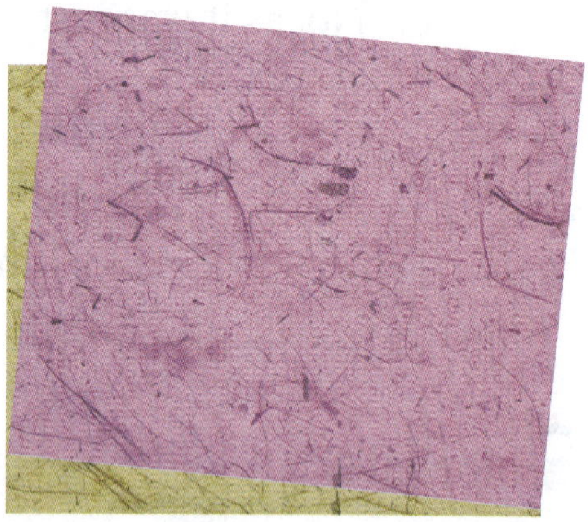

You need

- Old newspapers
- Big tub
- Water
- Wire mesh
- two trays
- Rolling pin

Steps

1. Take old newspapers and tear them into small pieces.
2. Soak them overnight in water.
3. Blend the soaked paper, in a blender, to make a fine paste.
4. Place the wire mesh in a tray.
5. Spread the paper pulp in a very thin layer over a wire mesh. Wait for all the water to drain out.
6. Gently remove the wire mesh from the tray and transfer the paper layer to a dry tray.
7. Cover it with another sheet of paper and roll with the help of a rolling pin.
8. Leave it to dry.
9. After 2–3 days, when it dries, you will have handmade paper.

Remember

- Plant more trees. Make people aware of the importance of trees and the need to care for them.
- Do not pluck flowers or leaves from trees.
- Water your plants every day and take care of them.
- Keep your garden and the park where you play, neat and clean.
- Use tree products like tissue paper, paper, paper plates, toothpicks, rubber, etc. very carefully. The more you use these, the more trees will have to be cut down to make these.

Enjoy

Find out about the festival of trees or *Vanamahotsava*. It is a day that reminds us all that we should take care of our priceless forests. Ask your teacher to tell you more about *Vanamahotsava* or learn about it from the Internet. Celebrate it in school.

Be smart

Look at the equations. Complete them by understanding the relationship between the words.

1. Deforestation—less trees, afforestation—________________
2. More plants—clean air, less plants—________________
3. Water plants—grow, do not water plants—________________
4. Waste paper—more trees cut down, do not waste paper—________________

Teaching tips

- Talk about the things nature gives us that we cannot see, like the air we breathe and utilities like natural gas.
- Also talk about how plants clean the air.
- Stress on how different the world would be if things we take for granted went missing even for a day.

Project I: Dr APJ Abdul Kalam

1. Read about the life of Dr APJ Abdul Kalam from either your school library or the Internet. Now answer the questions based on his life history.

    a. He was born on ____________________.

    b. The full name of Dr APJ Abdul Kalam was ____________________________________.

    c. His father's name was ____________________ and his mother's name was ____________________.

    d. He was the ____________________ child in the family.

    e. He had ____________________ brothers and ____________________ sister.

    f. At an early age, Dr APJ Abdul Kalam sold ______________ to help his family income.

    g. He had dreamed of becoming a ____________________.

    h. He has received the ____________________, India's highest civilian honour.

    i. He was the ____________________ of India from 2002 to ____________________.

    j. He was also known as the ____________________.

    k. He died on ____________________.

2. Collect pictures of Dr APJ Abdul Kalam from various stages of his life and make a collage.

Notes

Notes